Sara Alemán, PhD
Tanya Fitzpatrick, DSW
Thanh V. Tran, PhD
Elizabeth Gonzalez, PhD
Editors

Therapeutic Interventions with Ethnic Elders
Health and Social Issues

*Pre-publication
REVIEWS,
COMMENTARIES,
EVALUATIONS . . .*

"**D**r. Alemán and her colleagues are to be congratulated for providing health and social service providers with a fresh and comprehensive set of guideposts for geriatric services in preparation for the coming Ethnogeriatric Imperative. The unique ethnic histories and cultural values of elders from subpopulations of Hispanic, Asian, American Indian, and white immigrant elders provide an understanding that is critical for effective services.

Especially valuable are the chapters reviewing relevant information for newer immigrant elders, such as Russian, Jewish, and Vietnamese, and those that provide new insights into two Southwestern American Indian cultural groups, the Diné (Navajo) and Yaqui. This book will be especially useful for social work faculty and students interested in the issues of aging."

Gwen Yeo, PhD
*Director Emeritus,
Stanford Geriatric Education Center,
Stanford University School of Medicine,
Stanford, CA*

"This highly readable text is an excellent resource for professional caregivers, service providers, health workers, and others who come into contact with elders of ethnic backgrounds. It presents research and theory on cultural distinctiveness, the process of assimilation, and specific guidelines to sensitize readers to the needs of elders from diverse and potentially marginalized populations now living in the United States.

In this burgeoning new area of gerontology, there are intriguing contradictions, e.g., not all cultural groups are heterogeneous vs. 'traditional Japanese attitudes toward age,' 'Native American elders are the fastest growing segment of the population,' vs. 'African-American elders are the fastest growing segment of the minority population.' Some of these seeming inconsistencies simply point out to us that all human beings, regardless of their folkways, family traditions, and historical cohort, have strengths that can be appreciated. This resource presents a context for understanding Japanese, Vietnamese, Russian, African-American, Puerto Rican, Mexican-American, Yaque, and Navajo elders. Particularly interesting is the chapter by Peña, Alemán, and Beyal on modern-day aging on the Navajo Reservation.

The book is highly readable and authoritative. As service providers are made aware of the unique and shared characteristics of various ethnic populations, they will come to value the stories and histories of these individuals. It is hoped that many students and professionals in gerontology will make use of this text to begin a fascinating journey to better communicate with and touch the lives of our ethnically diverse elders."

Mary Alice Wolf, EdD
Director,
Institute in Gerontology
and Professor of Human
Development/Gerontology,
Saint Joseph College,
West Hartford, CT

"A practical and informative guide for clinicians who serve a diverse population. Clinicians will be especially interested in the discussion of obstacles experienced by clients in utilizing services.

An important contribution of this volume is the explanation of how past discrimination carries forward to the present day, making it difficult to establish a trusting relationship with a client."

Regina O'Grady-LeShane, PhD
Director of Academic
and Student Services,
Graduate School of Social Work,
Boston College,
Boston, MA

More pre-publication
REVIEWS, COMMENTARIES, EVALUATIONS . . .

"This book focuses on the needs of particular ethnic groups of older Americans and the way the service system responds to them. The groups range from the 'oldest' of older Americans—the Native American population, to the most recent of older Americans—Vietnamese and Russian immigrants. It also includes African Americans, Japanese Americans, and Hispanic Americans. Each chapter provides basic demographic information, family and cultural attributes, elders' experience with the service system, and conclusions and recommendations.

The reader's understanding of ethnicity considerations is enriched both by observing ethnic factors at play across so many different groups, and by the detailed presentation of each population. The book is particularly useful because it disaggregates the experiences of Hispanics by including separate chapters on Puerto Ricans, Cuban Americans, and Mexican Americans—distinctions not usually made in much of the literature on the Hispanic population. This book belongs on the bookshelf of academics, providers, and policy makers who wish to better understand how ethnic factors affect both the behavior of the older person and the response of the service system."

James J. Callahan Jr., PhD
Director,
Policy Center on Aging,
Heller Graduate School,
Brandeis University,
Waltham, MA

The Haworth Press, Inc.

Therapeutic Interventions with Ethnic Elders
Health and Social Issues

Therapeutic Interventions with Ethnic Elders
Health and Social Issues

Sara Alemán, PhD
Tanya Fitzpatrick, DSW
Thanh V. Tran, PhD
Elizabeth Gonzalez, PhD
Editors

Routledge
Taylor & Francis Group

NEW YORK AND LONDON

First published 2000 by The Haworth Press, Inc.

Softcover edition published 2001.

Published 2013 by Routledge
605 Third Avenue, New York, NY 10017
2 Park Square, Milton Park, Abingdon, Oxon OX14 4RN

Routledge is an imprint of the Taylor & Francis Group, an informa business

Cover design by Marylouise E. Doyle.

The Library of Congress has catalogued the hardcover edition of this book as:

Therapeutic interventions with ethnic elders : health and social issues / Sara Alemán ... [et al.], editors.
    p. cm.
    Includes bibliographical references and index.
    ISBN 0-7890-0272-8 (hc : alk paper)
    1. Minority aged—Medical care—Cross-cultural studies. 2. Minority aged—Medical care—Social aspects. 3. Minority aged—Health and hygiene. I. Alemán, Sara, 1944-
RA564.8.T49 1999
362.1'9897'0089—dc21   99-045998
                                                                 CIP

ISBN: 978-0-7890-0272-3 (hbk)
ISBN: 978-0-789-00273-0 (pbk)
ISBN: 978-1-315-82175-7 (eISBN)

CONTENTS

ABOUT THE EDITORS

Sara Alemán, PhD, is Associate Professor and Director of Gerontology in the Sociology and Social Work Department at Northern Arizona University in Flagstaff, Arizona. Her research articles have been published in several journals, including the *Journal of Gerontological Social Work* (The Haworth Press, Inc.), the *Journal of Aging and Ethnicity,* the *Journal of Case Management,* and *Women & Criminal Justice* (Haworth).

Tanya Fitzpatrick, DSW, RN, is Assistant Professor of Gerontology at Saint Joseph College in West Hartford, Connecticut. Dr. Fitzpatrick received the Harriet M. Bartlett Award from Simmons College Graduate School of Social Work in March 1999. She has presented her research on cultural and ethnic issues, leisure activities and health, and bereavement and health among older men at several national conferences.

Thanh V. Tran, PhD, is Professor and Chair of the PhD program at Boston College Graduate School of Social Work in Chestnut Hill, Massachusetts. Dr. Tran is Consulting Editor of *Social Work Research* and a reviewer for many professional journals. He is the author of more than fifty articles that have been published in journals such as *Social Work in Health Care* (The Haworth Press, Inc.), *Health & Social Work, Journal of Social Service Research* (Haworth), and *Gerontological Social Work.*

Elizabeth Gonzalez, PhD, is Associate Professor of Nursing at MCP-Hahnemann University and Tract Coordinator of the Psychiatric Mental Health Practitioner Program at the School of Nursing in Philadelphia, Pennsylvania. Dr. Gonzalez also has a private practice in New Jersey. She is the author or co-author of a number of articles that have appeared in the *Journal of Cultural Diversity, Issues in Mental Health Nursing,* and *Issues in Mental Health.*

CONTRIBUTORS

Charlotte Beyal is a City Magistrate in Flagstaff, Arizona. She was born in Greasewood, Arizona, on the Navajo Reservation. Her clan is Redhouse (from her mother) and she was born into the Salt Clan (from her father).

Raymond Bossè, PhD, has served as Associate Director of the Normative Aging Study since 1979. He is a Fellow of the Gerontological Society of America and has authored or co-authored more than fifty articles in scientific journals. He is also the author of books on aging and several book chapters.

Mary Damskey, MSW, ACSW, is Associate Professor at Northern Arizona University. She has twenty years of experience in practice with an emphasis on health issues, bereavement, and group work.

Anne O. Freed, MSW, is an Emeritus Adjunct Professor who taught in the Boston College Graduate School of Social Work and at Smith College in both the master's and doctoral programs. She was awarded two Fulbright Scholarships to teach in Bulgaria and has done research in Japan in the field of gerontology.

Neala C. Melcer, EdD, is the chairperson for the Health Education/ Health Promotion section of the Massachusetts Public Health Association. She did a postdoctoral fellowship in cancer control at the Harvard School of Public Health and the Dana Farber Institute in Boston. She is currently writing a book about the cultural dimensions of hypertension.

Dung Ngo, MS, is a doctoral candidate in clinical psychology at Saint Louis University, St. Louis, Missouri.

Juan Paz, DSW, has focused his research on aging and health issues among indigenous populations of the Southwest. For the past few years, he has held a national conference that addresses issues of wellness.

Sara Peña, MA, studied Navajo language, culture, and philosophy at Navajo Community College in Tsaile, Arizona. She is currently employed by the Bureau of Land Management in Washington, DC, as a Native American specialist.

Introduction

Sara Alemán

The purpose of the book is twofold. First, we aim to examine specific ethnic minority aging populations' culturally driven behaviors when seeking services, and second, to discuss appropriate interventions and strategies for health personnel and social service case workers. Also, when appropriate, therapeutic interventions with specific aging populations will be explained to assist with identified service delivery strategies.

Research suggests that many ethnic elders utilize services proportionate to their need only when the service providers are able to speak to them in the client's native language or when the office environment reflects a cross-cultural sensitivity by the use of music, decorations, and/or available literature (Hodges, 1990). Unless some of these items are in evidence to suggest to potential patients that they are welcomed, ethnic elders are less likely to use services. The ethnic elders will remain in their homes and/or community in spite of being functionally impaired (Bassford, 1995; Hing, 1987) or having higher rates of need (Stoller and Gibson, 1994). The authors propose that many ethnic elders will continue to underutilize services, in spite of their higher levels of need (Gerontological Society of America, 1994; Stoller and Gibson, 1994), because many service providers simply are not aware of methods, information, or cultural-specific factors that will more appropriately address the bicultural needs of elderly ethnic clients. This means that many services for elders who have been disenfranchised historically will need to receive more attention from service providers because of the increase in number of elders (Cuellar, 1990; National Association of Social Workers, 1993; The Commonwealth Fund Commission, 1989) and to the more severe needs and challenges that they present.

The most common recommendation for improving the rate of service participation by ethnic elders is for service providers to be from the same ethnic group as the population being served (*JAMA,* 1991). While this is the preferred approach to culturally sensitive service delivery, not many professionals are bilingual and bicultural, in spite of attempts to attract more ethnic students to the helping professions (*JAMA, 1991*). Therefore, the most realistic alternative may be to teach majority-culture service providers to respond to ethnic elders in a culturally appropriate manner—hence the need for this book.

Because of the need to be responsive at all levels of interactions, it is important to inculcate service providers with the knowledge that many elders are culturally different and need to have services provided with culturally appropriate strategies. For most people, regardless of ethnicity, it is difficult to ask and then to accept services from strangers. Therefore, in addition to being sensitive to the fact that elders are hesitant to ask for and to receive assistance, all service providers need to be aware of the even more intense feelings that ethnic elders experience. These feelings are evident when it comes to asking for (National Association of Social Workers, 1993) and receiving services from strangers who may also speak a different language and in many instances have different values, eating habits, religions, and so forth.

Demographic data reflect a changing world of elders. For example, Native American elders are the fastest-growing segment of that population. Between 1970 and 1989, the over-age-sixty-five population grew by 65 percent (Bassford, 1995; Butler, Lewis, and Sunderland, 1991). These data hold true for several ethnic groups (Bassford, 1995; National Association of Social Workers, 1993). Additionally, these elders are heterogeneous both within and between groups. As a result, the elderly population requires that professionals look at various factors before attempting to assist an elder who has a different ethnic or cultural background.

Aging demographics that show an increase in the age group over sixty-five years (Butler, Lewis, and Sunderland, 1991; National Association of Social Workers, 1993) are forcing researchers and service providers to seek and develop strategies for effective communication, more appropriate interventions, and better use of resources with diverse populations. Therefore, it is imperative to begin exploring how these factors affect our work with the aged population. The cultural diversity found among our aged citizens brings a greater need for culturally relevant information. This book adds such information to the current available literature that addresses the needs of our ethnic and racial minority elders. It provides an in-depth view of aging ethnic populations that encourages all interactions with elders to incorporate an appreciation for a variety of values, family interactions, and norms of acceptable behavior. All of these factors may reflect a divergence from what we know and appreciate about the majority white elderly population.

Each following chapter addresses a specific ethnic group of elders. As the elderly population grows and becomes more diversified, the authors believe this information is necessary for effective service delivery. It is important for all health and service providers to have knowledge that is useful as they assist and work with older ethnic people.

DEMOGRAPHICS

Older men and women tend to be seen as homogenous by health and social service providers who receive little, if any, training that considers racial or cultural norms in the delivery of services or medical care. Most older people of color are compared to the majority white population based on the premise that the latter is the prototype for all peoples' needs and behaviors during the life span but particularly during old age. This comparison is often unfair since ethnic elders have a history that is very different from the white people that they are compared to and measured against. Furthermore, long-standing prejudices, stereotypes, and discriminatory practices are perpetuated by bureaucratized and rigid systems. The end result is that service providers are overwhelmed by a minority aging population that is increasing in numbers and whose needs are becoming more evident.

Among the aging minority populations, African-American elders represent the largest group, and the elderly represent the fastest-growing segment of this minority group (Hopper, 1993; Kulys, 1990). Of all the Latino elderly, Mexican-American elders account for 50 percent of all the over-sixty-five members of the larger group, and Puerto Ricans and Cubans are the next two largest groups. Census data show that the over-sixty-five age group is the largest growing population for all groups, and ethnic elderly are included in this statistic.

REFERENCES

Bassford, T.L. (1995). Health status of Hispanic elders. In Espino, D.V. (guest ed.), *Clinics in geriatric medicine.* Philadelphia: W.B. Saunders Company, pp. 25-38.

Butler, R.N., Lewis, M., and Sunderland, T. (1991). *Aging and mental health: Positive psychosocial and biomedical approaches.* New York: Macmillan Publishing Company.

Commonwealth Fund Commission, The (1989). *Poverty and poor health among elderly Hispanic Americans.* Baltimore, MD: Author.

Cuellar, J. (1990). *Aging and health: Hispanic American elders.* Stanford, CA: Stanford Geriatric Education Center, SGEC Working Paper Series, Number 5.

Gerontological Society of America (1994). *Minority elders: Five goals toward building a public policy base.* Washington, DC: Author.

Hing, E. (1987). *Use of nursing homes by the elderly: Preliminary data from the 1985 national nursing home survey.* Washington, DC: U.S. Department of Health and Human Services. Number 135. May 14, 1987.

Hodges, V.G. (1990). Providing culturally sensitive intensive family preservation services to ethnic minority families. In E.M. Tracy, D.A. Haapale, J. Kinney, and P.J. Pecora (eds.), *Intensive family preservation services.* Cleveland, OH: Case Western Reserve University, pp. 95-116.

Hopper, S.V. (1993). The influence of ethnicity on the health of older women. In Kaiser, F.E. (guest ed.), *Clinics in geriatric medicine* 9(1). Philadelphia: W.B. Saunders Company, pp. 231-259.

JAMA (1991). Council on Scientific Affairs Hispanic health in the United States. 256(2), 248-252.

Kulys, R. (1990). The ethnic factor in the delivery of social services. In Abraham Monk (ed.), *Handbook of gerontological services.* New York: Columbia University Press, pp. 629-662.

National Association of Social Workers (1993). *Social work with older people: Understanding diversity.* Washington, DC: Author.

Stoller, E.P. and Gibson, R.C. (1994). Inequalities in health and mortality: Gender, race, and class. In E.P. Stoller and R.C. Gibson (eds.), *Worlds of difference.* Thousand Oaks, CA: Pine Forge Press, pp. 209-223.

Chapter 1

Culture-Specific Theoretical and Conceptual Models of Aging

Sara Alemán
Tanya Fitzpatrick

In this chapter, various theoretical and conceptual models that have been utilized to explain aging in the United States are discussed. This is necessary to provide a foundation for understanding how theories may apply to ethnic and racial groups. These theories have a common thread: they all attempt to explain the process of aging in an American society that generally marginalizes elders of color. The majority of current theories on aging contribute negligible understanding or exhibit little support for ethnic elders or for the strengths that they bring from their life experiences. Further, when aging occurs within a culture that is different from the majority culture, ageist behavior may become intolerable. The following theories represent the more popular perspectives that have been developed and used to explain the aging process. The authors attempt to relate the models to aging processes in ethnic minority groups.

Some researchers believe the *double jeopardy* hypothesis is perhaps the best example of a theory developed to accommodate differences and disparities between whites and blacks (Butler, Lewis, and Sunderland, 1991). When developed, this hypothesis was applied primarily to older blacks, yet is applicable to other ethnic minority groups. In essence, the theory asserts that being black and old is a double problem, as prejudice and discrimination are associated with both states of being. Dowd and Bengston (1978) characterize the double jeopardy position of the minority aged as a double burden resulting from devaluation in status in our society. This hypothesis may also represent a triple or quadruple problem in discussing older ethnic people who are also females (gender issue) and poor (low socioeconomic status), whose lives contrast sharply with those who are white, rich, young, and male (Lightfoot, 1982). The theory is used to explain issues that arise with being ethnic and old and the impact of that phenomenon on the larger society.

This is important because Dowd and Bengston (1978) found no relationship to the double jeopardy theory in the area of family and social interaction or life satisfaction; therefore, one may assume that double jeopardy is particularly potent in interactions that elderly ethnic people experience with the world outside their family and same-group social contacts. As in younger years, the jeopardy for ethnic elders is not within their group or culture but with the larger majority culture that is oftentimes hostile, repressive, and alien.

Markides (1983) found a narrowing of differences from middle to old age between aging blacks and whites on income and health, thus providing evidence of nonsupport for the double jeopardy hypothesis. However, most research supports findings that elders experience a decline in resources as they age and, therefore, the double jeopardy idea gains validity when applied to ethnic elders.

Theories may focus on individuals as points of impact and study or may look at family systems, culture, or changes that occur over time and ultimately impact individuals. All of them attempt to further our understanding of how aging impacts all of the aforementioned systems. The double jeopardy theory looks at groups of elders and may be seen as a microanalysis of what the aging experience is for ethnic elders. By contrast, the theory of modernization looks at the aging experience from a macro perspective.

Modernization theory postulates that as each society modernizes and becomes more industrialized, the less status the elders' position in the family carries (Cowgill and Holmes, 1972). This theory emphasizes the fact that minority or more traditional cultures place a higher value on and give more respect to their elderly. Critics question this theory in regard to the Japanese, who continue to value elderly relatives within the family system, yet are fast becoming one of the most highly technical societies in the world. (See Markides and Mindel's [1987] discussion of Rosenthal's [1983, 1986] new dimension of modernization theory.) In general, modernization theory views traditional families as providing more support to elderly members, whereas the opposite is true of more modernized families in which assistance and support has decreased. However, Rosenthal views ethnicity and culture as a source from which people may draw different meanings depending on their situation and their stage in life.

Assimilation theory, also a more macro theory, views ethnicity and minority status as a temporary situation (Gordon, 1964; Park, 1950, in Markides and Mindel, 1987). After some time living in the United States, one gradually rises up the socioeconomic ladder toward a middle-class position, producing loss of "cultural distinctiveness" (Markides and Mindel, 1987, p. 38). The expectation is that everyone will eventually become assimilated. With respect to family implications, the younger members would quickly lose their traditional values and replace them with values and patterns from the dominant culture.

The theory of assimilation is counter to research that identifies some ethnic groups who have been in the United States for generations, but continue to follow ascribed cultural norms. This is particularly true among Native American tribes in the Southwest and Mexican Americans. In many of these cultures, younger family members are educated but remain active in family ceremonies, tribal politics, and native religions. The area of health care also defies assimilation in that it is not uncommon for younger family members to go to their elders for medical advice and subsequently follow native or culture-specific ceremonies to deal with both mental and physical illnesses.

The theories that are discussed and others not discussed are important because they allow us to connect dynamics to processes which occur so slowly that on a daily basis there is little, if any, perception of what is happening. As gerontologists and service providers to elders of color, it is particularly important to put theories within the context of the culture of ethnic elders. It is important to view expected behaviors and changes with jaundiced eyes and not be prejudiced by the expectations that theories, based on the majority population, set into motion. Additionally, ethnic elders are different from the white majority elders but also from each other. Therefore, what may be an effective strategy for one may not work for another from the same ethnic group. This knowledge encourages service providers to view each elder as an individual and not as a stereotype of what has been read or heard. This is important for the reason that it will lead to relationships with ethnic elders that give them dignity and respect that is often lost when we deal with them as stereotypes of some preconceived paradigm.

REFERENCES

Butler, R.N., Lewis, M., and Sunderland, T. (1991). *Aging and mental health: Positive psychosocial and biomedical approaches*. New York: Macmillan Publishing Company.

Cowgill, D.O. and Holmes, L. (1972). *Aging and modernization*. New York: Appleton-Century-Crofts.

Dowd, J.J. and Bengston, V. (1978). Aging in minority populations: An examination of the double jeopardy hypothesis. *Journal of Gerontology, 33*, 427-436.

Gordon, M.M. (1964). *Assimilation in American life*. New York: Oxford University Press.

Lightfoot, O.B. (1982). Ethnic and cultural variations in the care of the aged. Psychiatric interventions with blacks: The elderly—A case in point. *Journal of Geriatric Psychiatry, 15*(2), 209-223.

Markides, K.S. (1983). Minority aging. In M.W. Riley, B.B. Hess, and K. Bond (eds.), *Aging in society: Reviews of recent literature*. Hillsdale, NJ: Lawrence Erlbaum, pp. 115-138.

Markides, K.S. and Mindel, C.H. (1987). *Aging and ethnicity*. Newbury Park, CA: Sage Publications.

Park, R.C. (1950). *Race and culture*. New York: Free Press.

Chapter 2

Therapeutic Interventions with Elders of Japanese Ancestry

Anne O. Freed

A place in the sun for most tends to obscure the reality that for minorities that place may be in the shadows. (Sata, 1973, p. 153)

As is true when intervening therapeutically with people of all cultures, human services providers who serve individual elderly people of Japanese ancestry in the United States must address their problems in light of that particular subgroup's unique cultural characteristics. This chapter is designed to help such providers by identifying the many special cultural features of elderly Japanese that can be pertinent when offering social and health services and conducting therapeutic interventions.

In addition to applying professional skills, human services personnel must be generally knowledgeable about the last stage of the life cycle, as well as traditional Japanese attitudes toward old age and how they may be modified by their acculturation in the United States. Although professionals of Japanese ancestry might be aware of these cultural factors, most non-Japanese professionals should become sensitive to the customs and values inherited from Japan as well as how they have been modified by their experience in the United States.

This chapter discusses several important facts about people of Japanese ancestry that effective professionals should know:

1. Who they are; how they identify and define themselves
2. Their history and experiences in the United States

9

3. Their inherited culture and behavior, assimilation, acculturation, and culture conflicts
4. How they handle health, mental health, and social and personal problems; what services are available; where they seek help
5. Considerations in therapeutic interventions

Foreigners in Japan inevitably hear, "We Japanese are unique; we
are different from other people in every way." As evidence of their
claimed uniqueness, they point out that they were isolated for
hundreds of years on their small island chain; that they have unique
history, rituals, beliefs, values, religions, and ceremonies; and that
only since 1853, when America's Admiral Perry opened their country to the West, have they been seriously exposed to outside influences, industrialization, and urbanization, after centuries of feu-
dalism and militarism. They hasten to add that, despite the fact that
after the American Occupation following World War II, they rapidly westernized and modernized their political and economic systems, their approach to family, religion, problem solving, interpersonal relations, and emphasis on group identity and consensus,
rather than individualism, remained thoroughly Japanese.

Knowledge of these factual and attitudinal differences should
help American professionals recognize basic Japanese cultural values and note how much acculturation has occurred in order to help
Japanese Americans.

HOW PEOPLE OF JAPANESE ANCESTRY
IN THE UNITED STATES IDENTIFY
AND DEFINE THEMSELVES

Although Japanese-American roots extend back to Japan ethnically, culturally, and historically, the strength of those roots, in the
process of assimilation and acculturation, inevitably is diluted with
each generation. Moreover, although the Japanese insist that they are
ethnically homogeneous, Japanese Americans are actually almost as
diverse as people of other foreign backgrounds in the United States.
In large numbers, they are either marrying people of other Asian
groups or Caucasians, or they are offspring of such unions (Kikimura

and Kitano, 1980). Like other ethnic minorities, they are either immigrants or native born, and speak English with varying degrees of proficiency. Although Japanese ethnicity and culture is increasingly being diluted, they are not rejecting their Japanese identity.

Japanese Americans refer to themselves by successive generations numerically. Because their immigration to the United States started toward the end of the nineteenth century, there are four generations here thus far. They are the *issei*, born in Japan and, hence, the first generation in the United States; the *nisei*, the first generation born in this country and, hence, the second generation; the *sansei*, the children of the nisei and, hence, the third generation; and the *yonsei*, their children and the fourth generation. Those terms are derived from the Japanese numbers of *ichi* (1), *ni* (2), *san* (3), and *yon* (4). Most of the pre-World War II issei have died, and relatively few issei have come to the United States even after the 1965 law opened immigration to Asians. Thus, the overwhelming numbers of elderly Japanese are nisei.

Demography

In 1990, there were 847,562 people of Japanese ancestry in the United States, more than half of whom lived in California and Hawaii. Of these, 12 percent were over sixty-five (Sakauye, 1993), and 63 percent were American born. California had 213,280, and Hawaii had 217,290. Forty-three percent of the elderly were men and 56 percent were women, 40 percent of whom lived alone. All but 6 percent of the elderly had been or were still married and 4.5 percent were in institutions (U.S. Bureau of the Census, 1992).

However, census figures generally understate the numbers of Asian elderly. They often are "apt to be underrepresented because they are among the most mistrustful of government agencies, suffer the greatest language handicaps, and are often poorly informed" (Kalish and Yuen, 1973, p. 9). Their World War II experiences in the United States continue to feed this mistrust.

Older Japanese women are the most proficient in English among Asian Americans in the United States (Burr and Mutchler, 1993). Primarily urbanites and suburbanites, 85 percent of the elderly now live in the metropolitan areas of Honolulu, Los Angeles, San Francisco, Chicago, New York, and Seattle (Fujii, 1980).

Myth and Reality

A common myth in the United States suggests that people of Japanese ancestry, along with the Chinese, are models of financially and educationally successful minorities and, therefore, suffer no adjustment problems, as presumably demonstrated by their apparent low juvenile delinquency rate and little use of mental health resources (Kitano, 1973a). Some even claim that the Japanese have overcome past discrimination and have no residual problems. However, in fact, a number of Japanese elders have low incomes; they have more two-wage-earner families than Caucasians; college graduates do not earn salaries equal to their Caucasian colleagues; and those living in Japantowns or Little Tokyos suffer from ghetto-type environments (Kitano, 1973b).

It is also questionable that their low reported rate of mental illness is a reliable indicator of good adjustment. This myth reflects a cultural reluctance to admit to emotional problems, as well as certain physical illnesses, because of the disgrace this will bring upon the family and the harm it will cause to their children's marital eligibility. Therefore, such problems are kept secret within the family (Fujii, 1980; Kitano, 1973b). As a community analyst with the War Relocation authority during World War II, this author observed this phenomenon among families in the Tule Lake Relocation Center.

History and Experiences of the Japanese in the United States

At the start of Japanese immigration to the United States in the 1880s and early 1900s, most were young, unskilled males, poor farmers and laborers, who sought work in farming, gardening, canneries, mines, and railroad construction. Later came the traders and small entrepreneurs. Their history was one of toil and struggle, severe discrimination, low economic status, and poor education. In addition, they remained isolated and "different" because of their religion, their unique language, their special writing system, and their physical appearance.

Being poor single males, after a number of years they sent to Japan for younger picture brides. Thus, a considerable age gap existed within the issei families, and especially between issei fathers and their nisei children.

Before World War II, racist attitudes led to self-contained, cohesive urban and rural Japanese communities where many had become successful farmers who were perceived as economic competitors by their Caucasian counterparts (Kalish and Yuen, 1973; Spicer et al., 1969; Takaki, 1989). The Japanese established extensive protective mutual aid associations, credit unions, religious institutions, newspapers, language schools, and cultural and recreational groups.

From the beginning, they suffered severe discrimination. In fact, the Alien Land Law of 1913 forbade aliens to own land; issei could only lease agricultural tracts. Furthermore, issei were legally barred from American citizenship. The Immigration Act of 1924 forbade Japanese immigration entirely. When the attack on Pearl Harbor occurred, the antagonism against Japanese living on the West Coast rose to a fury, declaring them un-American, enemies, and an international menace (Ogawa, 1973) who belonged to a "strange and inassimilable culture" (Kikimura and Kitano, 1980, p. 3). The culmination of the hostility and prejudice was Presidential Executive Order 9066, which ordered the evacuation of 120,000 Japanese citizens and aliens from the West Coast, for detention in ten relocation centers, which was a migration "more than the whole population of the Five Civilized Indian Tribes who were similarly dealt with a century ago—[and] has become, like the Indian 'Trail of Tears' before it, a theme of our literature" (Spicer et al., 1969, p. 1). They spent the next three years behind barbwire fences, living in tar paper barracks, which they referred to as "concentration camps," located in remote swamps, deserts, or wastelands.

Camp life was communal; family roles were reversed as nisei were designated community leaders by the War Relocation Authority, and the social and psychological pressures of the community became more influential than that of the issei head of the family. Previous family solidarity, loyalty, and standards could no longer be maintained. In fact, some parents, fearing ultimate deportation to Japan, clung to their children, demanding that they declare themselves "disloyal" to the United States. Some obeyed, while others joined the all-nisei 442nd Regiment of the United States Army (Spicer et al., 1969). Actually, no people were deported.

Twenty years later, a study by Morishima (1970) found that one-fourth of those interviewed stated that, because of the evacuation, they "made conscious efforts after the war to be more American because they thought the pre-war isolation of the Japanese-American community contributed to their being seen as alien and they should 'act more like Americans and raise their children as Americans'" (Morishima, 1970, p. 15). In contrast, others were more cynical about American democracy and refused to discuss the evacuation with their children. Some even felt that in the centers they had been "Japanized" by their peers. Clearly, the evacuation left its psychological scars on the nisei, creating for some "a cultural paranoia" (Sata, 1973, p. 157).

Many of today's elderly nisei Japanese still feel scarred by their residence in the camps. To help them today, professionals must be aware of this trauma. It is a great irony that, in light of the experience, today they are considered to be model Asian-American citizens.

After the war, the Japanese Americans recreated their former communities, rebuilt economic and social institutions, established small businesses, and entered service occupations and professions. They also addressed community issues of poverty, health care, housing, crime, and delinquency, and offered support services through churches, credit unions, prefectural associations, and social and cultural organizations employing professionally trained Japanese Americans (Murase, 1995).

CULTURAL INFLUENCES
ON AMERICANS OF JAPANESE ANCESTRY

The Individual, the Family, and the Group

Many Japanese traditions and customs are still evident in the Japanese-American community, however diluted by American culture. From the Japanese culture its members inherited rigidly defined rules and roles of loyalty and responsibility to the family, respect for the elders and immediate ancestors, and the filial duty of the older son to care for his elderly parents; subservience of women; the patriarchal and patrilineal family structure; and expectations that women will help care for their mothers-in-law and bear a male child (Christopher, 1983; Lebra, 1986; Murase, 1995; Reischauer, 1978). The group, which might be the immediate family, the extended family, or the community, is more important than the individual and demands loyalty and conformity because each member's behavior reflects upon the group. Guilt and shame are methods of control over the individual.

Because conflicts within the family must be minimized to avoid disrupting family relations, family values stress "the need to approach problems subtly and indirectly rather than openly" (Sue, 1981, p. 121). Family members are expected to submerge aggressive tendencies, prolong dependence, suppress independent desires, and conform to the group in order to preserve the family reputation (Burr and Mutchler, 1993; Kikimura and Kitano, 1980; Lebra, 1986; Murphey and Murphey, 1968). "Bad behavior is handled in the privacy of the family. Deviations are suppressed and mental illness hidden or denied. Obligations and responsibilities stress that children must always be grateful for what their parents have done or are doing for them, and they must not be selfish and inconsiderate" (Sue, 1981, p. 121). Traditional Japanese therapies are based on these premises.

The nisei family here, as in Japan, consists of one or two children with the "education mother" pressuring the children to study hard and get a college education. Divorces are rare (1.6 percent). Unlike in Japan, where outmarriages are discouraged, in the United States, over 50 percent have outmarried (Kikimura and Kitano, 1980). In both countries, traditional women's roles are being challenged, with the nisei women favoring more egalitarian roles, while nisei males still prefer male dominance (Sue, 1973). Nevertheless, the tradition of women presenting themselves as proper, unaggressive, modest, and passive persists in both countries (Fujitomi and Wong, 1973; Murase, 1995).

Respect-the-Elderly Tradition

Respect-the-Elders Day is celebrated annually in Japan, reflecting the fact that 41 percent of elders live with married sons and 34 percent with married daughters (Asano and Saito, 1988). However, they join their children's household well after the traditional age of sixty. Most elders still live with a spouse; only 5.7 percent live alone (Asano and Saito, 1988).

In contrast, in the United States, the issei and nisei favor having elderly parents live nearby; only 12.6 percent of the parents and 7.6 percent of the daughters feel that they should share a household (Goodman, 1990). Nevertheless, 50 percent actually live with one of their children.

Government programs for the elderly in Japan are more generous than in the United States. All are entitled to pensions, free medical care, and homemaker and home health services. Nursing homes, homes for the aged, and assisted-living apartments are expanding, and senior and community welfare centers and respite and day care services have proliferated. Many elderly belong to senior clubs and attend educational programs. However, a study of institutionalized aged found that those with psychiatric disorders received inadequate treatment (Hasegawa, 1982). By good fortune, planning is underway to prepare new resources for the elderly, because by 2020, one-fourth of the population will be over sixty. The pressure for increased services also arises in response to the fact that many Japanese married women are working and cannot care for seriously frail elders (Sodei, 1986).

Despite the traditional views that aged are revered and wise (Palmore and Maeda, 1985), considerable ambivalence and negativism on that notion is found (Koyano, 1989; Tobin, 1987). Koyano's study of attitudes toward the aged confirmed that there have always been two faces to claims of respect for the elderly in Japan: the overt or professed *(tatemae)* and the covert or actual *(honne)*. "The Japanese respect for the elderly is merely *tatemae*" (Koyano, 1989, p. 343). *Tatemae* respects the wisdom of aged, while *honne* thoughts view the aged with indifference and scorn and consider them infantile and silly (Doi, 1986).

Religion

Of the 100,000 Buddhists in the United States (U.S. Bureau of the Census, 1992), the Japanese Americans are only a small percentage. Non-Buddhists generally belong to Japanese-Methodist, Japanese-United, or Catholic churches. The younger Japanese generally join American churches or remain unaffiliated. Even the Japanese-American Buddhist churches model their procedures and social organizations after Christian churches. There are no Shinto shrines in the mainland United States.

The Japanese Buddhist and Shinto religions do not have a conception of a God that exists abstractly, separate from the human world. Sin and reward or punishment in an afterlife are alien concepts (Christopher, 1983). Buddhism stresses meditation, self-discipline, the philosophy of pure thought, and the importance of achieving Nirvana (World Almanac, 1991). However, women can never attain this ultimate state of being. Shintoism, based on animism, focuses on worshiping natural phenomena and mythological ancestors and, until the end of World War II, included Emperor worship and militarism (Nakane, 1973). Interestingly, Reischauer (1978) observes that Buddhism in Japan ". . . is not for many a leitmotif in either their intellectual or emotional lives" (p. 217). In fact, while in Japan few are Christian, the Japanese are attracted by its Western concepts, ethics, and emphasis on education and social work. But religion occupies a "peripheral position" in this secular society as a result of its Confucian philosophical background that emphasizes "right thinking and right living, loyalty to the ruler, filial piety to one's father, and strict observations of proper social ritual and etiquette" (Reischauer, 1978, p. 213).

Because the Japanese believe in an afterlife but not in reincarnation, there is no heaven or hell for them. Instead, the dead retain a continuing powerful presence to which one can pray for help in bad times. Suicide is not frowned upon; cremation is practiced; death is part of the continuity of life; and each Buddhist and Shinto household in Japan has an altar to remember and communicate with dead relatives who are considered residents to be fed, greeted, and consulted. The dead are believed to become Buddhas. Thus, because the Japanese are reluctant to share their problems with the living, some talk to the dead. Death is accepted with serenity, not fear. However, they tend to deny that they might die; they do not make wills; and doctors rarely tell dying patients they are terminally ill (Kristof, 1996).

Language and Communication

According to former ambassador Reischauer (1978), "It is more difficult for Japanese to learn English than it is for many other people" (p. 381). Not only is the Japanese language different in grammar and construction, but the culture and customs encourage ambiguity, vagueness, and unclarity in communication, rather than directness and openness (Christopher, 1983).

> The Japanese, with their suspicion of verbal skills, their confidence in non-verbal understanding, their desire for consensus decisions, and thus eagerness to avoid personal confrontation, do a great deal more beating around the verbal bush than we do and usually try to avoid the "frankly speaking" approach so dear to Americans. They prefer, in their writing as well as their talk, a loose structure of argument rather than logical reasoning, and suggestion or illustration rather than sharp, clear statements. (Reischauer, 1978, p. 386)

Given the linguistic complexity and cultural inhibitions, even Japanese-speaking professionals need to develop interviewing skills that bring out facts and feelings, clarify ambiguities, and sensitively recognize that omissions need not reflect resistance, evasion, or confusion. Problems of communication are more difficult when using interpreters who translate too literally, make errors, distort, and do not recognize subtleties and nonverbal communications, given that elders try to mask anxiety and are reluctant to share inner feelings (Freed, 1988).

Mental Health of the Aged of Japanese Ancestry

Lacking scientific data about the mental health of Japanese, Americans sing their praises for having no mental health problems. Kitano (1973b), a nisei social work professor, researching the use of therapeutic resources in the Japanese-American community, found that the three generations seldom used these resources, including hospitalization. Also, it was primarily the nisei who sought other Japanese community services. However, 60 percent of the professionals he surveyed thought that the three generations needed help, but did not seek it because acting-out behavior in public was generally suppressed by the strong, cohesive community, which shaped members' behavior in order to minimize acting-out and maintain a strong group identity. In their practice, these professionals did note many expressions of underlying anxieties, tensions, and conflicts between husbands and wives and parents and children that were defended against by politeness and withdrawal in response to these social controls.

Kitano (1973b) stated that the Japanese Chamber of Commerce in the United States reported that in the 1970s about sixty cases of schizophrenia were referred annually to public facilities. These were mostly issei men over fifty-five living on Social Security or public assistance and that, once hospitalized, they remained longer because they were severely disturbed. Kitano (1973b) and Murase (1995) conclude that although mental illness is not a serious problem among Japanese Americans, they suffer from emotional difficulties and handle pain and frustration by turning inward.

Because they reject individualism, older Japanese Americans think only in terms of group identification with the family and the community. They blame themselves rather than external forces when things go wrong, are fatalistic, accept what exists, and tolerate frustration. Finally, Japanese in general tend to sacrifice personal creativity and leadership to avoid being different and standing out.

In Japan, psychiatric problems are considered primarily physiological or neurological, treatable by psychopharmacology and shock therapy rather than psychotherapy. Fear of hereditary taint leads to hiding emotional problems from the public. Mental illness among the aged is ignored, hidden, or denied. Even mental health clinics in Japanese-American communities must repeatedly interpret the need to acknowledge emotional problems and change these cultural inhibitions in order to treat their illnesses (Sue and McKinney, 1980).

Some of the maladaptive behavior seen in the United States is a response by Japanese Americans to their past marginal position in the American society that led them to internalize their rage and frustrations. They defend against stress by denial, repression, and somatization. Younger nisei are obsessed with educational achievements, while the older are consumed with hard work. Some escape from stress through alcoholism and gambling (Baker, 1994).

Mental health programs for Japanese elderly are directed to two distinct populations, the 37 percent foreign-born and those who speak English. Even the nisei elderly have differences in attitudes toward expressing emotional distress and seeking help outside the family depending upon levels of acculturation. This is important because the elderly have the highest suicide rate of older ethnic Americans, from 9.93 per 100,000 population for those ages fifty-five to sixty-four to as high as 62.59 for those eighty-five and older (Baker, 1994). The rate for males is much higher than for females. Historically, Japanese culture-sanctioned ritual suicide in reaction to failures or loss of face. Baker (1994) further reports that, "In the 1980s, Japanese men in the United States who are depressed by material competitiveness of their economy select suicide as a way to opt out of the 'rat race'" (p. 258). The high rate for women is due to isolation after loss of family members, loss of the traditional family role, and conflict between cultures over the role of women. Therefore, Baker (1994) recommended more resources, such as midday meals, group socialization, and "adopted grandparent" programs for those who have no families.

Japanese-American mental health professionals agree that it is difficult to establish diagnoses of elders highly identified with the Japanese culture because of Eastern values of stoicism and self-sacrifice (Reischauer, 1978) as well as the inadequacy of using interpreters (Freed, 1988; Sakauye, 1993). It is particularly difficult and confusing to distinguish culturally "normal" behavior from psychopathology, especially when diagnosing schizophrenia and clinical depression. Elders with those conditions generally are overdependent upon their families, have difficulty learning English, and lack social involvements. New immigrants suffer the highest incidence of mental illness (Sakauye, 1993).

Many American-born Japanese adopt a learned helplessness stance (Sakauye, 1993; Sue 1980; Walsh, 1995) in adapting to the American culture because of confusion and conflict in ethnic identity. They blame their difficulties on the Japanese culture rather than accepting their personal inhibitions or limitations. As a result, they are overly cautious, inhibited, deferential to authority, and unsure of when to be active or passive. When requesting help outside the family, they tend to withhold and act paranoid out of insecurity. Even though, after World War II, the Chicago Psychoanalytic Institute offered therapy to nisei who had been in relocation centers and suffered from deficits in self-esteem and "cohesion of the self," thirty years later, these affects persisted. Even sansei, who had not been in the camps, showed extreme anger and bitterness about prejudice against Japanese, yet were unempathic with their parents' and grandparents' helplessness or indifference (Walsh, 1995).

In treating health and emotional problems of elderly Japanese, practitioners use a combination of acupuncture, herbal medications, Western medicines, and Western or Japanese Morita and Naikan psychotherapy. Naikan therapy (Lebra, 1986), which is based on the *moral* concept of social conformity and the motivation to change one's behavior, involves intense reflection on reciprocal relations between the patient and others, and the importance of gratitude and human interdependence. It stresses confrontation of guilt, unworthiness, and the need to be loved in spite of weaknesses and failings. Morita therapy teaches anxious, perfectionistic, phobic, and self-preoccupied patients to accept their symptoms and attribute them to personal strong ideals and to participate in life without waiting for anxiety to dissipate. Anxiety is reduced through the treatment relationship, which directs them away from self-preoccupation (Lebra, 1986; Makinodan and Harada, 1996).

HEALTH ISSUES AMONG JAPANESE ELDERLY

Very few Japanese-American health studies are reported in the literature. The University of California's Medical Treatment Effectiveness Program Center for Asian and Pacific Islanders, established in 1992, did find that Asian community members have better or equal health compared with non-Latino American whites, "but are less satisfied and feel less a partner in doctor-patient relationships compared to other ethnic groups" (Freed, 1990, p. 10). They report that Asians changed medications twice as often and reported side effects twice as frequently, compared to non-Latino American whites. Other studies indicate problems among Japanese elderly of osteoporosis, hip fractures, somatization, hypertension, and overconcern with bodily functions, although they have better health than non-Latino whites. However, because Japanese use health facilities sparingly, are reluctant to reveal personal health information, and carry a lower level of health insurance, they "may have a different perception of health-related quality of life as compared to other groups" (Sakauye, 1993, p. 103).

Until recently, elderly Japanese rejected nursing homes, assuming that they would be cared for by their families. It was considered shameful for children to place a parent in a nursing home (Yeo, 1993). However, intergenerational solidarity, especially between foreign parents and their Japanese-American children, has been weakened by acculturation and situational stresses, and in both Japan and the United States, use of nursing homes is increasing (Yeo and McGann, 1986). In the United States, Japanese Americans are building their own or joining with other Asians, given their "cultural aversion" to utilizing American institutions. They prefer their own ethnic foods, programs, activities, volunteers, religious practices, traditional holidays, and family participation in the nursing home, as well as an ethnic staff that understands and adapts to their non-Western dietary preferences and value system of duty and respect, and understands the residual effects of their internment in relocation centers (Burr and Mutchler, 1993).

Finally, Yeo and McGann (1986), concerned with minority elderly health services, recommended that more family physicians should receive culturally sensitive geriatric training, know community resources to which to refer patients for ancillary health and social services, and work as members of a multidisciplinary team when serving ethnic elderly.

SOCIAL AND HEALTH SERVICES
AVAILABLE TO JAPANESE ELDERLY

Social and health services* are provided by Japanese and Asian-American agencies and clinics in large American cities and in a number of smaller West Coast communities. The elders are drawn primarily to such concrete bilingual services as senior centers, Japanese lunch, nutrition, recreation, education, home aide, companion, friendly visitors programs, meals-on-wheels, case management, caregiver support groups, information, long-term planning, transportation, telephone reassurance, and escort services. Larger cities offer shared-living homes, independent-living apartments, and nursing homes. Many social agencies assist non-English-speaking Japanese to prepare for citizenship

---

*The following information was received by the author from Japanese-American agencies' reports across the country, particularly from the West Coast, where the largest number of Japanese elders live.

and obtain Social Security, Medicare, housing, passport applications, and public welfare. Japanese family service agencies and clinics provide much needed counseling and health services by professionally trained staff. Even when nisei and sansei professionals do not speak Japanese, the elderly feel more comfortable with them. It is, therefore, imperative that Japanese Americans obtain professional training, and non-Japanese who serve Japanese elders must learn about Japanese culture, behavior, and attitudes.

Because 50 percent of the Japanese-American elderly live with their children (Burr and Mutchler, 1993; Goodman, 1990; Kamo and Zhou, 1994), the entire family inevitably is involved when the elderly need health and counseling services. They require the bicultural experience of asserting their needs because it is necessary in order to preserve culture. The professionals of Japanese ancestry and those of non-Japanese background, in counseling elderly Japanese Americans, need to be aware of the Japanese culturally prescribed personality that expects internalization of conflicts and discourages acknowledgment or sharing of these with others, even sometimes within the family. By understanding this process and the culture, and by empathizing with them in recognition of their struggle with this cultural mandate, hopefully it will make it possible for them to express their feelings to be free to find another aspect of the self, one that is more cohesive (Sue, 1980, p. 300).

Because of these cultural inhibitions, professionals must be aware that, when elders of Japanese ancestry come for help, "The presenting problem is likely to be a severe dysfunction beyond the coping capacity of the individual and family and likely involves severe family breakdown, acute psychopathology, addiction, or stress" (Murase, 1995, p. 246). In working with such families, professionals must be aware of the client's guilt and shame, generalize the problem, support family and group roles, agree upon the goals and plans, and remain family focused. Murase even suggests that a directive and "professionally authoritative" approach is appropriate with these families.

More research is needed on Japanese health and emotional problems, on how to overcome their denial and repression of such problems, and on appropriate outreach methods to counteract their resistances. In addition, while a good deal is known about the Japanese cultural heritage, research on the influence of American culture on the Japanese family, as well as studies of these influences on their approach to health, mental health, interpersonal relations, and interpersonal conflict, will teach us a great deal about adaptation and acculturation.

In conclusion, it is understandable that many American-born Japanese elderly, having lived through severe discrimination and having inherited from their parents and grandparents a reliance on the family, will prefer to turn to their own ethnic group for help and empathy. However, both Japanese-American and non-Asian professionals, whether offering counseling, health care, research, or public services, or formulating public policies relevant to minorities, must know Japanese history, psychology, and culture. "By attempting to understand today's older Asians, who were yesterday's pioneers and folk heroes, we may be better prepared to provide for those who will be elderly in the future" (Fujii, 1980, p. 222).

REFERENCES

Asano, H. and Saito, C. (1988). Social service delivery and social work practice. *Journal of Gerontological Social Work, 12* (1/2), 131-151.

Baker, F.M. (1994). Suicide among ethnic elderly: A statistical and psychosocial perspective. *Journal of Geriatric Psychiatry, 27* (2), 258.

Burr, J. and Mutchler, J. (1993). Nativity, acculturation and economic status: Living arrangements in later life. *Journal of Gerontology: Social Sciences, 48* (2), 55-63.

Christopher, R. (1983). *The Japanese mind.* New York: Fawcett Columbine.

Doi, T. (1986). *The anatomy of self: The individual versus society.* New York: Kodansha International.

Freed, A. (1988, July-August). Interviewing through an interpreter. *Social Work, 33* (4), 315-319.

Freed, A. (1990). How Japanese families cope with fragile elderly. *Journal of Gerontological Social Work, 15* (1/2), 39.

Fujii, S.M. (1980). Elderly Asian Americans and the use of public services. In R. Endo, S. Sue, and N.N. Wagner (Eds.), *Asian Americans: Social and psychological perspectives.* Vol. 2. Palo Alto, CA: Science and Behavior Books; 217-222.

Fujitomi, I. and Wong, D. (1973). The new Asian-American woman. In S. Sue and N. Wagner (Eds.), *Asian Americans: Psychological perspectives.* Palo Alto, CA: Science and Behavior Books; 252-263.

Goodman, C. (1990). The caregiving roles of Asian American women. *Journal of Aging and Women, 2* (1), 109-120.

Hasegawa, K. (1982). Psychiatric investigation of the institutionalized aged people. *Japanese Journal of Gerontology, 4,* 29-51.

Kalish, R.A. and Yuen, S.Y. (1973). Americans of East Asian ancestry: Aging and the aged. In S. Sue and N. Wagner (Eds.), *Asian Americans: Psychological perspectives.* Vol. 2. Palo Alto, CA: Science and Behavior Books; 236-251.

Kamo, Y. and Zhou, M. (August 1994). Living arrangements of elderly Chinese and Japanese in the US. *Journal of Marriage and the Family, 56* (2), 544.

Kikimura, A. and Kitano, H. (1980). Interracial marriage: A picture of Japanese Americans. In R. Endo, S. Sue, and N. Wagner (Eds.), *Asian Americans: Social and psychological perspectives.* Vol. 2. Palo Alto, CA: Science and Behavior Books; 26-35.

Kitano, H. (1973a). Japanese Americans crime and delinquency. In S. Sue and N. Wagner (Eds.), *Asian Americans: Psychological perspectives.* Palo Alto, CA: Science and Behavior Books; 161-170.

Kitano, H. (1973b). Japanese Americans mental illness. In S. Sue and N. Wagner (Eds.), *Asian Americans: Psychological perspectives.* Palo Alto, CA: Science and Behavior Books; 181-201.

Koyano, W. (1989). Japanese attitudes toward the elderly: A review of research findings. *Journal of Cross-Cultural Gerontology, 4* (4), 335-345.

Kristof, N. (1996, September 29). Don't break family ties. *New York Times,* p. 1, col. 1.

Lebra, T.S. (1986). *Japanese patterns of behavior.* Honolulu: University of Hawaii Press.

Makinodan, T. and Harada, N. (1996). Medical health outcome studies in the Asian and Pacific Islander American population. *Asian American and Pacific Islander Journal of Health, 4* (1-3), 10.

Morishima, J.K. (1970). The evacuation: Impact on the family. In S. Sue and N. Wagner (Eds.), *Asian Americans: Psychological perspectives.* Palo Alto, CA: Science and Behavior Books; 3-12.

Murase, K. (1995). Asian Americans: Japanese. *Encyclopedia of social work.* Vol. 1 (Nineteenth edition). Washington, DC: NASW Press; 246.

Murphey, G. and Murphey, L. (1968). *Asian psychology.* New York: Basic Books.

Nakane, C. (1973). *Japanese society.* Rutland, VT: Charles Tuttle Co.

Ogawa, D. (1973). The Japanese Image. In S. Sue and N. Wagner (Eds.), *Asian Americans: Psychological perspectives.* Palo Alto, CA: Science and Behavior Books; 3-12.

Palmore, E. and Maeda, D. (1985). *Honorable elders revised.* Durham, NC: Duke University Press.

Reischauer, E. (Ed.). (1978). *The Japanese.* Cambridge, MA: Belnap Harvard University Press.

Sakauye, K. (1993). The elderly Asian patient. *Journal of Geriatric Psychiatry, 25* (1), 85.

Sata, L. (1973). Musings of a hyphenated American. In S. Sue and N. Wagner (Eds.), *Asian Americans: Psychological perspectives.* Palo Alto, CA: Science and Behavior Books; 150-160.

Sodei, T. (1986, January). Older women in Japan. Paper delivered at Women's Initiative of American Association of Retired Persons, Washington, DC.

Spicer, E., Hanson, A., Luomola, K., and Opler, M. (1969). *Impounded people.* Tucson, AZ: University of Arizona Press.

Sue, D.W. (1973). Ethnic identity: The impact of two cultures on the psychological development of Asians in America. In S. Sue and N. Wagner (Eds.), *Asian Americans: Psychological perspectives.* Palo Alto, CA: Science and Behavior Books; 140-149.

Sue, D.W. (1981). *Counseling the culturally different: Theory and practice.* New York: John Wiley and Sons.

Sue, S. (1980). Psychological theory and implications for Asian Americans. In R. Endo, S. Sue, and N.N. Wagner (Eds.), *Asian Americans: Social and psychological perspectives.* Vol. 2. Palo Alto, CA: Science and Behavior Books; 288-303.

Sue, S. and McKinney, H. (1980). Asian Americans in the community mental health care system. In R. Endo, S. Sue, and N.N. Wagner (Eds.), *Asian Americans: Social and psychological perspectives.* Vol. 2. Palo Alto, CA: Science and Behavior Books; 223-230.

Takaki, R. (1989). *Strangers from a different land.* Boston: Little, Brown and Co.

Tobin, J. (1987), The American idealization of old age in Japan. *The Gerontologist, 27,* 53-58.

U.S. Bureau of the Census (1992). *1990 Census of population—General population characteristics.* Washington, DC: U.S. Government Printing Office.

Walsh, R. (1995). Asian psychotherapies. In R. Corsini and D. Wedding (Eds.), *Current psychotherapies.* Fifth edition. Itaska, IL: F.E. Peacock Publishers.

World almanac (1991). New York: Pharos Books.

Yeo, G. (1993). Ethnicity and nursing homes: Factors affecting use and successful components for culturally sensitive care. In C. Barresi and D. Stull (Eds.), *Ethnic elderly and long-term care.* New York: Springer Publishing Co.; 168.

Yeo, G. and McGann, L. (1986). Utilization of family physicians in support services for elderly patients. *Journal of Family Practice, 22* (5), 431-434.

Chapter 3

Vietnamese-American Elders

Dung Ngo
Thanh V. Tran

There is no doubt that elderly Vietnamese Americans have suffered from many economic, health, psychological, and social problems. This chapter aims to address the Vietnamese immigration experience and the clinical approaches to the elderly Vietnamese population.

A BRIEF HISTORY
OF VIETNAMESE IMMIGRATION

During the decade from 1960 to 1970, the number of Vietnamese living in the United States was less than 4,000 individuals (*Statistical Yearbook of the INS,* 1991). This population, however, has increased rapidly within the last two decades. The influx of Vietnamese into the United States can be classified into two cohorts: the first arrived in the spring of 1975; the second began to arrive in the late 1970s and the early 1980s.

The First Wave

When the government of South Vietnam was defeated by the North Vietnamese Communist forces on April 30, 1975, approximately 65,000 Vietnamese immediately fled the country for safety (Gall and Natividad, 1995). Many of these individuals had little or no time to prepare for the rushed evacuation. As a result, thousands of families were separated and many family members perished during the chaos. Many risked their lives to flee Vietnam on small boats or by whatever means were available, hoping to be rescued by U.S. Navy ships. By the end of 1975, approximately 125,000 Vietnamese refugees had arrived in the United States (Office of Refugee Resettlement, 1993).

Until they could find a stable living arrangement, the Vietnamese refugees were housed temporarily at the following military bases: Fort Indiantown Gap in Pennsylvania, Eglin Air Force Base in Florida, Fort Chaffee in Arkansas, and Camp Pendleton located in California. At these locations, they were offered English classes and cultural orientation workshops. The United States government aimed to minimize the disruption of economic resources on local communities by dispersing Vietnamese refugees around the nation. However, the policymakers failed to recognize that once the Vietnamese refugees resettled in their new communities, they had the freedom to move wherever they liked.

Secondary Migration

Shortly after their resettlement in the assigned states, the Vietnamese began their "secondary migration" (Office of Refugee Resettlement, 1993). Family reunification, better employment opportunities, and warmer climates were the most common reasons leading many Vietnamese to undertake this second migration movement. Extended family members moved closer together for emotional and financial support. In addition, many Vietnamese, especially the elders, soon realized that the harsh winter environment in the northern states was unbearable. They gradually found their way to more comfortable climatic regions. As a result, the Vietnamese population has concentrated among the southern states and the West Coast, with particularly high concentrations in California and Texas.

Vietnamese refugees who escaped from their native land during the first wave possessed characteristics that are different from their subsequent compatriots. For example, many adults of the first wave generally had attained higher levels of education. For the most part, they were educators, doctors, lawyers, high-ranked military officials, and government personnel who had political ties with the United States. Additionally, many of these individuals were urban habitants. They were more affluent and possessed a better command of the English language compared to their subsequent refugee compatriots. These characteristics—previous exposure to Western ways of life, familiarity with the English language, better education, and transferable professional skills—were critical for the initial adjustment process to the new country. Indeed, a decade later their economic achievements are comparable with the majority of the U.S. population (Hanes, 1992).

The Second Wave

It was during the late 1970s and the early 1980s that the second wave of Vietnamese immigration began. Immediately after the war ended, the communists began mass persecution of thousands of former Vietnamese government personnel, military officials, and those who had connections with or had worked for the U.S. government. A large number of these individuals were forced into reeducation camps where they underwent terrifying and inhumane treatment, including severe torture, malnutrition, illness without medical care, indoctrination, and manual labor. In addition, the Vietnamese communist government forced thousands of people into the so-called "economic zone." These "zones" often were located in remote and underdeveloped areas.

Another important factor for the second exodus of Vietnamese refugees was the involvement of Vietnam in the Cambodian war in the late 1970s. Many adolescents and young adults were forced to fight the war in the foreign land. Thousands of Vietnamese citizens, unable to bear the harsh oppression, persecution, and war, poured to the open sea in overcrowded boats. Although the price for freedom was high, it did not discourage these individuals from risking their lives for the taste of freedom—a freedom they might not live to enjoy if they remained in Vietnam. Out of desperation, many would rather risk death than continue to live under brutal communist rule.

Unlike their first-wave counterparts, the second-wave refugees escaped in secret for fear of being caught by communist officials. The boats were often unequipped for crossing the perilous sea. The poorly planned escapes often resulted in food and fuel shortages. Many overloaded boats capsized. Thousands of men, women, and children were robbed, kidnapped, raped, and killed by pirates in the Gulf of Thailand. Many boats were denied entry into neighboring countries, leading to higher death rates. The phenomenon of second-wave refugees, known as the "boat people," consequently captured international attention (Kleinman, 1990).

As the Vietnamese boat people phenomenon became desperate, the United Nations and the United States felt morally obligated to confront this tragedy. Within the span of only four years (1978- 1982), the United States granted residency status to approximately 280,500 second-wave Vietnamese refugees (Gall and Natividad, 1995).

Many neighboring countries of Vietnam, which had once closed their eyes to these vulnerable refugees, now contracted with the United Nations to establish temporary asylums on their own soil. From these asylums, the Vietnamese awaited to be sponsored by relatives from the first wave, churches, charity organizations, and voluntary agencies (VOLAG). Many of these asylums were overcrowded, unsanitary, and not well-equipped medically. The stay in these camps for many was exhausting and hopeless. Some individuals waited for as long as seven years before they were granted permission to resettle in the United States, Canada, or Europe. The waiting period was often emotionally draining for many individuals who were without a sponsor.

In sharp contrast to the Vietnamese who left in 1975, members of the second wave were less educated and possessed fewer professional skills that could be readily transferred in the host country. A large number of the second-wave refugees had less formal education and limited command of the English language. Many had been farmers or fishermen in Vietnam. Consequently, they encountered greater difficulty in adjusting to the new country than their predecessors. The number of the second-wave refugees increased steadily until the mid-1980s. Immigration of Vietnamese almost came to a halt in the early 1990s due to more stringent criteria for refugee status. A new screening procedure was implemented to differentiate between "political refugees" and "economic refugees." As a result, those who did not qualify for political refugee status and those without a sponsor were forced to repatriate to Vietnam.

Special Groups of Vietnamese Refugees in the United States

Due to the constant increase of Vietnamese refugees risking their lives on the treacherous sea, the U.S. Congress passed the Refugee

Act in 1980 (Office of Refugee Resettlement, 1992). Under this law, the Orderly Departure Program was quickly established and implemented to give the Vietnamese a safer route to freedom. Within less than a decade (1980-1989), about 165,000 Vietnamese were admitted into the United States, and another 25,000 applications were approved in 1992 under this new program (Wieder, 1995). Many Vietnamese in the United States took this opportunity to bring their family members here. The new law also provided an opportunity for other groups of Vietnamese to come to the United States.

Vietnamese Amerasians

The term Vietnamese Amerasian refers to children born to a Vietnamese mother and an American father. Most of them were conceived during the Vietnam War. They were often mistreated and ostracized from their community in Vietnam because of their physical differences. Many Amerasian adolescents grew up without parental support or role models, lacked educational opportunities, and received limited employment training (Hanes, 1992). For different reasons and motivations, the Vietnamese communist government was reluctant to allow Amerasians to immigrate to the United States. However, in response to their desperate situation, the U.S. government passed the Amerasian Homecoming Act in 1988 (Office of Refugee Resettlement, 1993). The mission of this policy was to bring Amerasians and their family members to the United States. Since its inception, the Amerasian Homecoming Act of 1988 has brought more than 56,000 Amerasians and their immediate family members to the United States.

Vietnamese Former Political Prisoners

When the Vietnam conflict ended in 1975, thousands of Vietnamese politicians, military officials, and employees of the former government who were unable to escape were prosecuted and forced into reeducation camps. Many former soldiers of South Vietnam were imprisoned because of their political views and ties to both the United States and former government of South Vietnam. During their long-term internment, these individuals were often tortured, starved, and overworked, and also lacked nutritional and medical care. Many died as a result of physical and mental abuse. Those who survived their imprisonment were left with nothing to hope for after their release.

In the late 1980s, the United States established the Humanitarian Operation Program. Under this program, the Vietnamese communist government agreed to release the political detainees and their family members so that they might immigrate to the United States. Since its inception, this program has brought more than 70,000 individuals to the United States (Office of Refugee Resettlement, 1993). Once they arrived in the United States, these former political prisoners have been found to have the lowest rate of adjustment (Hanes, 1992) and are at a much higher risk for psychiatric disorders (Mollica and Son, 1989). The majority of former political detainees were in their fifties or older when they arrived in the United States. This group of Vietnamese is growing old with very little preparation—economically, psychologically, and socially.

DEMOGRAPHIC INFORMATION

As mentioned earlier, the presence of Vietnamese in the United States before 1975 was virtually unnoticeable. The reported number of Vietnamese in America until the mid-1970s was less than 4,000 persons (Gall and Natividad, 1995). Within the span of only two decades, the Vietnamese population in the United States has grown significantly. Among Asian-American ethnic groups, the Vietnamese population is considered to be the third largest, following the Chinese and Filipino groups. The 1991 Census data estimated the total number of Vietnamese Americans to be about 850,000; approximately 250,000 were born in the United States since 1975 (Wieder, 1995). The Vietnamese Americans are not as homogeneous a group as traditionally thought; they also include ethnic Chinese and Montagnards, who are members of ethnic tribes that live in the mountain areas of South Vietnam.

As a group, the Vietnamese age composition is comparable to that of the general population, except for the age group forty-five years and older (see Table 3.1). While over 50 percent of the group is between the ages of eighteen and forty-four, those who are forty-five and over represent roughly 14 percent. When using the American standard of aging (i.e., sixty-five years and over), the Vietnamese aging population is relatively small, representing only 2.6 percent of the Vietnamese population in the United States. The discrepancy in age structure among the Vietnamese refugees can be explained through the nature of their history of emigration. The Vietnamese elderly population was most likely to come to the United States at a later date through the family reunification program.

The concentration of Vietnamese in America can be identified easily in terms of geographical location. Due to a variety of factors including warmer climates, family reunification, better business and employment opportunities, better education, and better social and cultural support networks, the Vietnamese generally resettle in the southern states and on the West Coast, with the largest concentrations in California and Texas. As of 1990, the ten states with ten thousand or more Vietnamese persons included California, Texas, Virginia, Washington, Louisiana, Florida, Pennsylvania, New York, Massachusetts, and Illinois (see Table 3.2). In terms of distribution of Vietnamese Americans by region, about 10 percent resettled in the Northeast; 8.5 percent in the Midwest; 27.5 percent are in the South; and more than 50 percent resettled in the West.

With regard to gender distribution, one would expect to see significantly more males than females because of the emigration pattern of the Vietnamese. It has been observed that, among the second wave of immigration, more males fled the country for fear of being drafted to fight in Cambodia during the late 1970s. Furthermore, among the boat people, the eldest male in the family or the

TABLE 3.1. Age Structure and Percentage of Vietnamese in the United States

Age	Percentage
1-17	33.3
18-24	15.4
25-44	36.9
45-64	11.7
65 and over	2.6

Note: Data adapted from J. H. Lewis (1994).

TABLE 3.2. Vietnamese Population by State, 1990

State	Number (in thousands)	% Distribution
California	280	45.6
Texas	70	11.3
Virginia	21	3.4
Washington	19	3.0
Louisiana	18	2.9
Florida	16	2.7
Pennsylvania	16	2.6
New York	16	2.5
Massachusetts	15	2.5
Illinois	10	1.7

Source: U.S. Bureau of the Census (1990). Internet Web Site, http://www.census.gov.

husband was usually the one to embark on the dangerous voyage; survivors would eventually sponsor other family members to join them in the United States.

In comparison to other Asian ethnic groups, Vietnamese Americans comprise the highest percentage of foreign-born. For instance, more than 97 percent of Vietnamese Americans eighteen years of age or older are foreign-born (U.S. Bureau of the Census, 1990). Virtually 100 percent of the Vietnamese elderly population were born in their native country.

Education

The Vietnamese reserve the highest respect for education. Education is viewed not only as a means to better one's life economically and a sign of social status, but also is viewed as a sign of personal strength and is highly admired. Financial accomplishment is secondary to education and knowledge. By attaining higher education, one is assumed to possess a broader range of knowledge and moral character. To Vietnamese parents in the United States, their children's educational attainment is also the family's greatest joy and honor. For this reason, it is easy to understand why most parents sacrifice tremendously and invest in their children's education. Furthermore, Vietnamese parents relate their children's educational achievements to their own. Perhaps it was because of their deep respect for education that many Vietnamese parents overcame the vicissitudes of life for their children's future.

Asian Americans, as a group, have been noted to be generally better educated than the U.S. general population (Russell, 1996). In 1994, approximately 41 percent of the Asian population were college graduates, compared to only 22 percent of the total U.S. population. According to the U.S. Census (1990), over 90 percent of Vietnamese Americans ages five to nineteen attended school. Nearly 60 percent within the age range from twenty to twenty-four were enrolled in school, and 24 percent of the population within the age range from twenty-five to thirty-four remained in school. As a group, about 45 percent of the Vietnamese Americans enrolled in one type of school or another.

In terms of gender differences of high school and college graduates for Vietnamese twenty-five years of age or older, the 1990 U.S. Census reported approximately nearly 70 percent (68.5 percent) of Vietnamese males and over 50 percent (53.3 percent) of Vietnamese females to be high school graduates. On the other hand, only approximately 22.3 percent males and 12.2 percent females attained a college degree, respectively.

It should be noted that the educational and socioeconomic data represent only the achievements of those who are young and those who are in their thirties and forties. For those who are sixty years of age or over, their educational and financial accomplishments are irrelative because the majority of them are dependent on their adult children. A large number of Vietnamese elderly reported very little education in their native country and very few received postsecondary education (Tran, 1990). This finding is particularly common among Vietnamese elderly females. With regard to language proficiency, nearly 90 percent of individuals sixty-five years of age and over do not speak English "very well" (U.S. Bureau of the Census, 1990).

Employment Status and Earnings

Some of the salient characteristics recognized among Vietnamese Americans include perseverance, resilience, and a strong work ethic (Hanes, 1992). Although life in their new country is full of obstacles and challenges, the living standards are much improved when compared to life in their native land. Furthermore, the Vietnamese are known for their perseverance during a long history of foreign occupation, wars, and recent immigration experiences. Through such a unique history, the Vietnamese have developed special coping mechanisms to deal with adverse circumstances in the new land. For many Vietnamese, the initial goal and priority in the host society was to achieve basic needs such as housing, food, and clothing for their family members. Once in the United States, they would work at any job available to them. These jobs were often considered menial and not wanted by the general population.

According to the Bureau of the Census (1990), 72.3 percent of Vietnamese males aged sixteen or older and 55.8 percent for women of the same age category participated in the labor force. These figures indicate relatively higher rates of men who were in the labor force than women. This gender difference can be accounted for by the fact that men were traditionally the breadwinners. With regard to the earning power of men and women, the same trend that exists in the general U.S. population also appears to be true among Vietnamese Americans; that is, Vietnamese men tend to earn more than Vietnamese women.

Traditional Vietnamese Households

For the Vietnamese, family is the most important social as well as spiritual unit. The family is where bonding occurs; it is where one finds love, comfort, and emotional and financial support. The composition of a Vietnamese family may include grandparents, parents, children, grandchildren, and sons- or daughters-in-law. This definition of family that includes all of these relatives is different from an American family. However, many Vietnamese families are also organized as a nuclear unit, which consists of only parents and young children.

As a result of the process of acculturation, the Vietnamese household composition in the United States is changing; fewer family members live together as a family unit. Due to economic independence and employment opportunities, young adult children tend to move out and establish their own homes. According to the 1990 Census, 55 percent of Vietnamese householders are within the age range twenty-five to forty-four. Approximately 10 percent of individuals sixty-five and over reported to be heads of households. Many elders, however, still rely heavily on their children for support.

Marital Status

With regard to gender differences in marital status, relatively more Vietnamese women were married compared to Vietnamese men, at 53 percent and 44 percent, respectively. Additionally, a relatively higher percentage of men (51 percent) reported never having been married compared to women (35 percent). These different rates may be explained from the Vietnamese cultural perspective. While Vietnamese males are expected and encouraged to pursue higher education as well as to attain economic stability before marriage, females are expected to marry at a much younger age. Rates of widowhood among females are significantly higher than among males, with 5.9 percent and 0.9 percent, respectively. This phenomenon may be due to the fact that many husbands lost their lives during the wars, in communist prisons, or on the journey escaping from their homeland.

ADJUSTMENT EXPERIENCES

Several studies have examined both psychological and social adjustment of Vietnamese immigrants and refugees in the United States (Masuda and Holmes, 1967; Lin, Tazuma, and Masuda, 1979). Being uprooted from one's traditional culture and society is traumatic for most immigrants and refugees. Many Vietnamese refugees have also encountered difficulties in adjusting to American culture and society. A general pattern of problems is experienced by Vietnamese Americans including personal losses and culture conflict. Many Vietnamese left their native land either in such a hurry or so secretively that they were unable to bring along many of their possessions. Common losses reported by refugees include loss of properties, homeland, social status, and interpersonal relationships. Many refugees not only had to start a new life from scratch, they had to do it without support from extended family members as well.

Health and Mental Health Status

Currently there are no epidemiological data on the health and mental health status of Vietnamese immigrants as a group, let alone the Vietnamese elderly population. While the National Center for Health Statistics for Asian Americans (NCHSAA, 1992) reported that Asians as a group experience fewer health problems than the total U.S. population, this generalization might be misleading to health care providers. Although a number of health conditions, including heart disease, infant mortality, and cancer, occur less frequently among Asian groups compared to the mainstream population, tuberculosis is observed more frequently among Asian Americans (NCHSAA, 1992).

The health statistics reviewed earlier inadvertently have promoted the stereotype that Vietnamese, as an Asian group, also have good health status. In contrast to this popular misconception, previous studies on the psychological well-being of Vietnamese refugees have consistently reported that this population is at high risk for psychological disorders (Pham, 1986; Hauff and Vaglum, 1990). A high prevalence of depression, anxiety disorder, and post-traumatic stress disorder have been reported among Southeast Asian refugees, including the Vietnamese (Mollica, Wyshak, and Lavelle, 1987; Kinzie et al., 1990; Kroll et al., 1989). Emigration often causes many important changes in a person's social support network including multiple losses that cause psychological distress (Beiser, 1988). Immigrants and refugees have to overcome, for example, culture shock, language differences, and finding employment and adequate housing. Brown and Harris (1978) identified six life events that correlate significantly with depression: (1) death of loved ones, (2) separation, (3) unemployment, (4) loss of material possessions, (5) illness, and (6) loss of hope for the future. Due to the nature of their life experiences and history of wars, the majority of the Vietnamese in the United States encountered these life events. In addition, Vietnamese refugees have undergone mass trauma including torture, rape, witness of murder, and separation from loved ones (Mollica and Son, 1989), and the risk increases even more since they have to deal with additional stresses in the country of resettlement. The most powerful risk factors that are believed to correlate highly with psychological distress are unemployment and separation from family members or spouses.

VIETNAMESE ELDERLY

Vietnamese elders, like elders from other cultures, have been losing their social status due to changes in social structure caused by industrial revolutions and technological advancements. Furthermore, even migration from one village to another within Vietnam could be psychologically devastating for many older Vietnamese who had spent all their lives in one village or town. Nevertheless, they were still surrounded by people who spoke the same language and shared the same national identity, history, and culture. However, immigration to the United States stripped many elderly Vietnamese of all the power and social status that they enjoyed in their homeland. Although it was the only option for many, the process of immigrating to a strange country was definitely terrifying and stressful for the elderly Vietnamese.

Unlike many members of the mainstream elderly population, many Vietnamese elders do not have the opportunity to participate in the workforce in order to be financially independent. Thus, they will continue to be overly dependent on their adult children for financial support. Social and economic dependency of Vietnamese elders have become sources of family stress and disruption for their own children.

In-depth interviews with a small sample of Vietnamese elderly in the United States (Tran, 1997, unpublished data) suggest that a subjective sense of isolation and depression is highly prevalent among these individuals. Almost all participants still have loved ones (usually a spouse, parents, children, or grandchildren) in Vietnam. In addition, the majority of the participants reported that they feel lonely due to lack of friends in the new country. There are at least two distinct groups of elderly Vietnamese Americans: those who were already old upon arriving in the United States, and those who have been growing old in the United States. The first group appears to suffer from more economic, psychological, and social problems than the second group. The second group arrived in the United States in the 1970s during middle age and now have already entered or are entering retirement. To a certain degree, many in the second group have worked and may have some savings for their retirement. The first group is totally dependent on public assistance and family support. Some members of this group have been abandoned by their children or relatives and are living sorrowfully in public housing complexes or nursing homes throughout the United States. Some of the common difficulties that the Vietnamese elders face in the United States are discussed in the following sections.

Language Problems

Due to their age, Vietnamese elderly experience much more difficulty learning the new language than their children and grandchildren. For many elders, the process of acquiring a working knowledge of English not only is slow but can be impossible. Learning English becomes even more difficult due to the fact that many of these elders did not have adequate formal schooling in their native country, especially Vietnamese women. Even with an extended length of residency in the United States, learning English is still an impossible mission to many Vietnamese elders. These individuals will continue to find their new lifestyles difficult to adjust to, especially those who are living in urban settings that are drastically different from where they had lived in their native land. The lack of adequate command of the English language prevents these individuals from various daily activities such as food shopping, utilizing public transportation, making new friends, and seeking health and mental health services in times of need.

Isolation

Many Vietnamese elderly individuals have experienced isolation. When uprooted from their native land, they left behind a lifelong social support network. Many of their friends are either still in Vietnam or living in dispersed areas in the world. Without an adequate command of the English language, the elders find it extremely difficult to make new friends and to communicate with their U.S.-born grandchildren who prefer to use English rather than Vietnamese. Due to their inability to drive or utilize public transportation, these individuals find themselves staying at home all day long while their adult children and grandchildren are at work or at school. In Vietnam, their neighbors were their friends; in America, their neighbors are strangers. As a result, these individuals not only feel isolated from their extended family but also from their own community.

While Vietnamese women can find things to do at home such as babysitting, cooking, and cleaning, many Vietnamese men find themselves useless around the house. Men who once maintained a respected social status or occupation may experience a sense of demoralization from being idle all day. Their adult children and grandchildren are too preoccupied with everyday responsibilities to pay attention to what the elders are enduring.

Adjustment Issues

Language proficiency is emblematic of a successful adjustment to a foreign country. Thus, Vietnamese elders who have no English language skills appear to suffer from emotional distress and other forms of psychological problems. For many of these individuals, the spiritual tie to their native land and ancestors is so strong that the thought of breaking away from old traditions is unbearable. As a result, the search for a common ground between the old and new cultures is not an easy one. The potential impact of this issue may produce negative effects on their mental health. In our focus group study, we found that elderly Vietnamese participants often express common symptoms of depression, including having problems with their sleep, eating habits, or physical activities.

Successful adjustment to the mainstream culture requires regular interaction and participation in various social and cultural activities. Vietnamese elders, however, find themselves incapable of participating in these events due to language and cultural barriers. This condition may have a significant negative impact on their perceived self-efficacy (Bandura, 1977). Bandura's social learning theory suggests that individuals who were once capable and efficacious may develop a sense of self-doubt and low self-esteem when faced with difficult situations that cannot be resolved using the skills and knowledge they have acquired.

SOURCES OF WORRY OR ANXIETY

Health

Vietnamese elders who are newcomers to the United States are particularly at risk for physical problems. One of their central concerns is health. Many elderly Americans rated their current health as very poor (Tran, 1997, unpublished data). The most common physical complaints include fatigue, headaches, arthritis, insomnia, back pain, poor appetite, and hypertension. Ethnic Vietnamese health care professionals and facilities are available in most Vietnamese communities. However, for elderly Vietnamese persons who live outside the Vietnamese communities, availability and accessibility to culturally appropriate health care are a problem. Like other elderly Asian groups, elderly Vietnamese often do not seek mental health services nor services provided by a nursing home (Kobata, Lockery, and Moriwaka, 1980). Many elderly Vietnamese are also reluctant to tell their children about their health problems because they do not want to be a burden. The physical illnesses endured by these individuals may adversely affect their psychological well-being.

Intergenerational Concerns

The second source of concern has much to do with their children and grandchildren. Many elders fear that their children will grow up and become too Americanized and may neglect or abandon them in their old age. In Vietnam, children are expected to care for their parents when they become frail. The thought of being abandoned by their children and having to live their final years in a nursing home is frightening to these individuals. Many Vietnamese elders experience a sense of helplessness since they are totally dependent on their children for financial support.

Vietnamese elders also worry about how their grandchildren may turn out in the future. One of the greatest fears is that their grandchildren will be pulled into the materialistic world or come under the influence of "bad" peers. The fact that the young Vietnamese generation has become more independent in their thinking and behavior is most vexing to grandparents, for this is a sign that their grandchildren are gradually breaking away from their traditional culture. Although many grandparents expressed the desire to talk to their grandchildren about their life experiences, they find it impossible to do so because they cannot speak fluent English and their grandchildren cannot understand Vietnamese well enough to appreciate what their grandparents want to pass on to them.

Furthermore, many grandparents have expressed dissatisfaction with their grandchildren for being disrespectful to the elders. In their process of acculturation, Vietnamese youths have been taught at school and have learned from friends to speak their minds and to stand up for their individual rights. Moreover, since the elders are most likely to experience language difficulties and are ignorant of the new culture, their children and grandchildren will be reluctant to seek their advice. Their knowledge and wisdom are no longer useful and, hence, are obsolete. Furthermore, due to the lack of adequate English, many parents and grandparents heavily rely on their young children's language skills for tasks such as translation and filling out paperwork. The loss of authority due to role reversal generates much distress among the elders. These individuals often feel helpless and useless. This is particularly demoralizing for those who once held respected positions in Vietnam.

The Future

Vietnamese elders not only worry about their children and grandchildren's future and the loss of respect for elderly individuals, but the thought of their own future also brings much discomfort. Although many Vietnamese elders believe in and accept the inescapable stages of life, which include birth, aging, sickness, and death, the thought of dying far away from their homeland and their ancestors' graves is frightening. In fact, some Vietnamese elders have requested that their bodies be taken back to Vietnam to be buried next to their relatives or other loved ones.

Although many Vietnamese elders expressed satisfaction with current living conditions that provide adequate necessities and health care services, a considerable number of these individuals wish to return to their homeland. The majority of Vietnamese elders still have children and grandchildren living in Vietnam. Some have parents who are still alive. These individuals often spend time thinking and worrying about the difficult life their loved ones have to face. They spend a great deal of time reminiscing about relatives in Vietnam, which distracts their energy and concentration from daily tasks.

THERAPEUTIC INTERVENTIONS

The fields of psychology, psychiatry, and social work are rather unfamiliar to many Vietnamese because these fields have not yet been systematically developed and organized in Vietnam. In general, the concept of mental illness or psychological disorders in Vietnamese culture implies "abnormality" or "craziness." To lay people, a psychologist or psychiatrist is one who works with or treats "crazy" people. The word "crazy" is often used pejoratively to describe the abnormality of a person's mind rather than his or her behavior. Individuals who are labeled as "crazy" are often ostracized from their community, and their family feels a great sense of shame and failure.

Psychotherapy is still a foreign concept to the majority of Vietnamese. Vietnamese culture does not have an equivalent role for a mental health specialist (i.e., psychologist or social worker) who conducts psychotherapy to deal with emotional or behavioral problems. In addition, the American concept of mental illness and psychotherapy is not conceived of in the same way as in Vietnamese culture. Problems such as marital conflicts, family disputes, children's behavioral problems, and psychological disorders are considered internal affairs and should be handled within the family system. Similar methods of problem-solving and help-seeking patterns are still maintained by many Vietnamese in the United States. Consequently, mental health professionals are usually last on the list for help. Unfortunately, by the time the problem is brought to the attention of a mental health specialist, the individual is usually in a crisis state.

According to Vietnamese culture, maintenance of emotional equilibrium is highly valued and expected of every individual. Emotional problems should be contained and resolved individually "behind the closed door." When the problems become severe, one may seek support from extended family members, friends, or clergy. These differences in the conceptualization of mental illness may discourage many Vietnamese from seeking mental health services in the United States.

The condition becomes even more complicated because many of these individuals do not have adequate English proficiency to participate in psychotherapy, the traditional Western "talking therapy." As a result, they often deny the existence of family or personal problems, and may delay or avoid mental health services altogether. The family is often hesitant to admit the existence of a "crazy" person in the home for fear of negative reactions such as rejection or ridicule from the community.

To effectively assess and treat Vietnamese-American clients, a competent therapist must be sensitive to a number of important factors, including the understanding of the immigration experiences, the type of traumas these individuals have experienced, their cultural values, belief systems, socialization experiences, and their perspective on mental health. Western mental health professionals who treat Asian clients often lack knowledge on these important issues (Sue, 1994). Thus, their therapeutic interventions fail to work effectively, which may account for high rates of attrition among Asian clients.

In the late 1950s, only about thirty-six psychotherapy systems were recognized (Harper, 1959). Within the span of only three decades, the number has increased exponentially to more than 400 psychotherapy systems (Karasu, 1992). The rapid increase of therapies is confusing not only to the general public but among the professionals who practice them as well. Which method is most effective? Which therapy is useful to treat a particular disorder? Which therapy model has a stronger theoretical foundation? Which method is applicable to non-Western cultures? These questions have been widely debated over many years. Yet, there seems to be no universal consensus to some of the questions. The following section will discuss several prominent Western therapeutic techniques that may be applicable to the Vietnamese population. The competent therapist, however, also must be flexible and tailor his or her techniques to meet the specific needs of the clients.

Interventions at the Individual Level

Behavior Therapy

Behavior therapy was traditionally founded on behaviorism and on social-learning theory. Several underlying assumptions of behavior therapy include:

1. both desirable and undesirable behavior can be learned;
2. by applying social-learning principles, maladaptive behavior can be changed or modified;
3. methods of intervention can be modified according to the individual personal styles and types of problems; and
4. treatment methods are precisely prescribed by the therapist (O'Leary and Wilson, 1987).

In general, the basic tenet of behavior therapy is that maladaptive behaviors can be unlearned through counterconditioning, systematic desensitization, operant conditioning, cognitive-behavior modification, and systematic problem solving. Behavior therapists concentrate on the pertinent stressors and do not attempt to explore the client's unconscious motivations.

Behavior modification can be effectively applied via individual therapy. This method may have potential benefits for Asian clients since its central focus is to reduce symptoms and change undesirable behavior. Asian clients who come to see a doctor often expect immediate or quick results since their presenting problem is usually somatic rather than psychological in nature. Remedies to their problems must be direct, brief, and simple step-by-step procedures. One ubiquitous technique of behavior therapy is progressive relaxation procedures. This technique may be helpful to these elders in alleviating symptoms of anxiety, stress, and physiological arousal. Controlling physical symptoms may alleviate their somatic complaints, which will lead to better emotional and psychological well-being.

Psychopharmacological Therapy

Psychopharmacological therapy is another common type of non-insight-oriented therapy, which was founded on the medical model of psychopathology. The basic assumption of this model is that certain psychological disorders (e.g., depression, schizophrenia) are genetically linked and/or caused by an imbalance of chemicals (e.g., low level of neurotransmitters) in the brain. The common treatment method of psychopathology within this model involves using psychotropic medications to reduce or control undesired symptoms (e.g., depression) and stabilize the level of neurochemicals. It has been reported that antidepressants are quite effective in regulating depressive symptoms among Southeast Asian refugees (Kinzie, 1989). The effectiveness of this method may increase significantly if used in conjunction with individual psychotherapy or "talk therapy." However, psychotherapy should still be brief, focusing on the presenting problems and avoiding emphasis on past experiences and any unconscious conflicts.

Cognitive Therapy

The cognitive therapy model emphasizes the influence of individual perceptions, beliefs, and thoughts on one's psychological problems. This model proposes that the origin and the perpetuation of psychological problems result from the individual's distortions about the self, the problem, the environment, and the future. Thus, the application of this approach involves the modification of the client's distorted schema or misinterpretations of the activating events, irrational beliefs, and emotional consequences (Ellis, 1991). It is believed that through the process of psychotherapy, clients will gain insight into their problems, which can lead to positive cognitive change.

Cognitive therapy may be most helpful to individuals who have become more acculturated to the Western lifestyle and ways of thinking, including the young, the educated, and financially stable persons. Although many elders lack these characteristics, cognitive therapy can offer a useful psychoeducation to these individuals. It may be beneficial to teach the elders about their new lifestyles and expectations in the host country, the effect of changing social roles, utilization of public services, and how to discipline their children and grandchildren in the new culture. Cognitive therapy can help these individuals with new practical skills to cope with the demands in their new life by teaching them to think practically in accordance with life in the new culture.

Systems Therapy

The basic principle of systems therapy maintains that, to fully understand a person, we must take into consideration the social context or system in which that person operates. The system here is defined as "a set of units or elements that stand in some consistent relationship with one another" (Prochaska and Norcross, 1994, p. 348). For instance, a family is a system in and of itself. However, the interrelationships among units or members of the family are critically important to consider. Thus, in family therapy, therapists must not only assess each individual client separately but also the interrelationships between the units, i.e., relationships between husband and wife, parents and children, and the relationships among siblings. From this viewpoint, individual intervention is not as effective as collective intervention that includes the whole family in the treatment process.

Since the Vietnamese family is closely connected as a system, it is logical to think that a systems approach should be selected as a treatment method. While it may be a good idea for therapists to include all family members in the treatment process, Paniagua (1994) suggests some critical factors should be considered to maximize therapeutic effectiveness and to avoid high dropout rates. It should be noted that the custom of "saving face" is particularly important in Vietnamese culture. Systems therapy sometimes may not be as productive as we may have thought, because every member is consciously trying to preserve a good image for the other family members. Blaming others or attributing one's problem to other family members is not something that a Vietnamese client is comfortable doing. Furthermore, Vietnamese are often reluctant to express feelings or personal problems in the presence of others. This is particularly difficult for parents to do in front of their young children. Children, on the other hand, will not dare reveal negative things about their parents in their presence. Therefore, the following suggestions are presented should systems or family therapy be selected as a treatment method.

First, consider the degree of acculturation of the family and of the potential client to be treated. At the same time, assess the system's degree of adherence to traditional beliefs and problem-solving methods. Second, it is advisable to meet with the identified client and appropriate family members separately to collect background information and to learn about the perceptions of the problem that each member may hold. Third, when using individual therapy with an identified client, other family members should be invited to participate in psychoeducation sessions to learn about the nature of the problem or illness, the rationale for treatment strategies, and to ask for support from all family members during the treatment process. Only when there is an agreement among all parties involved should the therapist call a collective meeting with the family as a treatment unit. Finally, treatment should be brief, direct, and aimed at relieving presenting problems.

Which Intervention Method Is Most Effective?

A number of authors working with culturally diverse groups suggest that the treatment modalities discussed above may be applicable for Asian Americans (Ho, 1992; Paniagua, 1994; Uba, 1994). However, it should be emphasized that traditional Euro-American psychotherapy techniques cannot be readily transplanted and applied to other cultures. The array of Western therapy systems may have significant potential benefits to Asian clients with appropriate modifications to meet the individual's cultural background. Matsushima and Tashima (1982) reported that 46 percent of Asian-American therapists often used the integration of cognitive-behavioral therapy and 18 percent used psychopharmacological therapy as the treatment method with their Asian clients. Although there are no prescribed treatment methods for mental health professionals who are working with Asian groups, a number of useful suggestions have been proposed.

GUIDELINES FOR WORKING
WITH VIETNAMESE AMERICANS

As previously mentioned, psychotherapy is a foreign concept in Vietnamese culture. When a Vietnamese individual comes to see a doctor, he or she often expects the doctor to make a quick diagnosis and prescribe a practical treatment, such as medication (Sue and Sue, 1990). Therefore, talk therapy may not be easily accepted by most Vietnamese as a method of direct intervention. In selecting the best treatment methods for these individuals, some demographic variables such as age, socioeconomic status, and level of acculturation must be considered.

Paniagua (1994) provided the following suggestions for therapists who work with Asian ethnic groups:

1. demonstrate expertise and authority;
2. maintain a formal therapist-client (or doctor-patient) relationship;
3. allow and respect clients' cultural beliefs about the causes to their problems and their expression of the problems (e.g., somatically as opposed to psychological in nature);
4. be patient with the clients because shame and guilt may prevent them from revealing their emotions;
5. anticipate crises and thoroughly assess for risk of suicidal behaviors;
6. avoid discussing psychiatric hospitalization and recommend alternatives such as outpatient care or a community service center;
7. avoid talk therapy or prolonged verbal-exchange-type therapy, and provide concrete and practical advice on how to solve the presenting problem;
8. refrain from collecting an exhaustive history of the client as most therapists do during the clinical interview; and
9. avoid delving too much into the client's past traumatic experiences and unconscious feelings.

This last item is particularly applicable to Southeast Asian refugees as also suggested by Mollica, Wyshak, and Lavelle (1987).

Interventions at the Community Level
As Preventive Measures

Besides helping the Vietnamese elderly at the individual level, it is also critically important to consider some preventive measures at the community level. The elderly Vietnamese show a great desire to have a community center where they can come for social and other activities. In large communities such as southern California, senior centers offer services only to elderly Vietnamese. In Boston, Massachusetts, older Vietnamese have participated in local senior centers, but many have expressed that they would rather come to a center designed specifically for elderly Vietnamese. These individuals may benefit greatly from having a community center designed to address their specific needs. For instance, such a center or club may incorporate various activities such as cultural events, recreational activities, physical education and exercises, education about life in the new country, and learning new practical skills such as food shopping or riding a bus so that they do not feel a sense of uselessness from having nothing to do all day.

An ethnic Vietnamese community center is an ideal place for socialization and for making new friends, which will extend the support network for these individuals. A large proportion of elders from our data (unpublished) reported that they have suffered or experienced horrific experiences in war, migration, or in concentration camps. Thus, the center can also be a place for these elders to gather and share life experiences with one another.

Since religion plays a profound role in the spiritual life of elderly Vietnamese, it is crucial to help these individuals establish a place (e.g., church or pagoda) to practice their faith. Elderly Vietnamese who live within Vietnamese communities are able to attend Vietnamese churches and temples. For many elderly Vietnamese, the churches and temples are the only places where they can interact with others. Those who live outside the Vietnamese communities are often completely isolated from ethnic Vietnamese religious services and activities. One may wonder how these individuals could successfully cope with such a history of horrific migration experiences and many years of war, not to mention a very difficult life in the new country. The simple answer, perhaps, is strong faith.

The thought of being abandoned by their children and placed in an American nursing home is terrifying to most Vietnamese elders. The differences in culture and language will not only create stresses for the elders but for the service providers as well. A low quality of care for these individuals is inevitable since there will be a big gap in communication between the elders and the staff. When possible, nursing home administrators should recruit staff who are familiar with the Vietnamese culture and who are able to speak the Vietnamese language to provide care for elderly Vietnamese.

In this chapter, we present and discuss several historical and current characteristics of elderly Vietnamese. Although the lack of empirical data prohibits us from drawing any definitive conclusions about the social, psychological, and health conditions of elderly Vietnamese, we believe this chapter can make a modest contribution to our understanding of this unique population. Health care and social service professionals should continue to evaluate the effectiveness of various treatment models for elderly Vietnamese.

The Vietnamese-American community should be prepared to confront the problems of aging. Young Vietnamese Americans should be exposed to various aspects of aging including preparation for retirement, health care, and long-term care. Alternative housing and long-term care facilities should be explored and developed to meet the needs of Vietnamese elders and their families. Researchers and practitioners should work together to find appropriate services and treatments for this unique elderly population.

REFERENCES

Bandura, A. (1977). *Social learning theory.* Englewood Cliffs, NJ: Prentice-Hall.

Beiser, M. (1988, January). Influences of time, ethnicity, and attachment on depressive Southeast Asian refugees. *The American Journal of Psychiatry, 145*(1), 46-51.

Brown, G.S. and Harris, T. (1978). *The social origin of depression: A study of psychiatric disorder in women.* New York: The Free Press.

Ellis, A. (1991). The revised ABC's of rational-emotive therapy. *Journal of Rational Emotive and Cognitive-Behavior Therapy, 9*(3), 139-172.

Gall, S. and Natividad, I. (Eds.) (1995). *The Asian-American almanac: A reference work on Asian Americans in the United States.* Detroit, MI: Gale Research.

Hanes, P.J. (1992). *The Vietnamese experience in America.* Bloomington, IN: Indiana University Press.

Harper, R.A. (1959). *Psychoanalysis and psychotherapy: 36 systems.* Englewood Cliffs, NJ: Prentice-Hall.

Hauff, E. and Vaglum, P. (1990, Summer). Integration of Vietnamese refugees into the Norwegian market: The impact of war trauma. *International Migration Review, 27*(2), 388-405.

Ho, M.K. (1992). *Minority children and adolescents in therapy.* Newbury Park, CA: Sage Publications.

Karasu, T.B. (1992). The worst of times, the best of times: Psychotherapy in the 1990s. *Journal of Psychotherapy Practice and Research, 1,* 2-15.

Kinzie, D.J. (1989). A three-year follow-up of Cambodian young people traumatized as children. *Journal of American of Academic Child and Adolescent Psychiatry, 28*(4), 501-504.

Kinzie, D.J., Boehnlein, J.K., Leung, P.K., Moore, L.J., Riley, C., and Smith, D. (1990). The prevalence of posttraumatic stress disorder and its clinical significance on Southeast Asian refugees. *American Journal of Psychiatry, 147*(7), 913-917.

Kleinman, S.B. (1990). Terror at sea: Vietnamese victims of piracy. *The American Journal of Psychoanalysis, 50*(4), 351-362.

Kobata, F.S., Lockery, S.A., and Moriwaka, S.Y. (1980). Minority issues in mental health and aging. In J. Birren and R.B. Sloan (Eds.), *Handbook of mental health and aging* (pp. 448-466). Englewood Cliffs, NJ: Prentice-Hall.

Kroll, J., Habenicht, M., Mackenzie, T., Yang, M., Chan, S., Vang, T., Nguyen, T., Ly, M., Phommasduvanh, B., Nguyen, H., Vang, Y. et al. (1989). Depression and posttraumatic stress disorder in Southeast Asian refugees. *American Journal of Psychiatry, 146*(12), 1592-1597.

Lin, K.M., Tazuma, L., and Masuda, M. (1979). Adaptational problems of Vietnamese refugees, Part I: Health and mental health status. *Archives of General Psychiatry, 36*(9), 955-961.

Masuda, M. and Holmes, T.H. (1967). Magnitude estimation of social readjustment. *Journal of Psychosomatic Research, 11,* 219-225.

Matsushima, N.M. and Tashima, N. (1982). *Mental health treatment modalities of Pacific/Asian American practitioners.* A report of the Pacific Asian Mental Health Research Project. San Francisco, CA.

Mollica, R.F. and Son, L. (1989). Cultural dimensions in the evaluation and treatment of sexual trauma: An overview. *Treatments of Victims of Sexual Abuse, 12*(2), 363-379.

Mollica, R.F., Wyshak, G., and Lavelle, J. (1987, December). The psychosocial impact of war trauma and torture on Southeast Asian refugees. *American Journal of Psychiatry, 144*(12), 1567-1572.

National Center for Health Statistics for Asian Americans (1992). *Chartbook on health data on older Americans: United States.* Hyattsville, MD: U.S. Dept. of Health and Human Services, Public Health Service, Centers for Disease Control Center for Health Statistics; Washington, DC: U.S. Government Printing Office.

Office of Refugee Resettlement (1992). *Refugee Resettlement Program.* Report to the Congress. Washington, DC: U.S. Dept. of Health and Human Services.

Office of Refugee Resettlement (1993). *Refugee Resettlement Program.* Report to the Congress. Washington, DC: U.S. Dept. of Health and Human Services.

O'Leary, K.D. and Wilson, G.T. (1987). *Behavior therapy: Application and outcome,* (Second edition). Englewood Cliffs, NJ: Prentice-Hall.

Paniagua, F.A. (1994). Guidelines for the assessment and treatment of Asians. In F.A. Paniagua (Ed.), *Assessing and treating culturally diverse clients* (pp. 55-72). Thousand Oaks, CA: Sage.

Pham, T.N. (1986, December). The mental health problems of the Vietnamese in Calgary: Aspects and implications for service. *Canada's Mental Health, 34*(4), 5-9.

Prochaska, J.O. and Norcross, J.C. (1994). *Systems of psychotherapy. A transtheoretical analysis* (pp. 1-24). Pacific Grove, CA: Brooks-Cole Publishing Company. 1-24.

Russell, C. (1996). *The official guide to racial and ethnic diversity.* New York: New Strategist Publications, Inc.

Sue, D.W. (1994). *Guidelines for counseling Asian American clients.* North Amherst, MA: Microtraining Associates.

Sue, D.W. and Sue, D. (1990). *Counseling the culturally different: Theory and practice* (Second edition). New York: Wiley and Sons.

Tran, T.V. (1990). Language acculturation among older Vietnamese refugee adults. *The Gerontologist, 30*(1), 94-99.

Tran, T.V. (1997). Focus group and in-depth interviews with older Vietnamese persons. Boston College: Unpublished raw data.

Uba, L. (1994). *Asian Americans' personality patterns, identity, and mental health.* New York: The Guilford Press.

United States Department of Justice, Immigration and Naturalization Service (1991). *Statistical Yearbook of the Immigration and Naturalization Service.* Washington, DC: U.S. Government Printing Office.

U.S. Bureau of the Census (1990). *U.S. Censuses of Population.* Washington, DC.

Wieder, R. (1995). Immigration. In S. Gall and I. Natividad (Eds.), *The Asian-American almanac: A reference work on Asian-Americans in the United States* (pp. 265-268). Detroit, MI: Gale Research.

Chapter 4

Elderly Russian Jewish Immigrants

Tanya Fitzpatrick

Russian immigrants and their elderly family members have a long tradition of migration to America based on their escape from religious domination and economic oppression. Adult children primarily have been motivated to migrate and they expected their elderly relatives to accompany them (Althausen, 1993). Elderly parents may have been reluctant to leave their homeland but feared separation from their children and grandchildren. Stress from immigration and resettlement has led to an increase in physical illness, depression, and intergenerational conflict for elderly Russian immigrants. Problems relating to inadequate housing and obtaining medical services are often experienced. Although some elderly continue to live with family members, they speak only Russian and they suffer from physical disabilities, isolation, and lack assistance and access to community services (Belozersky, 1990).

This chapter explores the physical and psychological health of elderly Russian immigrants with the ultimate goal of presenting implications for practice, policy, and future research. The aims of the chapter will be addressed by focusing on the following:

1. Demographic information regarding immigrant status
2. A review of the literature on: (a) cultural values; (b) intergenerational issues and family caregiving; and (c) health care utilization, access, and attitudes
3. Theoretical perspectives
4. Therapeutic interventions for health care professionals (social workers, nurses, gerontologists)
5. Implications for practice, policy, and future research

BASIC DEMOGRAPHIC INFORMATION

Numbers

This chapter will focus on Russian or Soviet Jews, as many immigrated before the decline and fall of the Soviet Union (Hule-wat, 1996). The number of Russian immigrants has dramatically increased to 181,000 (Hebrew Immigrant Aid Society [HIAS], 1991) in all areas of the United States from 1971 to the present day. Bychkov (1991) projects that another 200,000 immigrants may have arrived between 1991 and 1995. The majority of Russian Jews in the United States emigrated from the urban centers of central Russia and Ukraine and settled predominantly in New York City, Boston, Chicago, San Francisco, Cleveland, and Cincinnati. In the Boston, Massachusetts area alone, there are approximately 20,000 Russian people, of which 60 percent are elderly. Twenty percent of the total Russian immigrant population are older than sixty-five years, which has made them one of the oldest groups of immigrants in this country (Brod and Heurtin-Roberts, 1992). Persidsky and Kelly (1992) state that because families do not leave their elderly members behind when they immigrate, the percentage of elderly is roughly the same as in their country of origin. The elderly, age sixty-five years and over, who live in the former Soviet Union constitute approximately 17 percent of the general population.

Gold (1991) further states that only estimates can be made of the number of Soviet Jews from Israel or other locations. Gold discusses patterns of secondary migration (those immigrants who have left their original place of settlement and have resettled in secondary locations). He reports that approximately 40 percent of the Soviet Jewish population have arrived in the San Francisco Bay Area without family members who could assist them to access needed goods and services, as many children of the older adults remained in the former Soviet Union.

Age

Twenty-nine percent of Soviet Jews are fifty years of age or over (HIAS, 1991). As previously stated, they are older than most immigrant groups, especially those who arrived in the country between 1979 and 1989. Persidsky and Kelly (1992) report on additional statistics from HIAS indicating that out of a total of 23,300 resettled Jewish immigrants arriving between 1979 and 1989, the majority of the immigrants (58.9 percent) were between ages sixty-one and seventy-one years. The age group seventy-one to eighty constituted 31.2 percent of immigrants, and those eighty-one years and over, were 9.9 percent of the total.

Gender

Females also tend to be older than males due to their greater life expectancy and the impact of World War II (Orr, 1987). There were a total of 14,308 women compared to 9,992 men age sixty-one years and older at a 61.4 percent to 38.6 percent ratio of resettled Soviet immigrants in the United States. Yet the male-female ratio increases with age (0.59, 0.65, and 0.75) in groups of sixty-one to seventy, seventy-one to eighty, and eighty-one-plus years old, respectively. This is in contrast with the general population of the United States, the former Soviet Union, or other parts of the world (Persidsky and Kelly, 1992).

Marital Status

Previous research suggests that the number of elderly women (single, widowed, divorced, separated, or never married) outnumbered elderly men. The majority of single men and women age sixty years and over are widowed, yet the proportions of married men and women decrease with age, especially for women. Because women tend to outlive their husbands, married men outnumbered married women in the sixty to eighty-nine years of age group (Persidsky and Kelly, 1992). Recent research indicates that marriage has been a less significant institution in the Soviet Union than in America (Halbertstadt, 1996) due to the important role of friendship as a source of intimacy and moral support. Men and women are said to form "more intense and intimate relationships with friends of the same sex than with their spouses" (Halbertstadt, 1996, p. 304).

Other Factors Affecting Immigration

Several unique factors are worth mentioning to assist in broadening our understanding of the Russian immigration experience and its relationship to emotional and physical well-being and health among this population.

Family Size and Living Arrangements

In most of the former Eastern bloc countries, Russian families tend to consist of three generations living together in the same dwelling, which is the direct result of political and economic conditions (Althausen, 1993; Persidsky and Kelly, 1992). In America, the goal of most resettlement agencies is to eventually separate the generations into their own households. This has created difficulties in adjustment, especially for elderly members, because of separation anxiety (Schneller, 1981) and disruption in role status leading to an increase in depression and loneliness (Althausen, 1993; Gusovsky, 1995).

Education and Employment

Little information is available on the educational level of elderly Russian immigrants. In the few studies available, researchers have noted that Soviet immigrants report higher levels of education if they tended to live in urban centers (Gold, 1991; Healey, 1996; Persidsky and Kelly, 1992; Simon and Simon, 1985). Also, Soviet émigrés have a history of successful economic adaptation in the United States, though their annual average family income varies considerably depending on the geographic location (Gold, 1991; Healey, 1996). Nearly 70 percent of Russian émigrés in 1991 were employed full- or part-time, and again this depends on the time and the part of the country sampled. Despite this promising figure, many have not received equal status in the United States and have taken positions of lesser occupational status and prestige. Of particular importance is the high proportion of Soviet Jewish women having professional and technical skills versus other immigrant or native groups. Soviet Jewish women are also more likely than others to be employed in jobs requiring technical and professional skills. Sixty percent of Soviet Jewish women in the United States work in these jobs, compared to 16.5 percent of American women (Gold, 1991).

Recent figures are not available for the elderly population and their employment status; however, self-employment may be a factor influencing the lives of older immigrants as this group of people have a strong tradition of community building, philanthropy, and providing assistance to newly arrived immigrants (Gold, 1991). Persidsky and Kelly (1992) state that Soviet immigrants have not been considered a minority group in the United States but rather a refugee group that escaped an oppressive, rapidly changing, and unpredictable former Soviet Union as well as present-day political and environmental pressures. Although these immigrants do not receive the benefits of minority status, they have received considerable support from the American Jewish community.

Cultural Values and Views of Aging

Overall, Russian Jewish immigrants highly value music, arts, sciences, and medicine as well as strong and lasting family and friendship ties. These values originated in the Soviet Union. Also, Belozersky (1991) considers the "collectivism mentality" the major value by which the Russian Jewish population can be best understood.

Collectivism values the whole or the consolidated rather than the needs of the individual, which is basically the opposite of the American value system. Typically, collectivism is characterized by conformism, authority and power rather than compromise, aversion to organized activity, mistrust of authority, fear of autonomy and initiative, cynicism and lack of firm moral standards resulting in cheating and manipulation, high value of friendship, and reliance on informal ties (Belozersky, 1991). Friendship can certainly be considered the highest of values (Belozersky, 1991; Gusovsky, 1995; Zahler, 1991), despite the emphasis placed on the collective versus the individual, and the inward versus the outward personality, which is observed in modesty about sharing accomplishments and strengths.

There is a sense of "tight-lipped cautions, compliance and manipulation in the presence of anyone perceived as having some kind of power" (Belozersky, 1991, p. 11). Russian immigrants are extremely serious when they describe the nature and quality of their friendships and relationships, which are primarily based on a deep sense of trust and unwavering and faithful loyalty. Unlike American society, where friendship has a more independent nature and is less intrusive or invasive of privacy, Russian friendships include a total commitment to the needs of the other in which favors are exchanged along with money, baby-sitting, scarce goods and services, help with personal problems, social and religious needs, and providing living space to friends if necessary. Gusovsky's (1995) findings indicate that the immigration process itself has placed additional stress on elderly individuals as their close and intimate relationships have been disrupted in this country.

Religious Orientation

Russian immigrants of Jewish origin exhibit ambivalence about their Jewish identity, as the Communist regime erased almost all cultural and religious customs (Yaglom, 1994). Only 15 percent are able to speak Yiddish (Flanerty et al., 1986). They have little Jewish awareness and rarely go to the synagogue (Goldstein, 1979). They were educated in the Russian culture and by the Soviet system. To be Jewish was to be socially handicapped. They retain a negative sense of Jewish identity and have viewed themselves as second-class citizens. The host community (the United States) has experienced a Jewish identity that is religiously nonobservant and does not embrace their religion; however, the first wave of immigrants from the early 1970s, who originated from the European border, the Baltic states, and Russian Georgia, are considered to have a stronger sense of religion and cultural traditions than those from the heartland of Russia who have immigrated to the United States (Flanerty et al., 1986).

Family Values

Marriage and fidelity are core values. "The family was and is a centerpiece of Yiddish culture" (O'Krent, 1995). The extended family and the growth and development of successful offspring is of paramount importance. In this country, the elderly Russian experience can be best understood in terms of the separation and individuation between the elderly and their adult children. Althausen (1993) relates this to the experience and needs the elderly encounter in the health care setting. When the elderly leave Russia, they suffer significant losses associated with authority in their family and their professional status, and they experience cultural and language barriers. The losses are compounded by additional age and health-related illnesses that force their adult children to assume a position of responsibility for their parents, which can cause emotional and physical stress due to their own unresolved issues of separation.

The history of strong parental authority and power originates from the previous Russian political and economic system. It was nevertheless a "cherished and unchallenged value" (Althausen, 1993, p. 64). Regardless, a strong family tradition of reciprocity remains between adult children and their elderly parents in which exchange of goods and services is a two-way interaction. In return for grandparenting and financial contributions, adult children are expected to provide extended care for their aging parents. This care extends from the home to the hospital setting. However, in this country, they are viewed as two separate families. Attempts are made by resettlement workers to establish separate households, which may be extremely difficult for the elderly immigrant as, in Russia, the entire family system had shared a single dwelling. This geographic division is an ambivalent experience for the elderly as it may be the first time they are separated from their nuclear family and, as a result, they may experience increased feelings of isolation and loneliness.

INTERGENERATIONAL ISSUES AND FAMILY CAREGIVING

As stated earlier, immigration and resettlement are experiences often fraught with great conflict and ambivalence for elderly Russian immigrants. This can produce an increase in isolation, depression, and/or physical and emotional illness. In addition, grandparents lose their traditional roles and are frequently left alone during the day because their children work outside the home. Many have become a burden to their adult children as dependency from physical illness and disability has increased (Belozersky, 1990). Adult children, particularly women, are becoming less available to provide the twenty-four-hour-a-day supervision needed if their elderly relatives become disabled.

Furthermore, as discussed by Gelfand (1986), the elder must rely on younger family members, who are forced to learn English more quickly, for assistance in negotiating the health care system, government bureaucracies, and for help with personal problems after their arrival in the new country. Health and community services of better quality, easier access, and fair cost will be needed as a backup to supplement the family system and to address the special language, health, and social needs of the elderly Russian individual. Elderly family members may also witness and experience unresolved marital conflicts among their adult children upon arrival in the new country. A high incidence of separation and divorce may result from the added pressures associated with resettlement and adjustment (Belozersky, 1991). The adult children have not encountered marriage counseling in the Soviet Union and are not familiar with legal advice or divorce proceedings. This marital conflict can have a negative impact on elderly family members, as they are now more dependent on younger family members for stability, assistance, and direction in their new surroundings.

Role shifts are said to occur as a result of changes and losses associated with life transitions and, in particular, in the process of adjustment to a new country (Gusovsky, 1995). Often an elder has been in a position of authority and respect and has been responsible for child care and financial assistance. The transition for the elder involves an autonomous, yet dependent, relationship in which he or she moves from an undifferentiated stage in the old country and is forced to take on a more differentiated and independent function with other family members. The separation-individuation process, which forces greater intergenerational distancing between the elderly and their children, can be observed in the context of language acquisition and differences between the generations in values and needs (Gusovsky, 1995). Younger generations have greater opportunities to learn English and integrate themselves into the larger society, while their parents or grandparents remain more entrenched in the old-world values, customs, and norms that now seem obsolete to younger family members. As a result of these differences and changes, the older generation may react with feelings of depression and even hopelessness and despair, thus causing further conflict with adult children who feel burdened and pressured into providing continued emotional support plus safeguarding their elderly family members' medical care (Althausen, 1993). Additionally, conflict may develop when medical problems arise and family members are forced to make decisions regarding institutionalization of their elderly relative. The family's first choice would be to provide care in their homes similar to their practices in the old country. However, due to new responsibilities and pressures outside the home, adult children are not able to provide the care as readily as before. Nursing home placement, therefore, becomes the epitome of separation for the elderly immigrant. Younger family members are left with extreme feelings of guilt and regret.

Physical and Mental Health Status

The Soviet immigration to the United States began approximately twenty-five years ago. Among the first wave of immigrants, acculturation was not a prominent theme. However, for both the earlier immigrants and the more recent refugees, cultural expectations and beliefs about health have influenced their health behavior. For example, many immigrants magnify normal aches and pains while ignoring more serious health problems and failing to take responsibility for their health care (Brod and Heurtin-Roberts, 1992). Consequently, health and community services of better quality, easier access, and fair cost will be needed to supplement the family system and to address the special language, health, and social needs of elderly Russians.

Although the majority of Russian immigrants are emotionally healthy, 20 to 30 percent of all arriving refugees from the second wave of immigration and 10 percent from the first wave are distressed due to chronic health or emotional problems and are in need of long-term therapeutic services. In contrast to earlier findings on education and economic status (Gold, 1991; Persidsky and Kelly, 1992), a recent study by Kennedy, Kelman, and associates (1996) on the prevalence of depressive symptoms among older Jewish community residents found that Eastern Europeans (Russian, Polish, and Hungarian) reported greater disability, poorer health, and lower incomes than Jewish residents born in the United States and elsewhere. In addition, Soviet Jews were reported to be older, less educated, and to have more cognitive impairment, yet were more likely to attend religious services as a means of support than their Jewish-American counterparts. Also, narcissistic behavior caused by feelings of insecurity and inadequacy were reported to be the result of the rigid hierarchical structure of the Soviet society and the inability of the structure to provide its citizens with adequate emotional support (Halbertstadt, 1996). The findings suggest that as a result of these factors, depression is a major mental health issue and is more prevalent among Russian Jews born in Eastern Europe than those born in the United States.

The following is a case vignette illustrating the process of separation, adjustment, and acculturation issues experienced by a widowed Russian woman upon immigration to the United States.

Miriam is a sixty-eight-year-old widow who arrived in the United States in 1979 with her divorced forty-five-year-old daughter and thirteen-year-old granddaughter. Her husband was killed during World War II.

In Russia she lived in one apartment with her family. Prior to her immigration to this country, she worked as a physiotherapist. Miriam's paycheck was one of the major money sources for the whole family. After she began to receive her pension, she continued to work part-time. In the house she was the head of the family. She also loved to educate herself, which was expressed in reading books and going to plays and concerts.

After her arrival in the United States, she moved in with her daughter and granddaughter. In time, after completing an accounting course, Miriam's daughter began to work and moved into her own apartment. The daughter expressed that she was tired of living her life under her mother's pressure. She also believed that her divorce was the result of the Soviet life in which the whole family struggled in one apartment.

The move to the United States was very difficult for Miriam. She often said that she moved only for her daughter's sake. Back in Russia she left her friends, a brother, and the memory of a murdered husband. Now, everything seemed very strange and complicated. She could not communicate with people due to the language barrier. She was always dependent on someone to translate for her, and her daughter could not give her the attention she needed due to her work responsibilities. Being accustomed to Soviet-government medicine, she could not and did not want to understand the U.S. medical system. She was irritated by the fact that she had to make an appointment to see a doctor and could not visit him whenever she felt like it.

Miriam was constantly in disputes with her granddaughter because she could not accept how teenagers dressed or their use of makeup. In addition, she did not understand what her granddaughter was talking about with her English-speaking friends. When her daughter rented her own apartment to live independently, Miriam began to feel abandoned by her daughter in a strange country. She called her daughter on the phone constantly, complaining about her weak health and her loneliness. Shortly after, Miriam fell and broke her hip. She was taken to the hospital where she underwent emergency surgery for a hip replacement. After the surgery she was transferred to a nursing home for rehabilitation. Although she was a difficult and demanding patient, after a few weeks she was walking again. She was surprised to find a lot of people who gave her the best of care and found ways of communicating with her. After her return home she was encouraged to attend adult day care, where she made new friends and improved her English.

Once again, she began to enjoy life. Previously she had called her daughter daily with frequent complaints about her horrible life. She was now capable of expressing an interest in her daughter's and granddaughter's lives and had begun to exchange services and help in a reciprocal manner. (Smolkin, 1997)

THEORETICAL PERSPECTIVES AND KEY CONCEPTS

Schneller's (1980) findings indicate that the process of grief and mourning resulting from the loss of one's native country can be far greater than the mourning associated with the loss of a loved object or person. Severe grief reactions and depressive symptoms may occur in the first six months after the Russian immigrant has settled in America, which supports Bowlby's (1961) and Parkes' (1971) theories of the process of mourning. During the first phase of mourning, symptoms of fear, alarm, anger, confusion, somatic disturbances, and a preoccupation with memories of their past life in Russia can be experienced. In the second phase of mourning, disorganization and depression are representative. Disorganization occurs as a result of an inability to understand the English language or the behavior and expectations of the American way of life. Depression is derived from difficulties in establishing meaningful friendships and relationships in the new country, a need to reminisce about Russia, and from a decline in social status. Not only is the individual attempting to form new behavior patterns and coping skills, adjust to the loss of the object, and prepare to make new goals, as in Bowlby's perspective, but the individual is also faced with the challenge of adapting to a foreign and unfamiliar environment, thus remaining in the marginal position of balancing the past and the present way of life (Schneller, 1980). Gusovsky (1995) describes the traumatizing effect of immigration in terms of "a disrupted attachment to a primary parental figure" (p. 225). This concept can be compared to the somewhat normal process of mourning. The ability to grieve for the motherland depends on the degree of attachment to it. However, the last wave of Russian immigrants remains ambivalently connected to the past, which may result in a more complicated resolution of the loss as previously described by Schneller (1980).

THE PROCESS OF ASSIMILATION

The United States has historically emphasized the process of assimilation, in which former separate groups or cultures come together and a new and unique society is developed. This can be better understood in terms of the new group taking on the culture of the old or dominant group, followed by a decrease in differences between the two groups (Healey, 1995). The more popular image of the "melting pot" has always been experienced as a "sharing of elements from a variety of traditions" (Healey, 1995, p. 40). Assimilation has traditionally been a one-sided process in which some minority groups such as African Americans and Native Americans have been excluded.

Cultural Pluralism

Cultural pluralism must be differentiated from assimilation. Assimilation occurs when two distinct groups merge and become one in the sense that the differences between the groups cease to exist. Pluralism, on the other hand, exists when each group observes its own unique identity and the groups remain separate despite the passage of time (Healey, 1996). Both of these pathways for group development may remain in opposition yet can even be seen to coexist. For example, some segments of a minority group may assimilate into the larger population while others may remain distinct or even increase their differences (for a more detailed discussion, please refer to Healy, 1996).

Acculturation

Acculturation is a very different experience than assimilation. The goals of acculturation have become a priority due to the difficulties encountered with the first wave of Russian immigrants. Nasitar (1991) and Belozersky (1991) suggest that acculturation is a subtle process taking place over a long period of time and can be an individual experience which is also extremely diversified. Nasitar compares the turn-of-the-century Eastern European Jewish and Russian immigrants to the more recently arriving immigrants for whom the tasks of acculturation and adjustment are different. The earlier wave of immigrants may never have seen the modern technology of today's world, but they had a firm background in Jewish tradition and religious and cultural identity, and a familiarity with business and commerce. More recent arrivals may come with strong professional experience and educational background, but they lack basic knowledge about their Jewish heritage and the market economy. Despite the fact that Russian immigrants receive one of the most well-funded and professionally staffed resettlement systems for recent immigrants (United States compared to Israel), difficulties in adjusting to the loss of family and friends and major problems in learning English still persist (Gold, 1991). This suggests that the elderly individual would be equally or even more affected by these problems than the younger generations of family members. The literature, therefore, suggests that English language acquisition is a major component and aspect of the process of acculturation (Gusovsky, 1995; Hulewat, 1996; Tran et al., 1996). As described by Tran and colleagues, acculturation involves a complicated process that includes basic elements in the individual's personal background and the host society, such as language skills, familiarity with the host culture, education, and generational factors. Acculturation is operationally defined in terms of language skills and education, which are distinct but related variables.

Resettlement

Resettlement is primarily the initial phase and is a crucial step in the difficult and lengthy process of acculturation. Elderly immigrants face the tasks of learning a new language and adapting to the political and economic workings of the United States, along with attempting to "fit in" or belong to the American Jewish society (Kugelmass, 1988). As Kugelmass emphatically states, Russian immigrants view themselves and identify as Jews first and Russians second.

The resettlement experience focuses on the concrete tasks of immigration and can be described as a more acute cultural and psychological crisis: the actual journey into a new country (Hulewat, 1996). Hulewat believes that all immigrants experience several stages of psychological adjustment in the process of resettlement. The first stage is the preimmigration or preparatory phase in which the decision to leave one's country of origin is made. The defensive mechanism of "splitting" is used as a means of coping, which allows the individual to idealize the future and deprecate the present situation; thus, the decision to leave is easier. Hulewat further points out that although splitting can be a pathological defense in the context of certain psychiatric and emotional disorders, during the resettlement process it can become a more healthy way of preparing for the new and unknown future. "Splitting is a temporary defense against a temporary crisis" (Hulewat, 1996, p. 130). The second phase of resettlement is the actual departure or journey, and the length of the transition time can be crucial in the adjustment phase. The third phase of the process is the arrival in the new country and the new home, which entails considerable tasks and can be accompanied by a variety of emotions such as excitement, stress, fatigue, and disappointment. Most immigrants are faced with learning a new language, which is especially difficult for the elderly, while the younger members of the family must begin to look for employment. The resettlement worker faces many challenges in assisting family members during this phase, and splitting may occur again as the worker can be seen as either all good or all bad. The fourth stage of resettlement has been termed the "decompensation" and is described as a general sense of discouragement. The individual is faced with the dual task of confronting the reality of past losses and attempting to balance the present situation with the past. The final or fifth stage of resettlement is the transgenerational stage in which "unresolved conflicts from the immigration experience are passed on to the succeeding generations" (Hulewat, 1996, p. 131). This can become a point of tension and conflict between generations.

Although additional opportunities offer some economic and emotional freedom, the ultimate task of the immigrant group is to face new crises and manage their past losses. These losses are particularly difficult for the elderly Russian immigrant because resistance to change may continue for many years. Finally, these stressful situations point to one of the most important needs of the elderly, that of the provision of health and community services needed to address the elderly Russian immigrant's physical and emotional needs.

HEALTH CARE UTILIZATION AND ACCESS

The medical realities of aging and the stresses of immigration can result in hazardous problems for elderly Russian immigrants. Similar to other populations, these immigrants may experience problems with access and utilization of health care services, which can jeopardize their ability to live independently in the community. As discussed by Tran (1996) in a proposal assessing public health needs of elderly Russian immigrants, various health conditions such as hypertension, coronary disease, gastrointestinal problems, diabetes, and cancer are more severe among Russian immigrants than the general U.S. population (Massachusetts Department of Public Health, 1995). Language and cultural differences also interfere with access to and effective use of the U.S. health care system. The language barrier and difficulties in communication alone can create a tremendous roadblock to medical care for elderly Russians, as few bilingual staff are available to address and interpret their medical needs.

Cultural differences and previous health care expectations have a strong influence on attitudes and health care behavior in this country. The Russian medical system is described as authoritarian and paternalistic, in which medical care is not administered until one becomes very ill. Preventive medicine is not practiced and psychiatric illness and care have severe consequences "ranging from loss of social status to imprisonment" (Brod and Heurtin-Roberts, 1992, p. 334). After arrival in this country, their expectations are unrealistic; people expect miracles and believe that physicians will cure them immediately. Immigrants also exhibit a lack of recognition of the relationship between biological influences and health status. They do not perceive that social forces such as food and housing shortages contribute to their health problems. All these factors have an influence on their interaction with health care professionals and the U.S. medical system.

The purpose of this chapter is to explore the physical and psychological well-being of elderly Russian immigrants, drawing attention to the meaning of these dimensions through empirical research and theoretical perspectives. It is expected that the exploration of these dimensions will encourage further consideration and utilization of this material for future clinical practice and research. In conclusion, it is therefore appropriate to bring together and summarize the central topics of this chapter. A discussion and review of the major themes will be presented, including:

1. factors affecting physical and psychological well-being;
2. cultural and intergenerational issues; and
3. health, access, and utilization, integrating theories, and therapeutic recommendations for health care professionals and future research.

Factors Affecting Physical and Psychological Well-Being

In formulating interventions and recommendations for practice with elderly Russian immigrants, knowledge of factors such as family size, living arrangements, education, language acquisition, and employment is a basis for understanding their experiences and the relationship to physical and mental health. Theoretical perspectives such as attachment theory, separation and individuation, and the process of grief and mourning provide a background for successful intervention and understanding of how living arrangements and language acquisition influence elderly immigrants' acculturation and coping strategies in the new country. The literature reviewed indicates that Russian immigrants must be viewed in a totally different context than other minority and immigrant groups, yet the basic principles of clinical practice should be observed, such as establishing a warm and trusting relationship, acceptance and validation of the client's feelings, understanding of the client's frame of reference, and identifying the correct medical or psychosocial problem (Belozersky, 1991).

Appropriate Training for Practitioners

In the initial phase of entry into the new country, one of the most important considerations in working with elderly Russians is the ability to converse in their own language. There is a great need for professionally trained bilingual and bicultural health care professionals. Persidsky and Kelly (1992) suggest training professional interpreters to assist American professionals with the Russian-speaking population. American professionals, however, must be trained and informed about the former Soviet Union in relation to the demographic impact of social and health factors. Additionally, it is necessary to provide accurate information and guidance that address the family members' expectations and future tasks of resettlement. One of the underlying themes in the initial stages of resettlement is the separation process from the former homeland and the loss of familiar routines, activities, family, and friends. As previously mentioned, in the United States generations of families are separated and placed in single households, creating feelings of isolation, loneliness, and depression for older immigrants, as former roles have been changed or lost. Professionals must remain sympathetic to the needs of elderly immigrants by allowing the expression of feelings of grief and loss. In summary, the professional must address the diverse social and historical factors encompassing present social and medical needs, including an understanding of culture, family structure, language, education, and housing.

Relationship

Friendship is based on a deep sense of trust, loyalty, and long-lasting devotion. Yet friendships are frequently severed and disrupted upon immigration. The professional should understand that since friendship, marriage, and the extended family are core values among Russians, theoretical perspectives including attachment theory, separation/individuation, and grief and mourning, together with the concepts of assimilation, acculturation, and resettlement, are essential background knowledge to guide therapeutic interventions. Factors such as education, housing, and cultural and family values are combined with the normal stress of resettlement. The worker is frequently faced with these stressful conditions and must intervene and address adjustment reactions such as depression, anxiety, increased illness, intergenerational conflict, and even marital conflict.

RECOMMENDATIONS AND GUIDELINES

Conflict often arises for elderly immigrants when friendship and similar former roles are no longer appropriate in the new country. One of the goals of the resettlement worker or caseworker is to reinforce a new sense of independence and reciprocity between the generations, in which elderly members can still provide child care and household assistance to their children in exchange for assistance with language and other cultural necessities and tasks of establishing themselves in their new environment. This is particularly valuable when friends are not available. Gusovsky (1995) has outlined several recommendations for practitioners when treating and working with elderly Russian immigrants. For example, it is essential that the worker be familiar with the role of cultural values and norms, including the dynamics of the process of resettlement and acculturation. Addressing issues of overdependency between the generations requires a perceptive approach and understanding of the value system, thus allowing for greater mutuality and support. A thorough understanding of the process of acculturation and the stages of resettlement previously described are required of the practitioner during the initial phase of immigration. Assistance with learning English, basic tasks of daily living, and community service information, along with remaining patient and available to answer what the worker may perceive as mundane questions is extremely helpful in relieving anxiety and confusion. It is also important to provide ego-supportive treatment during the process of acculturation by reinforcing the elderly immigrant's past strengths and coping mechanisms rather than challenging and weakening the client's primary ego defenses (Gusovsky, 1995). Future research efforts might, therefore, include studies that address specific cultural issues and treatment or supportive measures that more directly address the new immigrant's particular needs and problems.

The Coalition of Limited English Speaking Elderly (CLESE) recently reported that among all the immigrant groups, the Russians and the Koreans are the most in need of case management assistance as they remain extremely vulnerable "to the imminent elimination of many services to legal immigrants under last year's federal welfare act, especially SSI" (Cooper and Kleyman, 1997, p. 13). The Russian elderly need a great amount of assistance, because they are now the least likely to live with family members and most likely to live in high-rise housing for low-income elderly. Simultaneously, they experience difficulty with English and with familiarizing themselves with the U.S. culture and health care system. The service providers have, therefore, become their families.

The material presented previously on the process of acculturation and resettlement repeatedly emphasizes the drama of attachment and separation the elderly Russian immigrants and their family members experience when they encounter the unfamiliar culture of the U.S. health care system and the professionals who are attempting to provide services. For example, close psychological ties frequently exist between elderly parents and their adult children, who upon immigration are faced with the task of separation if a nursing home placement becomes necessary. The hospital staff frequently experience a sabotaging response from the family (Althausen, 1993). The professional must recognize the intensity of the parent-child bond when attempting to obtain their permission and cooperation for various hospital and health services.

In dealing with the crisis of separation, Althausen (1993) provides several recommendations and guidelines to "better facilitate the client's understanding and smoother utilization of the health care system" (p. 73):

1. For the purpose of preventing and eliminating cultural misunderstandings, the worker must remain cognizant of his or her own ethical values in response to the client's stated medical needs, yet maintain necessary limits.
2. Despite a variety of health care issues experienced by elderly immigrants, the worker must recognize the extent and importance of the separation/individuation dynamic as an underlying issue in providing appropriate care and interventions.
3. The worker should respect the clients' "culturally-syntonic values" (p. 74) and view the overinvolvement between the elder and the adult child as a normal filial responsibility and bond.
4. Consistent limit setting in a firm but kind manner is necessary in reminding the client of the hospital's limitations and ability to fulfill all their needs and requests.
5. Physical health referral requests are frequently confused with psychosocial needs. It is necessary for the physician to refer the client to a social worker or other mental health worker to address mental health needs, as elderly patients may call a physician for a common cold when in fact they are experiencing far greater medical problems. Russian patients often complain about long waiting periods between the referral and their internist's appointments. In Russia they went to the physician more frequently for every type of ailment and did not need an appointment.
6. Support groups are suggested for the elderly as a means of providing much-needed peer support and sharing. They may reduce the sense of loneliness and isolation. Other important goals for the group process would include focusing on issues of separation and abandonment from their adult children. This may facilitate the differentiation process, thus ultimately im-

pacting and possibly preventing a crisis during a serious health problem.

To summarize, the practitioner must realize that the strong emotional bond between the adult child and the elderly parent may never or should never be completely severed. However, attempts can be made to introduce a balance between parental dominance and authority and a basic sense of mastery and control between each generation (Althausen, 1993).

CONCLUSION

American health care practitioners may initially have difficulty understanding the cultural and political realities that influence the older Russian immigrant's acculturation process and health care experience in this country. This chapter has explored several aspects of the physical and psychological well-being and health of elderly Russian immigrants and has attempted to address the conflicts and misunderstandings that tend to occur between elders, their family members, and the helping professionals. As stressed by Brod and Huertin-Roberts (1992), education for both immigrants and practitioners is essential to better understand first how the immigrant reacts to the American system and its philosophy toward the family and health care. Second, professionals must recognize the important role that cultural influences have played in this process.

The results of this review have further implications for social policy and future research. A proactive research approach should be taken to include studies addressing the health, socialization, and activity requirements of needy and immigrant populations. The results of these studies may contribute to and promote future therapeutic interventions directed toward the diverse medical and social needs of elderly Russian immigrants. Health care professionals should also focus their clinical interventions on the benefits of participation in community programs such as adult day health care centers. Helping elderly people remain in the community is one of the most important and primary goals when working with the elderly Russian population. Family members are extremely reluctant to institutionalize their elders despite stress and burden experienced as a result of increased disability or medical problems. Appropriate public policy and community interventions should enhance community supports such as adult day health care centers by including permanent bilingual and bicultural professional staff, thus targeting appropriate social supports, health services, and acculturation needs. Studies have demonstrated the benefits of adult day health care programs on the well-being of elderly participants among heterogeneous populations (Aaronson, 1983; Capitman, 1989; Gelfand, 1988; Lyman, 1989; Rothman et al., 1993; Weissert et al., 1989). Those who have been isolated and neglected due to separation from family members, physical limitations, lack of information regarding community health services, and inability to communicate their needs will gain increased access if future professionals are appropriately educated and trained, and thus more able to address the elderly immigrant's physical health and emotional needs. This will contribute to a more positive sense of life satisfaction and assist in allowing the elderly Russian individual to maintain a higher level of independence and to remain in the community longer.

REFERENCES

Aaronson, L. (1983). Adult day care: A developing concept. *Journal of Gerontological Social Work, 5,* 35-47.

Althausen, L. (1993). Journey of separation: Elderly Russian immigrants and their adult children in the health care setting. *Social Work in Health Care, 19,* 61-75.

Belozersky, I. (1990, January). New beginnings, old problems. *Journal of Jewish Community Service*, 124-130.

Belozersky, I. (1991). Therapeutic interventions with Soviet refugee families. Paper presented at the Jewish Family and Children's Services, Boston, MA.

Bowlby, J. (1961). Processes of mourning. *International Journal of Psychoanalysis, 11*(2), 317-340.

Brod, M. and Heurtin-Roberts, S. (1992). Older Russian immigrants and medical care. *Cross Cultural Medicine—A Decade Later, 157,* 333-336.

Bychkov, I. (1991, June). Role of the new Jewish Americans. Paper presented at the Wilstein Institute Conference, Stanford University, CA.

Capitman, J.A. (1989). Day care programs and research challenges. *The Gerontologist, 29,* 584-585.

Cooper, A.Y. and Kleyman, P. (1997). Aiding elders in a strange land. *Aging Today, 18,* 1-13.

Flanerty, J., Kohn, R., Golbin, A., Gaviria, M., and Birz, S. (1986). Demoralization and social support in Soviet-Jewish immigrants to the United States. *Comprehensive Psychiatry, 27,* 149-158.

Gelfand, D.E. (1986). Assistance to the new Russian elderly. *The Gerontologist, 26,* 444-448.

Gelfand, D.E. (1988). *The aging network.* New York: Springer Publishing Company.

Gold, S. (1991, June). Soviet Jewish émigrés in the US: What we know and what we don't know. Paper presented at the Wilstein Institute Conference, Stanford University, CA.

Goldstein, E. (1979). Psychological adaptations of Soviet immigrants. *The American Journal of Psychoanalysis, 39,* 219-234.

Gusovsky, T. (1995). New beginnings: Older Russian immigrants in the U.S. *Geriatric Psychiatry, 28,* 219-234.

Halbertstadt, A. (1996). A model assessment of an émigré family from the former Soviet Union. *Journal of Jewish Communal Services, 72,* 298-309.

Healey, J.F. (1995). *Race, ethnicity, gender, and class.* Thousand Oaks, CA: Pine Forge Press.

Healey, J.F. (1996). *Race, ethnicity, and gender in the US.* Thousand Oaks, CA: Pine Forge Press.

Hebrew Immigrant Aid Society (1991). *Report of annual statistics, 1979-1991.* New York: HIAS.

Hulewat, P. (1996). Resettlement: A cultural and psychological crisis. *Social Work, 41,* 129-135.

Kennedy, G.J., Kelman, H.R., Thomas, C., Chen, J., Katsnelson, N., and Efremova, I. (1996). Depressive symptoms among Jewish community residents of Eastern European origin. Paper presented at the annual meeting of the Gerontological Society of America, Washington, DC.

Kugelmass, J. (Ed.) (1988). *In between two worlds: Ethnographic essays on American Jewry.* Ithaca, NY: Cornell University Press.

Lyman, K.A. (1989). Day care for persons with dementia: The impact of the physical environment of stress and quality of care. *The Gerontologist, 29,* 557-560.

Massachusetts Department of Public Health (1995). *Refugees and immigrants fact sheet: An overview of selected communities.* Boston: Author.

Nasatir, S.B. (1991, May). The challenge of Jewish acculturation and integration. Paper presented at the Integration and Acculturation of Soviet Jewish Immigrants Professional Conference, Chicago, IL.

O'Krent, V. (1995). Eastern European Jews and Yiddishkeit. Unpublished Paper.

Orr, M. (1987). *Report to Congress: Refugee Resettlement Program.* Office of Refugee Resettlement; Washington, DC: U.S. Government Printing Office.

Parkes, C.M. (1971). Psychosocial transitions: A field for study. *Social Science and Medicine, 5,* 101-115.

Persidsky, I.V. and Kelly, J.J. (1992). Adjustment of Soviet elderly in the United States: An educational approach. In Celia Berdes, Adam A. Zych, and Grace D. Dawson (Eds.), *Geragogics: European research in gerontological education and educational gerontology.* Binghamton, NY: The Haworth Press, 129-140.

Rothman, M.L., Hedrick, S.C., Bulcroft, K.A., Erdly, W.W., and Nickinovitch, D.G. (1993). Effects of VA adult day care on health outcomes and satisfaction with care. *Medical Care, 31,* SS38-SS49.

Schneller, D.P. (1981). The immigrant's challenge: Mourning the loss of homeland and adapting to the new world. *Smith College Studies in Social Work, 51*(2), 95-125.

Simon, R.J. and Simon, J.L. (1985). Social economic adjustment. In R.J. Simon (Ed.), *New lives: The adjustment of Soviet Jewish immigrants in the U.S. and Israel* (pp. 13-46). Lexington, MA: Lexington Books.

Smolkin, L. (1997). A difficult journey for elderly Soviet immigrants to life in the USA. Unpublished manuscript.

Tran, T.V. (1996). Assessing public health care needs of elderly Russian immigrants and refugees. Funded proposal submitted to The Medical Foundation/ Charles H. Farnsworth Trust.

Tran, T.V., Fitzpatrick, T.R., Berg, W.R., and Wright Jr., R. (1996). Acculturation, health, stress, and psychological distress among elderly Hispanics. *Journal of Cross-Cultural Gerontology, 11,* 149-165.

Weissert, W.G., Elston, J.M., Bolda, E.J., Cready, C.M., Zelman, W.N., Sloane, P.D., Kalsbeck, W.D., Mutran, E., Rice, T.H., and Koch, G.G. (1989). Models of adult day care: Findings from a national survey. *The Gerontologist, 29,* 640-649.

Yaglom, M. (1994). Role of psychocultural factors in the adjustment of Soviet Jewish refugees: Applying Kleinian theory of mourning. *Journal of Contemporary Psychotherapy, 23*(2), 135-145.

Zahler, G. 1991. Acculturation: A two way street. Paper presented at the Integration and Acculturation of Soviet Jewish Immigrants Professional Conference, Chicago, IL, May 13-15.

Chapter 5

African-American Elders

Elizabeth Gonzalez

Unlike all other immigrants to the United States, the ancestors of African Americans did not come to the United States by choice. Historically, Africans were brought to this country as slaves for cheap labor. Because of their migration history, African Americans struggle to maintain their culture and traditions (Dixon, 1976). For this reason, researchers, educators, and clinicians need to view the cultural characteristics of African Americans in the context of their struggle to maintain African culture and traditions in this country.

African-American elders are a rapidly growing segment of the minority population. The majority of African-American elders (59 percent) live in the South; smaller numbers live in the north central, northeastern, and western regions of the United States (U.S. Department of Health and Human Services, 1991).

Although African Americans exhibit considerable diversity, they suffer disproportionate economic hardships, as evidenced by the high percentage of individuals living below the poverty line (Baker, 1995). In 1991, 29.3 percent of African-American families and 31.9 percent of African-American persons were below the poverty line (U.S. Department of Health and Human Services, 1991) in comparison with 8.1 percent of Caucasian families and 10.7 percent of Caucasian persons below the poverty line. The median income of African Americans was $21,423, which was below the national average of $35,262 and below that of Caucasians ($36,915) (U.S. Bureau of the Census, 1992). Income and poverty status also vary considerably among African Americans as a function of household living arrangements, with female-headed households exhibiting the greatest poverty rates. Compared with Caucasian women, a larger proportion of African-American women receive public assistance. Among unmarried women ages sixty-five and over, as many as 33 percent of African-American women are on public assistance, compared with only 8 percent of Caucasian women. In the last decade, at least 60 percent of African-American women lived alone and in poverty (Ozawa, 1995).

FAMILY SYSTEM

Residual characteristics of African traditions are seen in the African-American extended family. African-American families include both biological members (e.g., parents, children, sisters, uncles) and nonbiological members (e.g., friends, minister, godfather) (Boyd-Franklin, 1989). A systematic review of the caregiver literature reveals that the majority of studies that have included African Americans have reported biological and nonbiological caregivers among African Americans (Gonzalez, Gitlin, and Lyons, 1995).

Fictive kin were as important in the black family as those related by blood. This particular orientation has served the African-American community very well, especially in regard to creating a mutual-aid system that highly values reciprocity and social responsibility within the family.

Studies show that African-American elders receive support from their family networks (Mindel, Wright, and Starrett, 1986; Silverstien and Waite, 1993). The family support system of the elderly African Americans provides transportation, banking services, homemaker services, and administrative/legal services. Their adult children assist them when they are sick, help during financial crises and emergencies, and advise them on matters that impact their lives.

On the other hand, studies show that many aged African Americans are major contributors to young generations. Cantor (1979), Mutran (1985), and Silverstien and Waite (1993) report that elderly African Americans give advice and economic support to their adult children more often than do Caucasians and assist their children by providing services to their grandchildren. The support African-American elders give in the grandparent role has involved providing temporary and sometimes permanent homes for their grandchildren, serving as co-parents in their socialization and rearing, and frequently supporting them financially (Hogan, Hoa, and Parrish, 1990; Slaughter and Dilworth-Anderson, 1990).

African-American elders underutilize formal home services (Chadiha et al., 1995). Among African-American elderly and their families, the tradition of receiving care from informal sources and their continued underrepresentation in nursing homes (Yeo, 1993) suggest that African-American elders are more dependent on home care.

Religious Beliefs

For many African-American families, the church is considered an important aspect of family life and provides a special role in the support networks of older African Americans (Allen and Chin-Sang, 1990; Levin and Taylor, 1993). The church provides tangible services as well as emotional and social support in African-American communities. Ministers and parishioners are often involved in providing both instrumental and expressive care on a long-term basis for frail elders (Wood and Parham, 1990). Research shows that religion is associated with mental well-being among African-American women (Brown, Ndubuisi, and Gary, 1990). Therefore, an important guideline is to explore the role that the church plays in the life of an African-American client. If church members are essential in providing instrumental and emotional support for the client, clinicians need to ask the client if he or she wants to include these church members in the discussion of his or her concerns.

Folk Beliefs

Within the belief systems of many African Americans, health problems can be the result of physical (natural) causes or spiritual forces. Illness attributed to a physical cause is believed to be cured with herbs, teas, and other natural substances. If the illness is attributed to spiritual factors (such as evil spirits, supernatural forces, violation of sacred beliefs, or sin), folk healers are consulted for treatment (Dana, 1993). For example, serious mental illness may be viewed as "the wages of sin" or being "possessed by the devil" (Hines and Boyd-Franklin, 1996). African Americans may consult a spiritualist to drive the evil spirit out. The voodoo priest is another healer that African Americans may go to for help. The voodoo priest has more formal training in the process of traditional healing (including selecting plants for healing purposes, prescribing the ingestion of organs of parts of certain animals to treat the problem, and having the skills to deal with individual and family problems).

Many African Americans believe that through their involvement with Bible study groups, prayer meetings, and advice from a minister they will achieve solution to their problems (Dana, 1993). For this reason, it is essential that clinicians accept these beliefs regarding the client's understanding of causation and solution of mental problems in the assessment and treatment of African-American clients (Baker and Lightfoot, 1993).

ACCULTURATION AND PHYSICAL HEALTH

Acculturation is a process whereby the attitudes and/or behaviors of persons from one culture are modified as a result of contact with a different culture (Moyerman and Forman, 1992). Issues of acculturation are as salient for African Americans as they are for new immigrants. For example, Lambert and Taylor (1990) surveyed a large sample of African-American parents and asked them if they believed that African Americans should relinquish or should maintain their distinctive culture and traditions. The researchers found that African-American parents favored maintaining their cultures and they favored multiculturalism. This study suggests that clinicians, researchers, and educators should be aware not only of the client's ethnic background, but also the extent to which the client identifies with and practices the culture of his or her ancestors.

Health problems such as cancer, stroke, hypertension, and cardiovascular disease are foremost among the major health issues of African Americans (Anderson, 1988; National Center for Health Statistics, 1991). Smoking plays a major role in heart disease, stroke, and hypertension. Smoking remains as the single most preventable cause of death (U.S. Department of Health, Education, and Welfare, 1991), accounting for 30 percent of all deaths from cancer each year. Health problems related to smoking, such as cancer, stroke, hypertension, and cardiovascular disease, are foremost among the major health issues of

African Americans (Anderson, 1988; National Center for Health Statistics, 1991).

Klonoff and Landrine (1996) have examined the relationships between levels of acculturation and health behavior/health status among African-American adults. Specifically, they examined acculturation, smoking, and high blood pressure. Their findings suggest that African-American smokers tend to be more traditional than their nonsmoking counterparts. These data suggest that smoking prevention and cessation programs may need to target traditional African Americans (who are likely smokers).

Although hypertension is one of the most serious health problems among African Americans (Baker, Lavizzo-Mourey, and Jones, 1993; Hildreth and Saunders, 1992), only one study (Klonoff and Landrine, 1996), was found that examined the relationship between hypertension and acculturation in this population. The study found that African Americans who were hypertensive tended to be more traditional, while those who were not hypertensive were more acculturated. One possible explanation for this finding is that traditional African Americans consume traditional foods that tend to be high in salt. This finding suggests that efforts to prevent hypertension among African Americans may need to include educational programs that address hypertension and different ways of preparing traditional foods.

Older African-American women comprise a subgroup at risk. Older African Americans are more likely to be widowed or separated with at least three medical problems such as heart disease, stroke, and diabetes (Baker, Lavizzo-Mourey, and Jones, 1993). Although the prevalence of breast cancer among Caucasian women is greater than among African-American women, the age-adjusted death rate for African-American women is 14 percent higher than for Caucasian women (National Center for Health Statistics, 1991).

Epidemiological studies commonly demonstrate nutritional deficiencies in this elderly population. For example, in a study of African Americans ages seventy-four years and older, Bernard, Anderson, and Fogery (1995) found that 20 percent of the subjects had relatively low serum albumin levels, 14 percent had serum cholesterol levels below 160 mg/dy, and some reported low food intake during a twenty-four-hour dietary recall.

Conditions related to nutritional excess, such as obesity, are also common among African Americans. More than 60 percent of African-American women ages sixty-five to seventy-five years are obese, which is almost twice the prevalence among Caucasian elderly women (36 percent) (Conway, 1995). Bernard, Anderson, and Fogery (1995) reported that 40 percent of African Americans ages seventy-four years and older had a body weight that was at the 120th percentile or greater.

ACCULTURATION AND MENTAL HEALTH

Despite the improvements in the reliability of diagnostic criteria and advances in neuroimaging, which have increased the capacity to identify discrete disorders, the myth that mental illnesses are not real persists among African Americans. This myth has kept many African Americans from seeking help for mental health problems. In addition, many African Americans with mental disorders who do seek help are not accurately diagnosed because the frequency with which they report some symptoms differs from that in the overall population. This may be due to colloquial descriptions of symptoms that may not be consistent with mental health practitioners' understanding of diagnostic criteria.

Various studies have documented the increased presence of depressive symptoms in older African Americans with medical illness (Glik, Steadman, and Michels, 1990; Husaini and Moore, 1990). Although the Epidemiologic Catchment Area (ECA) study found that only 2 to 4 percent of community residents have a depressive disorder, a greater percentage of older community residents reported symptoms of depression (15 percent) (Blazer, Burchett, and Service, 1991), and depression increases across the life course in men. Among the medically ill, 25 percent were found to have depressive illness. The rates of depressive illness are higher among those with Parkinson's disease (40 percent), Huntington's chorea (50 percent), stroke (60 percent), and Alzheimer's disease (25 percent) (Blazer, Burchett, and Service, 1991; Yesavage, 1992).

In a recent study of general clinic patients, 32 percent of the sixty-three African-American patients with a mean age of seventy-four and at least three active medical problems screened positive on the Center for Epidemiologic Studies—Depression (CES-D) scale for depressive symptoms, but only 11 percent met the DSM-III-R criteria for depression, a rate of depression higher than that of the 2 percent from the ECA study (Baker, 1995).

Because depressive symptoms have been shown to be associated with specific disorders that affect the elder's quality of life (Blazer, Burchett, and Service, 1991; Delehanty, Dimsdale, and Mills, 1991; Husaini and Moore, 1990), health care providers need to be alert to monitor their patients for the presence of a treatable condition that can exacerbate existing medical illness.

Recently, Landrine and Klonoff (1996) found that the best predictors of psychiatric symptoms for acculturated African Americans differ from those of their traditional counterparts. Acculturated African Americans tended to blame themselves for problems (taking responsibility coping style), whereas traditional African Americans tended to deny problems (escape-avoidance, distancing coping styles), with both of these maladaptive coping styles predicting psychiatric symptoms. Additionally, the study also found that appraised generic stress played an important role in symptoms among acculturated African Americans, accounting for a significant percentage of the variance in four of the six (66.7 percent) symptom measures for this group (i.e., total symptoms, depression, obsessive-compulsive, and interpersonal sensitivity symptoms). Appraised generic stress played only a minor role in the symptoms of traditional subjects.

This study suggests that symptoms among acculturated subjects may be predicted by self-blaming and by ordinary stressors, whereas symptoms among traditional subjects may be predicted by various types of denial problems. These differences suggest that acculturation-specific models of African-American mental health are needed, along with acculturation-specific therapies that focus on the different, maladaptive coping styles used by some members of both acculturation groups. Further studies are needed to clarify the nature of the acculturation-stress-coping-symptom relationship.

Despite reports that African-American caregivers are subject to higher risks than Caucasian-American caregivers, because of generally poorer health and greater exposure to chronic stressors such as poverty, unemployment, crime, and racism (Belgrave, Wykle, and Chloe, 1993; Young and Kahana, 1995), there are indications that

African-American caregivers are resilient in the face of negative effects of the stress of caregiving. Studies found that African-American caregivers report less stress than Caucasian-Americans (Hinrichsen and Ramirez, 1992; Segal and Wykle, 1988-1989). In a recent study examining similarities and differences in learned resourcefulness and coping between African-American and Caucasian-American caregivers of relatives with Alzheimer's disease, African-American caregivers were found to be more resourceful than their Caucasian-American counterparts (Gonzalez, 1997).

CONCLUSION

Clinicians and researchers need to be cognizant that African Americans as a minority have a unique migration history. The history of racial discrimination has limited the access of African Americans to higher incomes, improved health care, adequate housing, and better education. Their struggle to maintain their tradition and culture is evident in their extended family networks, strong religious beliefs, and spirituality. The family solidarity among African Americans serves as a critical resource for African-American elders. Many elderly African-Americans are being cared for by informal support networks, a factor that delays and sometimes even prevents institutionalization. With the increasing life expectancy among older African Americans, family members will continue to need assistance in caring for their elders.

In working with African-American elderly, clinicians, researchers, and educators must be willing to develop innovative strategies that acknowledge the social, political, socioeconomic, and environmental conditions that affect this group. Advocacy in the form of guiding these families to negotiate complex bureaucratic systems becomes critical. Culture-specific interventions need to be conducted to provide directions in establishing guidelines for assisting families in providing support for their older family members.

REFERENCES

Allen, K. and Chin-Sang, V. (1990). A lifetime of work: The context and meanings of leisure for aging Black women. *The Gerontologist, 30*(6), 134-140.

Anderson, N. (1988). Aging and hypertension in blacks: A multidimensional perspective. In J. Jackson (Ed.), *The Black American elderly: Research on physical and psychological health.* New York: Springer Publishing Co.: 90-214.

Baker F. (1995). Mental health issues in elderly African Americans. *Clinics in Geriatric Medicine, 11*(1), 1-13.

Baker, F., Lavizzo-Mourey, R., and Jones, B. (1993). Acute care of African American elders. *Journal of Geriatric Psychiatry, 6,* 66-72.

Baker, F. and Lightfoot, O. (1993). Psychiatric care of ethnic elders. In A. Gaw (Ed.), *Culture, ethnicity and mental illness.* Washington, DC: American Psychiatric Press: 517-552.

Belgrave, L., Wykle, M., and Chloe, J. (1993). Health, double jeopardy, and culture: The use of institutionalization by African-Americans. *The Gerontologist, 33*(3), 379-385.

Bernard, M., Anderson, C., and Fogerty, M. (1995). Health and nutritional status of old-old African Americans. *Journal of Nutrition for the Elderly, 14*(2), 55-67.

Blazer, D., Burchett, B., and Service, C. (1991). The association of age and depression among the elderly: An epidemiologic exploration. *Journal of Gerontology, 46*(6), M210-M215.

Boyd-Franklin, N. (1989). *Black families in therapy: A multisystem approach.* New York: Guilford.

Brown, D., Ndubuisi, S., and Gary, L. (1990). Religiosity and psychological distress among blacks. *Journal of Religion and Health, 29*(1), 55-68.

Cantor M. (1979). The informal support system of New York's inner city elderly: Is ethnicity a factor? In D. Gelfand and J. Kutzit (Eds.), *Ethnicity and aging.* New York: Springer: 137-140.

Chadiha, L., Proctor, E., Morrow-Howell, N., Darkwa, O., and Dore, P. (1995). Post hospital home care for African-American and white elderly. *The Gerontologist, 35*(2), 233-239.

Conway, J. (1995). Ethnicity and energy stores. *American Journal of Clinical Nutrition, 62*(5), 1067S-1071S.

Dana, R. (1993). *Multiracial assessment perspectives for professional psychology.* Boston: Allyn and Bacon.

Delehanty, S., Dimsdale, J., and Mills, P. (1991). Psychosocial correlates of reactivity in black and white men. *Journal of Psychosomatic Research, 35*(4), 451-460.

Dixon, V. (1976). World views and research methodology. In L. King, F. Dixon, and W. Nobles (Eds.), *African philosophy: Assumptions and paradigms for research on the black person.* Los Angeles: Fanon Center: 102-108.

Glik, D., Steadman, M., and Michels, P. (1990). Antihypertensive regimen and quality of life in a disadvantaged population. *Journal of Family Practitioners, 30,* 143-149.

Gonzalez, E. (1997). Resourcefulness, appraisals, and coping efforts of family caregivers. *Issues in Mental Health Nursing, 18*(3), 209-227.

Gonzalez, E., Gitlin, L., and Lyons, K. (1995). Review of literature on African-American caregivers of relatives with dementia. *Journal of Cultural Diversity, 2*(2), 40-46.

Hildreth, C. and Saunders, E. (1992). Heart disease, stroke, and hypertension in blacks. In R. L. Braithwaite and S. Taylor (Eds.), *Health issues in the black community.* San Francisco: Jossey-Bass: 90-105.

Hines, P. and Boyd-Franklin, N. (1996). African-American families. In M. Goldrick, J. Giordano, and J. Pearce (Eds.), *Ethnicity and family therapy.* New York: The Guilford Press: 66-84.

Hinrichsen, G. and Ramirez, M. (1992). Black and white dementia caregivers: A comparison of their adaptation, adjustment, and service utilization. *The Gerontologist, 32*(3), 375-381.

Hogan, D., Hoa, L., and Parrish, W. (1990). Race, kin networks, and assistance to mother-headed families. *Social Forces, 68*(6), 797-812.

Husaini, B. and Moore, S. (1990). Arthritis disability, depression, and life satisfaction among black elderly people. *Health and Social Work, 24,* 253-260.

Klonoff, E. and Landrine, H. (1996). Acculturation and cigarette smoking among African-American adults. *Journal of Behavioral Medicine, 19*(5), 501-514.

Lambert, W. and Taylor, D. (1990). *Coping with cultural and racial diversity in urban America.* New York: Praeger.

Landrine, H. and Klonoff, E. (1996). *African-American acculturation.* Thousand Oaks, CA: Sage Publications, Inc.

Levin, J. and Taylor, R. (1993). Gender and age differences in religiosity among black Americans. *The Gerontologist, 33,* 16-23.

Mindel, C., Wright, C., and Starrett, R. (1986). Informal and formal health and social support systems of Black and White Elders: A comparative cost approach. *The Gerontologist, 26,* 279-285.

Moyerman, D. and Forman, B. (1992). Acculturation and adjustment: A meta-analytic study. *Hispanic Journal of Behavioral Sciences, 14*(3), 163-200.

Mutran, E. (1985). Intergenerational family support among blacks and whites: Response to culture or socioeconomic differences. *Journal of Gerontology, 40,* 382-389.

National Center for Health Statistics (1991). *Health, United States, 1990.* Hyattsville, MD: DHHS, Public Health Service.

Ozawa, M. (1995). The economic status of old women. *Social Work, 40*(3), 323-331.

Segal, M. and Wykle, M. (Winter 1988/Spring 1989). The black family's experience with dementia. *Journal of Applied Social Sciences, 13*(1), 170-191.

Silverstien, M. and Waite, L. (1993). Are blacks more likely than whites to receive and provide social support in middle and old age? Yes, no, and maybe? *Journal of Gerontology: Social Sciences, 48*(4), S212-S222.

Slaughter, D. and Dilworth-Anderson, P. (1990). Sickle-cell anemia, child competence, and extended family life. In H. Cheatham and J. Steward (Eds.), *Black families—Interdisciplinary perspectives.* New Brunswick, NJ: Transaction: 131- 148.

U.S. Bureau of the Census. (1992). *Statistical abstract of the United States.* Washington, DC: U.S. Government Printing Office.

U.S. Department of Health and Human Services. (1991). *Health status of minorities and low-income groups,* Third edition. Washington, DC: Health Resources and Services Administration.

Wood, J. and Parham, I. (1990). Coping with perceived burden: Ethnic and cultural issues in Alzheimer's family caregiving. *The Journal of Applied Gerontology, 9*(3), 325-339.

Yeo, G. (1993). Ethnicity and nursing homes: Factors affecting use and successful components for culturally sensitive care. In C. Barresi and D. Stull (Eds.), *Ethnic Elderly and Long-Term Care.* NY: Springer Publishing: 161-177.

Yesavage, J. (1992). Depression in the elderly. *Postgraduate Medicine, 91,* 255-259.

Young, R. and Kahana, E. (1995). The context of caregiving and well-being outcomes among African and Caucasian Americans. *The Gerontologist, 35*(2), 225-232.

Chapter 6

Elderly Puerto Ricans

Raymond Bossè

Elderly Puerto Rican immigrants to the United States are a unique case because Puerto Rico was annexed to the United States in 1898 and the natives were granted U.S. citizenship in 1917. As American citizens, Puerto Ricans are free to relocate to the U.S. mainland at will. Easy access to the mainland, the density of the population on the island (over 3.5 million in an area the size of Rhode Island), and the poverty (60 percent under the U.S. poverty level, according to the U.S. Bureau of the Census, 1993) prompted millions of Puerto Ricans to migrate to the mainland United States.

The first wave of immigrants began arriving in 1918 during World War I to work in factories and farms in the New York City area. East Harlem quickly became their barrio, and they replaced the Italians who preceded them in that neighborhood. Possibly the language, religion, and other cultural similarities with the Italians, such as the predominance of family relationships, attracted them to this location. The second wave of Puerto Rican migration occurred during World War II and continued through the 1950s and 1960s, supported by the industrial boom that also began to draw immigrants to other urban industrial centers. After the 1960s, better-educated, professional, middle-class, and upwardly mobile Puerto Ricans stopped leaving the island in large numbers because of new opportunities resulting from "Operation Bootstrap" (Donaldson and Martinez, 1980), which sought to develop jobs and opportunities in Puerto Rico that would make migrating to the United States less attractive.

While the approximately 350,000 elderly, ages sixty-five and older, constitute roughly 10 percent of the island population, the 1990 United

States census recorded another 2.5 million Puerto Ricans living in the continental United States, with roughly 100,000 or 4 percent of these sixty-five years of age and over. The previous 1980 census reported 2.3 million on the continent, with 3.6 percent ages sixty-five and over—a noticeable increase over ten years. Predictions are that the number of Puerto Rican elderly in the United States will more than double by the year 2050 (U.S. Bureau of the Census, 1993). This chapter will attempt to identify the factors that impact the health status and service utilization of Puerto Rican elders and thereby affect their ability to maintain daily functioning activities.

THEORETICAL PERSPECTIVES

Use of Services by Minority Elders in General

Minority elders do not utilize health care services the way the white majority does. However, assessing the true usage of services by various minorities can be difficult for several reasons: though numerous differences exist between them, much research combines minorities together; studies use different definitions or methodologies; baseline health status may vary; or differing cultural values are ignored (Damon-Rodriguez, Wallace, and Kington, 1994).

The problem is compounded by the fact that minorities tend to use emergency rooms for primary care, especially because they have no health insurance or a primary care physician. Unfortunately, emergency rooms are not equipped to care for the chronic conditions of elders; service is more expensive and does not provide for the continuity of care or for the frequent multiple chronic conditions of the elderly.

Even when minority elders have recourse to private physicians, they receive less aggressive treatment and diagnostic procedures than do whites with identical conditions (Escarce et al., 1993; Goldberg et al., 1992). Also, despite the fact that Medicare and Medicaid pay for almost 90 percent of hospital care of the elderly (Waldo et al., 1989), Latino minorities use hospital facilities significantly less than whites and blacks (Starrett et al., 1989), make less use of community-based services, and have dramatically lower admissions to nursing homes (Weissert and Cready, 1988).

Some barriers to service utilization are considered structural in that they are external to the elderly, such as racism and income. Others are considered cultural and internal to the elderly. These are based on cultural values and preferences, which are specific to each minority, such as familism, religion, and specific ideas about health.

The Acculturation Problem for Immigrant Minorities

In addition to the preceding, immigrant populations share a common problem—that of becoming acculturated into the dominant society. This may be accomplished with varying degrees of difficulty depending on several factors.

The elderly have an especially difficult time adapting to a new culture because they have lived for so long in their culture of origin. For them, acculturation severs ties to familiar networks, institutions, and lifelong values, beliefs, and expectations. The loss of everything familiar, combined with the diminished capacity to relearn, can jeopardize the elderly's ability to deal with new institutions such as the health care system.

In addition to age, the task is made more or less difficult depending on the degree of similarity between the culture of origin and the host culture. In that regard, factors such as language, religion, family structure, ghetto concentration, beliefs, and customs about health can all present obstacles to acculturation.

FACTORS HYPOTHESIZED TO IMPACT ELDERLY PUERTO RICANS

The acculturation problems of elderly Puerto Ricans are particularly relevant because they currently constitute one of the largest immigrant groups in the United States and are expected to double in size during the next two or three decades. It is therefore doubly imperative for social service and health care providers to identify, understand, and find solutions to the special problems of the Puerto Rican elderly in order to deliver their services in a more effective and efficient manner (Krause and Goldenhar, 1992). In light of the preceding, unidimensional explanations would surely be inadequate for understanding the health status and care utilization of the Puerto Rican elderly (Escovar and Kurtines, 1983). Among the factors that tend to be obstacles to the utilization of formal support systems by Puerto Rican elders are the following: (a) the traditional centrality of *the family* on the island and its possible breakup due to migration; (b) the use of *Spanish* on the island and English in the United States; (c) historical membership in the Roman Catholic *religion* confronted by active proselytizing on the mainland; (d) *race,* because of the centuries-long existence and acceptance of mixed-race families in Puerto Rico compared to the racist attitude that tends to prevail in the United States; and (e) the use of *spiritualists and folk healers* as traditional sources of social support and health providers within Puerto Rican communities (Delgado, 1982). We will briefly describe each of these factors and how they may impact the status of the Puerto Rican elderly.

The Family

As a culture of Hispanic origin, the Puerto Ricans, like all other Latinos, have very traditional families. Hispanic families are known to have strong bonds, with patterns of frequent interaction that are extremely important to their members. There is a deep sense of family obligation that often supersedes the needs or desires of the individual (Lockery, 1991). In that regard, the Puerto Rican family may be both a blessing and a curse. As a student at Fordham University during the late 1950s, the author remembers several cases of Puerto Rican students who felt pressured to drop out of college because other family members chided them for being "different" by going to college. (For more on school dropouts, see Delgado, 1974.)

As a blessing, the elderly have traditionally been held in high esteem. It is a family obligation to care for the elderly in their declining years and a source of comfort for the elderly to know that care will be provided (Cuellar, 1990; Delgado, 1982). However, it is important to recognize significant differences among Hispanic groups (Schur, Bernstein, and Berk, 1987). Escovar and Kurtines (1983), for instance, found that Cuban Americans tended to seek exclusively the help of their children when in need and not the help of other extended family members. Puerto Ricans, by contrast, more than any other Hispanic group, have been found to rely on themselves or on friends more than family members for assistance (Lacayo, 1980).

Lacayo's finding may result from the fact that among Puerto Ricans the definition of "family" is different from that commonly accepted in the United States. For them, family can go beyond the family of origin or of procreation to encompass not only other blood relatives and those related by marriage, but also others *(compadres)* tied to the family through custom. These others share in the same reciprocal obligations and support expectations in times of need (Mizio, 1978; Perez-Stable, 1987).

The negative aspect of Puerto Rican family centeredness with regard to elder care is that they are unable to individually care for themselves. Self-reliance is lacking, which differs from what is common in the dominant culture. This may be particularly important when younger family members did not immigrate, which may explain Lacayo's (1980) finding that immigrant Puerto Ricans tended to turn to friends and others more than to family members. On the other hand, if the local ageism or individualism captures the mind of the young, the traditional informal caregiving function of the extended family may fail the elderly (Delgado, 1982; Maldonado, 1975; Valle and Vega, 1980).

Language, Education, and Income

Although Spanish is spoken extensively in parts of the mainland United States, it is not the national language, nor is it likely to be the language spoken by doctors, nurses, other health care specialists, or social workers. It has been shown that for Hispanics, including Puerto Ricans, language can be a barrier to accessing formal community services (Andersen et al., 1981; Bullough and Bullough, 1982).

Education and income have been included in this heading because invariably the language deficiency of minorities is an obstacle to successful education, which in turn limits one's level of occupation and income.

Religion

In Puerto Rico, the dominant religion has been Roman Catholicism. Although Roman Catholic churches, parishes, priests, and schools are readily available throughout the United States, language has remained an obstacle to Puerto Ricans' active participation in church activities. In fact, since the early days of massive Puerto Rican migration to the mainland, they have been a ready target for the Pentecostal movement, whose storefront churches attracted them by speaking their language and by structuring services to include activities linking song and dance, which appealed to their Latin cultural background.

Race

Although race may not constitute a problem among Puerto Ricans themselves because of their long history of interracial marriage, race may constitute a difficulty for Puerto Ricans in general and for the elderly in particular when they attempt to obtain the assistance of services they require from public agencies.

Spiritualism and Folk Healers

As described by Delgado (1982), one can find up to four major types of folk healers in Puerto Rican communities: the medium (spiritualists); the *santero* (psychotherapist); the herbalist (pharmacist); and the *santiguador* (internist/chiropractor). These various forms of healers are all based on the same principle that illness or other misfortune can be the result of spiritual intervention. One manifestation of this thinking is the *azabache* or the "black-hand amulet" which Puerto Ricans attach to their newborns or display in the home as a protection from the evil eye (*el mal de ojo*). It is not uncommon for Puerto Ricans to turn first to these various forms of folk medicine or spiritualists for the health care of their elderly and to consider formal health care agencies only as a last resort. For insights into the extent and use of spiritualism among Puerto Ricans, see Delgado, 1974.

PHYSICAL HEALTH STATUS
OF ELDERLY PUERTO RICANS

Until fairly recently, very little was known specifically about the status of Puerto Rican elders in the United States (Angel and Angel, 1992; Markides and Mindel, 1987). Information about elderly immigrant Hispanics in general was attributed to elderly Puerto Ricans. Despite the absence of concrete research, Puerto Ricans, as a distinct ethnic group, were pictured as having lower education; being employed principally in service, blue collar, or agricultural occupations; living in substandard housing; and having poor health. (For a description of the status and living conditions of the Puerto Ricans during the early years of immigration to New York City, see Delgado, 1974.) Frequently, their years of work have not provided Social Security, medical insurance, or retirement pensions. Several surveys have found the Puerto Rican elderly least likely to have medical insurance coverage when compared to other groups in the community (Andersen, Giachello, and Aday, 1986; Perez-Stable, 1987). Elderly Puerto Rican women were particularly vulnerable to loss of income and to serious deprivation (Torres-Gil and Negm, 1980).

Because they tend to live in large metropolitan areas, Puerto Ricans invariably are affected by a number of problems common to the inner-city poor and minorities. Aside from street crime and vandalism, they are subject to poor living conditions, high taxes, and the risk of dispossession and relocation. Public services are likely to be few and of poorer quality compared to the more affluent communities. This latter situation is frequently compounded by prejudice on the part of the providers and by poor knowledge of English and of procedures for accessing services on the part of the Puerto Rican elders themselves (Torres-Gil and Negm, 1980).

Heavy concentration in specific areas may be prompted by the strong family bonds. The proximity of others with the same culture facilitates social support. For the elderly, younger members of the family may provide assistance in learning English or in dealing with local agencies (Angel and Angel, 1992; Biafora and Longino, 1990). The ghetto phenomenon, however, with its strong family and group bonds, may also be an obstacle to acculturation and therefore to accessing the formal services available only outside of one's protective ethnic or cultural network. As for the state of health of the elderly Puerto Ricans, a study conducted in New York City in 1970 began to shed light on the problem (Cantor and Mayer, 1976). It found 62 percent of Puerto Rican elderly with some form of disability. In contrast, blacks registered a 49 percent disability rate and the white majority was found to have a 48 percent disability rate.

Prior to the 1970 survey, there had been problems gathering data on Puerto Ricans because they were lumped with other groups of Hispanic origin. The difficulty in documenting the illegal immigrants among other Hispanics tended to extend to the Puerto Ricans and to discourage survey takers either from gathering data on Hispanics or from differentiating them (Espino et al., 1988). Puerto Ricans, however, are American citizens like anyone else born on American soil.

A 1986 survey of Puerto Rican elderly living in the New York City metropolitan area began to expand our knowledge and to specify how poorly the Puerto Rican elderly fared when compared to U.S. blacks or whites. (For details, see O'Donnell, 1989.) Focusing on functional ability, the survey measured six activities of daily living (ADLs): three personal care tasks (bathing, dressing, and trimming one's toenails) and three mobility tasks (climbing stairs, moving around indoors, and going outdoors). ADL measures were seen as more objective than self-reports of health status, which are more prone to cultural bias as to what constitutes good or poor health.

The survey found Puerto Rican elderly to be considerably more disabled than either blacks or whites. Only 41 percent of Puerto Ricans said they could climb stairs, and 46 percent could trim their toenails, compared respectively to 62 percent and 66 percent of blacks, 77 percent and 76 percent of whites. Even when controlling for income, education, marital status, sex, and age, significant differences were found between the Puerto Ricans and the other two groups in all of the ADLs. Blacks and whites did not differ significantly from each other. It should be noted that these findings also applied to Puerto Ricans ages fifty-five to sixty-four. In addition, the greater functional disability of the Puerto Rican elders was found to continue among those eighty years of age and older.

The researchers also reported a direct relationship between degree of functional disability and degree of language problems. They found that those with the greatest language problems also had significantly greater functional disability. Nevertheless, the functional disability status of the Puerto Rican elderly remained significantly greater than that of blacks and whites even after controlling the functional competence in English.

A number of relevant observations may be made regarding the functional disability of elderly Puerto Ricans in the New York City study:

1. They clearly revealed a greater level of disability than blacks or whites
2. Some of this difference can be attributed to acculturation difficulties and specifically to their knowledge of English
3. Part of the difference may also be explained by the lower socioeconomic condition
4. The greater disability of the elderly implies a greater need for services

Based on these findings, a study by O'Shaughnessy (1986) concluded that the social isolation of elderly Puerto Ricans, caused by the language barrier, qualified them for the special help described in Title III of the Older Americans Act.

Another large-scale study of elderly Hispanic Americans, including Puerto Ricans, Mexicans, and Cubans, was undertaken as part of the 1988 *National Survey of Hispanic Elderly People,* sponsored by the Commonwealth Fund Commission on Elderly People Living Alone (Andrews, 1989; Davis, 1990). Trained bilingual interviewers contacted 2,019 families in regions of heavy Hispanic concentrations. They interviewed 937 elderly Mexican Americans (46.4 percent), 714 Cuban Americans (35.4 percent), and 368 (18.2 percent) Puerto Ricans ages sixty-five and over. The study sought to determine self-assessed health, functional disability, and life satisfaction while taking into account age, year of migration, education, living arrangement in terms of size and composition of household, and household income including retirement benefits. (For details see Angel and Angel, 1992; Wallace, Campbell, and Lew-Ting, 1994; Tran and Dhooper, 1996.)

It is important to note that this study avoided the pitfall of lumping Hispanics together. It is widely recognized that these three principal Hispanic groups differ greatly in levels of acculturation, socioeconomic status, and economic mobility, as they do in their migration experiences (Angel and Angel, 1992). There also is ample evidence that these groups are as different from one another as they are from blacks or whites in the access and use of medical care

(Angel and Angel, 1992; Krause and Goldenhar, 1992; Schur, Bernstein, and Berk, 1987).

The Puerto Rican elderly were found to be extremely disadvantaged when compared to the Mexicans and Cubans. They were more likely to fall below the poverty line, to be less educated, and to have more children than the Cubans but the same number as the Mexicans. They were more likely to be married and living with children, an important determinant of social support. Puerto Ricans were more likely to have migrated in mid-adulthood, Cubans in adulthood, and Mexicans to have been born here or to have come as children (Angel and Angel, 1992). These facts are significant in terms of the more difficult acculturation process experienced by adults described earlier (Angel and Angel, 1992).

In terms of social support, Angel and Angel (1992) report that the three groups see their children at least once a day. The Puerto Rican elderly, however, are less active in religious or church activities or in any other outside activities such as going to sporting events, the movies, or clubs. In addition, these findings were reported to be particularly true for Hispanics who migrated as adults, which is the case with a majority of the Puerto Rican elderly.

On the three dependent variables investigated—self-reported health, functional disability, and life satisfaction—elderly Puerto Ricans were found to consistently have the poorest status (Wallace, Campbell, and Lew-Ting, 1994). Although all groups reported high levels of functional disabilities, the elderly who migrated in late adulthood reported more disability and lower life satisfaction than the native born or those who migrated before the age of twelve. The findings suggest that at least some of the association between poor health, life satisfaction, and age at migration is due to reduced social contacts evidenced by nonattendance at church, social, cultural, or sporting activities. The principal fact remains that elderly Puerto Ricans are more likely to have migrated in adulthood and consequently to have greater difficulty in adjusting to their new environment. This in turn leads to poorer health, greater functional disability, and lower life satisfaction. Of course, there is always the possibility of a reversal in cause and effect, namely, that unhealthy or depressed people are less likely to attend social activities.

Using data from the same 1988 *National Survey of Hispanic Elderly People,* Tran and Dhooper (1996) focused on the ten most common social service needs perceived by the elderly age sixty-five-plus:

1. transportation,
2. use of a senior center,
3. food stamps,
4. ability to eat at a senior center,
5. home-delivered meals,
6. homemaker services,
7. routine telephone calls to check on one's health,
8. use of a home health aide,
9. visiting nurse service, and
10. use of church-based services for the elderly.

The Puerto Rican elderly had significantly greater needs than the Cuban Americans on all ten of the measures and significantly more than the Mexican Americans on three: transportation, routine telephone calls to check on health, and food stamps. Mexican-American elderly also had significantly greater needs than the Cuban Americans on all but one measure. These findings held even when Tran and Dhooper (1996) controlled for education. The authors also reported significant gender differences between the men and the women in the three Hispanic groups, which space limitations prevent describing herein.

It is of interest that a much smaller study of Puerto Ricans residing in New York City was undertaken between 1986 and 1987 or at about the same time as the 1987 survey described above (Espino et al., 1988). The study in question included only nineteen elderly Puerto Ricans along with six other Hispanics. The principal outcome measures were also ADL functioning. The findings of this survey, undertaken in one specific nursing home, were basically identical to those of the larger survey. In addition, the Hispanics who needed nursing home care were younger than the non-Hispanic elderly in the control group, they had significantly less mobility, greater functional disability in all ADL categories, and had greater mental impairment, which was not examined in the larger survey. Comparable findings were reported by Mui and Burnette (1994) from data collected in ten diverse sites along the eastern seaboard from Maine to Miami, plus Cleveland and Houston. Unfortunately, these data compared whites and blacks with an undifferentiated group of Hispanics. Nevertheless, because of the geographic location of the study sites, a good percentage of the elderly had to be Puerto Rican, with the exception of Cubans in Miami and Mexicans in Houston (see Biafora and Longino, 1990).

In their attempt to explain the greater functional disability observed among the Puerto Ricans and the "other Hispanics" group, Espino and colleagues (1988) suggest a possible breakup of the immigrant Puerto Rican family and thus its inability to gather the economic or personal supports necessary to maintain impaired members at home. They see this as contrary to the generally recognized extended family caregiving function of traditional Puerto Rican and Hispanic families (Delgado, 1982; Maldonado, 1975; Valle and Vega, 1980).

Espino and colleagues (1988) refer to another possible explanation for the high rates of disability among the Puerto Rican elderly. Their view stems from a suggestion made by Eribes and Bradley-Rawls (1978) in their explanation of the high levels of disability among elderly Mexican Americans. It is suggested that both of these Hispanic groups share a cultural mandate that requires them to maintain their sick elderly in the community as long as possible so that they are only committed to institutional care as a last resort. In that case, the elderly Puerto Ricans as well as the Mexican Americans in nursing homes are considerably more ill than other elderly residents.

It should be noted, however, that in their study of Puerto Rican, Mexican, and Cuban-American elderly, from data collected in 1979-1980, Starrett and colleagues (1989) found a difference between Puerto Ricans and Mexican Americans with regard to the impact of family and friends on use of services. Mexicans with available family members were less likely to use formal services, whereas Puerto Rican elderly with more contact with relatives, friends, and neighbors made greater use of formal services. The authors suggest that friends and relatives act as a source of information and a referral service in the case of elderly Puerto Ricans.

Although this is speculative, it is quite possible that the sense of alienation felt by immigrants in dominant white institutions, combined with the cultural expectations of family care, lead to delayed institutionalization. It is understood that this is not only a reflection of an underlying cultural factor but of additional factors such as language, religion, and possibly race.

MENTAL HEALTH STATUS
OF ELDERLY PUERTO RICANS

Krause and Goldenhar (1992) used a cultural-assimilation approach in their study of Mexican, Cuban, and Puerto Rican Americans. They described a model wherein lower acculturation, indexed by poor knowledge of English, would result from lower education; this then would lead to poorer financial status and greater social isolation, which in turn would predict greater psychological distress.

Using data from the 1988 *National Survey of Hispanic Elderly People,* Krause and Goldenhar (1992) found general support for their model, but with important differences between the three groups. They found that despite lower levels of education, which inhibits their use of English, Puerto Rican elderly had a better command of English than Cuban Americans. Nevertheless, the Puerto Rican elderly experienced more financial difficulties and social isolation, which may coincide with their greater functional disability described earlier (O'Donnell, 1989). Also, we are reminded of the Eribes and Bradley-Rawl (1978) statement that the Puerto Ricans turn to committing their elderly to institutional care only as a last resort.

Concerning psychological distress, Krause and Goldenhar (1992) found Puerto Rican elderly to be significantly more distressed than elderly Mexican or Cuban Americans. They saw this as resulting from lower education, which leads to lower language acculturation and financial status, as well as greater social isolation. Their findings were supported by a study undertaken sixteen years earlier in New Jersey with seventy-two elderly Puerto Rican women (Torres-Matrullo, 1976). Like the Krause and Goldenhar study, this earlier study measured acculturation by length of residence in the United States, place and level of education, language preference, and responses to questions regarding sex-role attitudes. As in the Krause and Goldenhar study, this earlier study found that women low in acculturation were more likely to exhibit psychopathology. They scored significantly higher on scales of depression, withdrawal, and obsessive-compulsive disorder.

Comparable findings were reported by Tran, Fitzpatrick, Berg, and Wright (1996), based on data from the same 1988 *National Survey of Hispanic Elderly People.* Their structural equation model supported the hypothesis that degree of acculturation would have a significant indirect effect on psychological distress. The model concluded that age, gender, marital status, and ethnicity lead to poor education and poor English proficiency, which in turn lead to lower income and poor physical health; these then lead to lower acculturation and ultimately to psychological distress.

It should be noted that a study undertaken with Puerto Ricans ages seventeen to sixty-four on the island reported rates of psychiatric disorders similar to those found in comparable studies of non-Hispanics in the United States, with the exception of higher rates of cognitive impairment and somatization disorder among Puerto Ricans (Canino et al., 1987). Although the study found increases in symptoms with age, the upper age range of the sample was sixty-four, making it impossible to draw conclusions regarding the elderly. Nevertheless, although the rates of psychiatric disorders were similar in Puerto Rico and on the mainland, the difference in the size of the populations in the two studies means that one in six Puerto Ricans on the island was afflicted with a major psychiatric condition. These findings also coincide with the Alsina-Pomales and Rodrigues-Gomez (1995) findings of significant levels of depression and suicide among those sixty-five and older on the island compared to the population under sixty-five between the years 1980 and 1990.

The principal reason given for the high rates of suicide among the elderly on the island is depression. Other factors related to suicide, which may themselves have led to depression, were unemployment, poverty, retirement, and loss of loved ones or of social supports due to death or institutionalization. Although the reasons given by Krause and Goldenhar (1992) for the high rates of psychological distress appear somewhat different from the reasons given by Alsina-Pomales and

Rodriguez-Gomez (1995) for the depression, they are basically quite similar. What appears to be lacking is whether the experience of deprivation among Puerto Rican elders on the mainland causes as high a rate of suicide as it does on the island. Unfortunately, suicide rates specifically for the elderly Puerto Ricans in the United States do not appear to exist as they do for the island.

Certainly, we should be careful not to consider depression as endemic to Puerto Ricans. The higher rates of depression or of psychological distress are most likely due to the many sources of deprivation experienced by Puerto Rican elders. This is supported by a study of elderly Hispanics (mostly Mexican) in the Los Angeles area, which found higher rates of depression than of heart disorders, strokes, hypertension, and arthritis among elderly who were also poorly educated, spoke little English, and lived generally below the poverty line (Lopez-Aqueres et al., 1984).

In dealing with the mental health status of Puerto Rican elders, it is critical to consider one significant cultural factor frequently underscored in the research literature on Hispanics. The cultural issue in question is generally referred to as *nervios* (nerves) or *ataques de nervios* (attacks of nerves). *Nervios* is a nonspecific manifestation of emotional distress and is a generalized sense of psychological disturbance, which may even be chronic, experienced by Puerto Ricans and other Latinos (Angel and Angel, 1992; Guarnaccia and Farias, 1988; Guarnaccia, Good, and Kleinman, 1990; Low, 1981, 1989).

The experience of *nervios* may be accompanied by a number of psychosomatic symptoms such as headaches, heart palpitations, a sense of heat in the chest, generalized bodily pains, trouble sleeping, and persistent worrying. These are usually brought about by a variety of personal, familial, and social problems.

The term *ataque de nervios,* on the other hand, is a somewhat better defined and more dramatic episode. The most important component of an *ataque de nervios* is a culturally accepted response to an acute stressful experience stemming from grief, fear, or family conflict. The culturally accepted manifestations of an *ataque* include trembling, heart palpitations, a sense of heat in the chest rising into the head, faintness, and even seizurelike episodes. Because of their cultural component, an *ataque* traditionally occurs at culturally appropriate occasions such as a funeral, an accident, a family argument, or a fight. *Ataques* may also take on a vast variety of forms that deviate from the cultural norms. Nevertheless, an *ataque* elicits support from the sufferer's social network. Such episodes may even end with the person regaining consciousness without remembering the attack (Guarnaccia, Good, and Kleinman, 1990).

The significant point to be made is that the tendency for studies of mental health among Puerto Ricans and possibly other Hispanics to record high scores on standard psychiatric or mental health tests needs to be interpreted in the context of the culture. As was indicated by Rogler (1989), cultural factors are integral components of the research process, every bit as important to the successful understanding and interpretation of outcomes as are the more formal procedures codified in epidemiological and clinical research textbooks. In the case of the Puerto Rican elderly, therefore, it should be remembered that they have been enculturated into a pattern of behavior that not only accepts but expects a symptomatic response to specific stressful events.

For instance, during the 1950s and 1960s, several psychiatric studies in New York City consistently found that Puerto Ricans reported the highest number of psychological symptoms of any ethnic group studied. Angel and Angel (1992) suggest this may be due to the cultural influence of *nervios*. In their own analysis of data from the Hispanic Health and Nutrition Examination survey (Hispanic HANES) conducted between 1982 and 1984, Angel and Angel (1992) found much support for the effect of *nervios* among the Puerto Rican and Mexican elderly. The first indication of its effect was the fact that the Puerto Ricans reported more symptoms than the Mexican elderly and many more symptoms than were observed by the physicians. This was particularly true for those who took the examination in Spanish compared to those who did the interview in English, suggesting a cultural and linguistic effect as well as an effect of poor acculturation.

In addition, both Mexicans and Puerto Ricans who rated their health as poor tended to score higher on the Center for Epidemiologic Studies—Depression (CES-D) scale, while those who did the interview in Spanish scored even higher on depression. However, in both instances the Puerto Rican elderly scored higher than their Mexican peers. Angel and Angel (1992) view their findings as further evidence that individual experiences are labeled and acted on according to the symbolic and linguistic system provided by one's culture.

More recently, as indicated by Malgady, Rogler, and Cortés (1996), the significance of cultural factors has been recognized by the inclusion of culturally varied symptomatology in the DSM-IV (American Psychiatric Association, 1994). Malgady, Rogler, and Cortés (1996) found a significant relationship between anger and mental health symptoms among Puerto Ricans living in New York City. They suggest that expressions of anger through high levels of aggression, assertiveness, and vindictiveness are consistent with the low socioeconomic status of ethnic groups in the inner city. For a thorough anthropological, psychiatric, medical, and psychosocial review of the literature on this issue we suggest Guarnaccia, Good, and Kleinman (1990) and Guarnaccia et al. (1996).

Although we have not underscored gender differences in the mental health status of immigrant Puerto Rican elders, we should point out that significantly higher rates have tended to be reported for elderly Puerto Rican women than for men (Canino et al., 1987; Torres-Matrullo, 1976). As noted by Torres-Matrullo, there may be several reasons for this, not the least of which is the culturally prescribed subservient role of women compared to the machismo or dominant male role. Faced with the task of acculturation into American society with the increasing equality of the sexes, Puerto Rican women experience a more difficult task. This may even be true on the island because of the increasing universality of female liberation.

USE OF SOCIAL SERVICES
BY ELDERLY PUERTO RICANS

It is one thing to identify the physical and mental health status of elderly Puerto Ricans but quite another to describe and evaluate their utilization of community-based social services. Starrett and associates (1989) described a model for assessing such utilization based on a classificatory system proposed by Andersen and Newman (1973). The model suggests three sets of components to evaluate the use of formal social services. These are predisposing factors, enabling factors, and need factors. *Predisposing* factors are socio-demographic characteristics of individuals or groups and health-related attitudes that precede an illness episode and provide a greater propensity to use social services. This propensity is associated with variables such as ethnicity, age, sex, education, marital status, or specific attitudes. *Enabling* factors refers to variables such as knowledge or awareness of services, income, transportation, and availability and accessibility of services. Finally, *needs-for-care* are actual illnesses or impairments that individuals must recognize are in need of service before they take concrete steps to obtain that service (Burnette and Mui, 1995; Starrett et al., 1989).

Using the Andersen-Newman model, Starrett and his associates analyzed data from a national survey of Hispanic elderly collected in 1979-1980 (Lacayo, 1980), which included Puerto Rican, Mexican-American, and Cuban-American elderly. Among the Puerto Rican elderly, significant predictors of actual use of formal social services included one predisposing variable (number of children), three enabling variables (knowledge, income, and contact with friends and neighbors), and two need variables (needs-for-care and poor functioning with respect to ADLs). In short, those with lower incomes, less education, and poorer health were more likely to use social services. Also, children and contact with friends and neighbors appeared to be an informal social support network that facilitated access to social services (Starrett et al., 1989).

Burnette and Mui (1995) applied the Andersen and Newman (1973) model to the data from the 1988 *National Survey of Hispanic Elderly People* (Davis, 1990) described earlier. Outcome variables in the Burnette and Mui study were somewhat different from those in the Starrett and colleagues study in that they included in-home services such as meals-on-wheels, home health aides, and visiting nurses, in addition to community-based services including senior citizen centers, congregate meals, transportation, church programs, and telephone assurance programs.

Burnette and Mui (1995) found the Puerto Rican elderly were slightly younger, more likely to be unmarried (65.8 percent), to live alone, not to have medical insurance, to receive Medicaid and food stamps, and to be in poorer self-reported health. As regards the outcome variables, Puerto Rican elderly reported much higher use of homemaker services and visiting nurses, more transportation services, and more services at senior citizen centers during the past year. Mexican Americans reported greater use of meals-on-wheels and church programs, and reported having more children and more frequent contact with children each week. Cuban Americans had the poorest knowledge of English, but the best physical and functional health.

In the analyses that predicted the factors best related to use of services, Burnette and Mui created a dummy variable for the Hispanic groups by comparing the Puerto Ricans and the Mexicans against the Cubans. The analyses specified the predisposing, enabling, and needs-for-care factors that best predicted actual use of services. For the use of in-home services, the best predisposing factor was age—being eighty or older; the best enabling factors were living alone, number of children, being on public assistance (food stamps, Medicaid, or Supplemental Security Income), and use of community-based services; the best needs-for-care factors were ADL and Instruments of Activities of Daily Living (IADL) impairment, and hospital utilization. No differences were found among the three Hispanic groups.

For use of community-based services, age was again the best predisposing factor. The best enabling factors were living alone, being on public assistance, and use of in-home services. The best need-for-care factor was IADL impairment. In this model, the Puerto Rican elderly were significantly more likely to use community-based services than Cuban Americans. It should be noted that income data were not available, although being on public assistance may well serve as a proxy for low income. It is interesting that education, fluency in English, self-rated health, or length of residency in the United States were not significant predictors of use of services in these models.

In summary, the Andersen and Newman model tends to show that needs-for-care factors are stronger predictors of in-home services, followed by enabling and then predisposing factors. Enabling factors, however, make the greatest contribution to community-based services. Certainly the older individuals in the study who also lived alone and who were less likely to have an informal support system were at increased risk for need of services.

CONCLUSION

It has been made abundantly clear that elderly Puerto Ricans are in a poorer state of physical and mental health and have greater functional disability than blacks and whites in the United States. They are also worse off than Mexican and Cuban Americans regarding a variety of the factors that contribute to poor health. The Puerto Rican elderly are also generally worse off than elderly blacks and whites with regard to access to in-home or community-based care or social services. Their status varies in regard to use of services when compared to Mexican and Cuban Americans, with each of the three being worse off than the others on specific factors. All three of the major Hispanic groups, however, tend to be worse off in access to and use of formal social services than black and white elderly Americans.

It was suggested that a number of factors would undoubtedly be identified as significant contributors to the health status of elderly Puerto Ricans. Among these were level of acculturation, the family, language, religion, race, spiritualism, and use of folk healers. A low level of acculturation was in fact identified as one of the major reasons why elderly Puerto Ricans are lacking in necessary services. Poor acculturation itself was seen as resulting from older age at migration and poor knowledge of English. Poor acculturation in turn has led to low-level occupations with little or no benefits and low income. It should be noted that an exception to the significant negative effect of language acculturation on use of formal services was reported recently (Calderón et al., 1997). Calderón and colleagues reported findings from a study undertaken in Springfield, Massachusetts, which found language acculturation unrelated to use of services by Puerto Rican elders (see Delgado and Tennstedt, 1997 for a description of the Springfield Elders Project).

The role of religion in the access or utilization of health care services by elderly Puerto Ricans is somewhat ambiguous. Contrary to initial expectations, the historical prevalence of Roman Catholicism on the island did not appear to be an obstacle to the access or utilization of health care services by elderly Puerto Ricans, nor did religion appear to promote the use of services. Angel and Angel (1992) as well as Burnette and Mui (1995) found that elderly Puerto Ricans did not have recourse to services provided by churches in their neighborhood.

This finding coincides with suggestions made by Delgado and Tennstedt (1997) to the effect that historically, Puerto Ricans have been nominal Roman Catholics only. In fact, they have always had a deep-rooted suspicion of and antagonism for the Church because they viewed the clergy as siding with the aristocracy in opposition to the lower-class natives. Also, in opposition to the Roman Catholic Church, Puerto Ricans have tended to turn to spiritualism and otherworldly forces to seek answers to misfortunes. The Church and clergy have always frowned on that type of behavior. Delgado (1982) has also suggested that in addition to the use of spiritualists, Puerto Ricans also use a variety of folk healers, described earlier, which are all part of this complex culture and also may militate against the use of more modern health care services, including ordinary visits to the doctor.

Although race was not identified as a source of discrimination preventing Puerto Rican elderly from having access to or use of health care services, race should not be ignored as a strong secondary factor in the case of the Puerto Ricans. This is explained by the fact that Puerto Ricans are largely a mixed-race ethnic group. As such, instead of having the best of both worlds, they have the worst of both when it comes to many social factors such as jobs and housing. Massey and Bitterman (1985) provided ample evidence documenting the segregation of Puerto Ricans due to their low socioeconomic status and black ancestry, which closes off white neighborhoods to them and leaves them on the fringe of the black ones. This segregation has the added effect of limiting access to agencies that serve whites and those that serve blacks.

The Puerto Rican family, as indicated earlier, is a double-edged sword when it comes to access and utilization of formal health services for the elderly. There is ample evidence that members of the younger generation frequently provide the necessary assistance the elderly need to access local health care agencies, due to their greater knowledge of English, the neighborhood, and the procedures for obtaining community assistance.

On the other hand, because of the predominance of the family in the lives of Puerto Ricans and the culturally prescribed respect and esteem for the elderly, they have a tendency to care for their elderly at home. In fact, Espino and colleagues (1988) suggest it is a cultural mandate for Puerto Ricans to maintain their sick elderly at home as long as possible: Institutionalization is sought only as a last resort.

The negative side of familism is evidenced in the underutilization of formal services by elderly Puerto Ricans, which may have many dysfunctional side effects. Purdy and Arguello (1992) have argued, for instance, that reliance solely on informal family supports creates added stress in the lives of the caregiving children, which in turn has been found to correlate with higher levels of depression. In addition, reliance on children only perpetuates the cycle of poverty because children are frequently required to sacrifice economic opportunities for the sake of caregiving duties.

Another possibility suspected by Purdy and Arguello is that caregiving children act as a barricade against information reaching the elderly because of misconceived filial obligation. This notion suggests that the elderly under certain circumstances would opt for formal care services, rather than burden their offspring, if they were aware of their availability and accessibility. Use of formal services is infrequent, however, because the elderly are unaware of them and because of the multiple layers of informal caregiving within the Puerto Rican community. The typical Puerto Rican informal care system, which may need to be exhausted before turning to the formal system, includes the immediate family, the extended family, the *compadrazgo* (the extended family created by religious life events that require godparents), the barrio, and the larger Puerto Rican community.

In support of their argument, Purdy and Arguello refer to Starrett, Mindel, and Wright (1983), who found that knowledge of available social services had the strongest direct effect on usage. Frequent contact with family, friends, and neighbors had no effect on frequency of utilization of services. They also reference a Maldonado (1988) study, which found that elderly Puerto Ricans in fact resemble their white counterparts in preferring to be independent and not to burden their children with their care despite the long cultural tradition of doing so.

Recommendations

The major component of the Puerto Rican social support system is the extended family and the Puerto Rican community. Delgado (1995), as well as Purdy and Arguello (1992), suggest that this asset or natural support system could be better utilized in the care of the Puerto Rican elderly. The natural support system may be composed of individuals with or without institutional affiliation, such as family members, friends, religious groups, folk healers, and community institutions.

In essence, they note that the natural support system of ethnic groups such as Puerto Ricans is an untapped resource that can be most valuable toward providing for elder care both through informal as well as formal services while respecting the cultural or ethnic belief system. Natural support systems have many advantages, such as accessibility and mutuality, as well as feelings of love, affection, respect, trust, and loyalty. See Delgado's 1995 work for how the family may become a source for providing information on formal health care services instead of a roadblock. Recent research into Puerto Rican family caregiving underscored the importance of sons in that capacity, a possibility generally overlooked in the past (Delgado and Tennstedt, 1997).

One way to accomplish higher rates of utilization of services is dissemination of information. It was shown by Starrett and colleagues (1990) that knowledge is probably the most powerful determinant of utilization. It is important, therefore, for social workers, medical practitioners, and others who are likely to have contact with elderly Puerto Ricans to dispense information about available services. In that regard, it is important to assign bilingual Spanish-speaking workers in areas of high Puerto Rican concentration.

In their attempt to suggest strategies for overcoming barriers to use of community services, Yeatts, Crow, and Folts (1992) begin by underscoring the importance of knowledge. They identify three types of knowledge and indicate strategies used in Texas to provide the required knowledge. The first is the knowledge of or the perception of a need. Potential elderly clients need to be educated in recognizing symptoms that require help. The second type of knowledge is that of availability. Two strategies used successfully to provide or improve these two forms of knowledge are the use of public mass media (newspapers, radio, television, pamphlets, posters, billboards, and giveaway items such as pencils), use of group gatherings (at churches, senior centers, neighborhood picnics, political rallies), and the use of significant individuals. Use of significant individuals is a two-step process. The first is the identification of persons in the community whose opinions are generally respected by low-income minority elderly, such as physicians, clergy, hospital staff, personnel counselors, company representatives, and staff of social agencies. The second step is to provide these individuals with information on available elderly services and how to obtain them.

The third form of knowledge refers to accessibility: the elderly need to know how to access required services. It is important at this stage to have individuals available to assist potential clients in taking the necessary steps to access the service. Inability to read or write English, for instance, can be an insurmountable obstacle without help. In addition, there is the need to provide for physical access to the service.

Some successful solutions to physical access include locating service sites close to minority neighborhoods or establishing satellite centers close to such neighborhoods. Satellites have been established economically by using facilities at churches, schools, and other private or public halls. Meals can even be brought to such locations from a central facility. Transportation problems have been resolved by various arrangements with transit authorities or carpools (Yeatts, Crow, and Folts, 1992).

Additional solutions described by Yeatts, Crow, and Folts deal with problems stemming from cultural factors such as the discomfort felt by minority elderly in dealing with culturally different service providers, or negative attitudes toward receiving help, which are fostered in some minority cultures.

Other researchers (Sanchez-Ayendez, 1989) underscored the need for awareness of values such as familism, *respeto* (respect), and *personalismo* (individuality). Tradition promotes great respect for the elderly, manifested by deference. Caseworkers need to use the more polite *Usted* (the formal "you") when addressing them, rather than *tú* (the familiar "you"). *Personalismo* requires a degree of informality in providing services by accepting the traditional hospitality in the form of tea or coffee and something to eat, and a willingness to chat. Elderly Puerto Ricans expect these manifestations of *personalismo* or the establishment of a close personal relation rather than the formal relation of a functionary.

Also, in the case of in-home services in particular, because of their less formal nature, it is important for the success and continuity of the service for care providers to be sensitive to cultural factors. Knowledge of Spanish and of customs that are meaningful to the elderly is of utmost importance.

REFERENCES

Alsina-Pomales, S. and Rodrigues-Gomez, J.R. (1995). El suicidio en ancianos Puertorriquenos. *Revista Latinoamericana de Psicologi'a, 27*(2), 263-282.

American Psychiatric Association (1994). *Diagnostic and Statistical Manual of Mental Disorders,* Fourth edition. Washington, DC: Author.

Andersen, R.M., Giachello, A.L., and Aday, L.A. (1986). Access of Hispanics to health care and cuts in services: A state of the art overview. *Public Health Reports, 101*(3), 238-252.

Andersen, R.M., Lewis, S.Z., Giachello, A.L., Aday, L.A., and Chiu, G. (1981). Access to medical care among the Hispanic population of the Southwestern United States. *Journal of Health and Social Behavior, 22*(March), 78-89.

Andersen, R.M. and Newman, J.F. (1973). Societal and individual determinants of medical care utilization in the United States. *Milbank Memorial Fund Quarterly, 51*(1), 95-124.

Andrews, J. (1989). *Poverty and poor health among elderly Hispanic Americans.* Baltimore, MD: The Commonwealth Fund Commission on Elderly People Living Alone.

Angel, J.L. and Angel, R.J. (1992). Age migration, social connections, and well-being among elderly Hispanics. *Journal of Aging and Health, 4*(4), 480-499.

Biafora, F.A. and Longino, D.F. Jr. (1990). Elderly Hispanic migration on the United States. *Journal of Gerontology: Social Sciences, 45*(5), S212-S219.

Bullough, V.L. and Bullough, B. (1982). *Health care for the other Americans.* New York: Appleton-Century-Crofts.

Burnette, D. and Mui, A.C. (1995). In-home and community-based service utilization by three groups of elderly Hispanics: A national perspective. *Social Work Research, 19*(4), 197-206.

Calderón, V., Morrill, A., Chang, B.H., and Tennstedt, S. (1997). Acculturation of Puerto Rican elders and their caregivers, and the use of formal services. Presented at the annual meeting of the Gerontological Society of America, Washington, DC, November. *The Gerontologist, 36*(Special Issue II), 4.

Canino, G.J., Bird, H.R., Shrout, P.E., Rubio-Stipec, M., Bravo, M., Martinez, R., Sesman, M., and Guevara, L.M. (1987). The prevalence of specific psychiatric disorders in Puerto Rico. *Archives of General Psychiatry, 44*(8), 727-735.

Cantor, M. and Mayer, M. (1976). Health and the inner city elderly. *The Gerontologist, 16*(Part I), 17-25.

Cuellar, J.B. (1990). *Aging and health: Hispanic American elders.* Stanford, CA: Stanford Geriatric Education Center.

Damon-Rodriguez, J.A., Wallace, S., and Kington, R. (1994). Service utilization and minority elderly: Appropriateness, accessibility, and acceptability. *Gerontology and Geriatrics Education, 15*(1), 45-63.

Davis, K. (1990). *National survey of Hispanic elderly people, 1988.* Ann Arbor, MI: Interuniversity Consortium for Political and Social Research.

Delgado, M. (1974). Social work and the Puerto Rican community. *Social Casework, 55*(2), 117-123.

Delgado, M. (1982). Ethnic and cultural variations in the care of the aged Hispanic elderly and natural support systems: A special focus on Puerto Ricans. *Journal of Geriatric Psychiatry, 15*(2), 239-251.

Delgado, M. (1995). Puerto Rican elders and natural support systems: Implications for human services. *Journal of Gerontological Social Work, 24*(1/2), 114-130.

Delgado, M. and Tennstedt, S. (1997). Puerto Rican sons as primary caregivers of elderly parents. *Social Work, 42*(2), 125-134.

Donaldson, E. and Martinez, E. (1980). The Hispanic elderly of East Harlem. *Aging,* March-April, 6-11.

Eribes, R.A. and Bradley-Rawls, M. (1978). The underutilization of nursing home facilities by Mexican-American elderly in the southwest. *The Gerontologist, 18*(4), 363-371.

Escarce, J.J., Epstein, K.R., Colby, D.C., and Schwartz, J.S. (1993). Racial differences in the elderly's use of medical test procedures and diagnostic tests. *American Journal of Public Health, 83*(7), 948-954.

Escovar, L.A. and Kurtines, W.M. (1983). Psychosocial predictors of service utilization among Cuban-American elders. *Journal of Community Psychology, 11*(4), 355-362.

Espino, D.V., Neufeld, R.R., Julvihill, M., and Libow, L.S. (1988). Hispanic and non-Hispanic elderly on admission to the nursing home: A pilot study. *The Gerontologist, 28*(6), 821-824.

Goldberg, K.C., Harts, A.J., Jacobsen, S.J., Krakauer, H., and Rim, A.A. (1992). Racial and community factors influencing coronary artery bypass graft surgery rates for all 1986 Medicare patients. *Journal of the American Medical Association, 267*(11), 1473-1477.

Guarnaccia, P.J. and Farias, P. (1988). The social meanings of nervios. A case study of a Central American woman. *Social Science and Medicine, 26,* 1223-1231.

Guarnaccia, P.J., Good, B.J., and Kleinman, A. (1990). A critical review of epidemiological studies of Puerto Rican mental health. *American Journal of Psychiatry, 147*(11), 1449-1456.

Guarnaccia, P.J., Rivera, M., Franco, F., and Neighbors, C. (1996). The experiences of "ataques de nervios": Towards an anthropology of emotions in Puerto Rico. *Culture, Medicine and Psychiatry, 20*(3), 343-368.

Krause, N. and Goldenhar, L.M. (1992). Acculturation and psychological distress in three groups of elderly Hispanics. *Journal of Gerontology: Social Sciences, 47*(6), S279-S288.

Lacayo, C.G. (1980). *A national study to assess the service needs of the Hispanic elderly: Final report.* Los Angeles, CA: Asociación Nacional Pro-personas Mayores.

Lockery, S.A. (1991). Caregiving among racial and ethnic minority elders: Family and social support. *Generations,* Fall-Winter, 58-62.

Lopez-Aqueres, W., Kemp, B., Plopper, M., Staples, F.R., and Brummel-Smith, K. (1984). Health needs of the Hispanic elderly. *Journal of the American Geriatric Society, 32*(3), 191-198.

Low, S. (1981). The meaning of nervios. *Culture and Medical Psychiatry, 5*, 350-357.

Low, S. (1989). Health, culture and the nature of nerves: A critique. *Medical Anthropology, 11*(1), 91-95.

Maldonado, D. (1975). The Chicano aged. *Social Work, 20*(3), 213-216.

Maldonado, D. (1988). El barrio: Perceptions and utilization of the Hispanic neighborhood. In S.R. Applewhite (Ed.), *Hispanic elderly in transition: Theory, research, policy and practice.* Westport, CT: Greenwood Press.

Malgady, R.G., Rogler, L.H., and Cortés, D.E. (1996). Cultural expression of psychiatric symptoms: Idioms of anger among Puerto Ricans. *Psychological Assessment, 8*(3), 265-268.

Markides, K.S. and Mindel, C.H. (1987). *Aging and ethnicity.* Newbury Park, CA: Sage.

Massey, D.S. and Bitterman, B. (1985). Explaining the paradox of Puerto Rican segregation. *Social Forces, 64*(2), 306-331.

Mizio, E. (1978). *A conceptual framework and proposed model for mental health service delivery to the Puerto Rican family.* New York: Family Service Association of America.

Mui, A.C. and Burnette, D. (1994). Long term care service use by frail elders: Is ethnicity a factor? *The Gerontologist, 34*(2), 190-198.

O'Donnell, R.M. (1989). Functional disability among the Puerto Rican elderly. *Journal of Aging and Health, 1*(2), 244-264.

O'Shaughnessy, C. (1986). *Older Americans act: Participants in supportive and nutrition services* (Report no. 86-867 EPW, Congressional Research Service). Washington, DC: Library of Congress.

Perez-Stable, E.J. (1987). Issues in Latino health care. *Western Journal of Medicine, 146*(2), 213-218.

Purdy, J.K. and Arguello, D. (1992). Hispanic families in caretaking of older adults: Is it functional? *Journal of Gerontological Social Work, 19*(2), 29-42.

Rogler, L.H. (1989). The meaning of culturally sensitive research in mental health. *American Journal of Psychiatry, 146*(3), 296-303.

Sanchez-Ayéndez, M. (1989). Puerto Rican elderly women: The cultural dimension of social support networks. *Women and Health, 14*(3-4), 239-251.

Schur, D.L., Bernstein, A.B., and Berk, M.L. (1987). The importance of distinguishing Hispanic subpopulations in the use of medical care. *Medical Care, 25*(7), 627-641

Starrett, R.A., Bresler, C., Decker, F.T., Walters, G.T., and Rogers, D. (1990). The role of environmental awareness and support networks in Hispanic elderly persons' use of formal social services. *Journal of Community Psychology, 18*(3), 218-227.

Starrett, R.A., Mindel, C.H., and Wright, R. (1983). Support networks among the Hispanic elderly. *Social Work Research and Abstracts, 19*(4), 35-40.

Starrett, R.A., Wright, R. Jr., Mindel, C.H., and Tran, T.V. (1989). The use of social services by Hispanic elderly: A comparison of Mexican American, Puerto Rican and Cuban elderly. *Journal of Social Service Research, 13*(1), 1-25.

Torres-Gil, F. and Negm, M. (1980). Policy issues concerning the Hispanic elderly. *Aging,* March-April, 2-5.

Torres-Matrullo, C. (1976). Acculturation and psychopathology among Puerto Rican women in mainland United States. *American Journal of Orthopsychiatry, 46*(4), 710-719.

Tran, T.V. and Dhooper, S.S. (1996). Ethnic and gender differences in perceived needs for social services among three elderly Hispanic groups. *Journal of Gerontological Social Work, 25*(3/4), 121-147.

Tran, T.V., Fitzpatrick, T.R., Berg, W.R., and Wright, R. Jr. (1996). Acculturation, health, stress, and psychological distress among elderly Hispanics. *Journal of Cross-Cultural Gerontology, 11*(2), 149-165.

U.S. Bureau of the Census. (1993). *Statistical Abstract of the United States: 1993,* 113th edition. Washington, DC: author.

Valle, R. and Vega, W. (1980). *Hispanic natural support systems: Mental health promotion perspectives.* Sacramento, CA: Department of Mental Health, State of California.

Waldo, D.R., Sonnefeld, S.T., McKussick, D.R., and Arnett, R.H. (1989). Health care expenditures by age group, 1977 and 1987. *Health Care Financing Review, 10*(4), 111-120.

Wallace, S.P., Campbell, K., and Lew-Ting, C.-Y. (1994). Structural barriers to the use of formal in-home services by elderly Latinos. *Journal of Gerontology: Social Sciences, 49*(5), S253-S263.

Weissert, W.G. and Cready, C.M. (1988). Determinants of hospital-to-nursing home delays: A pilot study. *Health Service Research, 23*(5), 619-647.

Yeatts, D.E., Crow, T., and Folts, E. (1992). Service use among low-income elderly: Strategies for overcoming barriers. *The Gerontologist, 32*(1), 24-32.

Chapter 7

Cuban-American Elders

Thanh V. Tran
Neala C. Melcer

The purpose of this chapter is to provide readers with a review of historical and demographic information on Cuban elders, to present and discuss various issues of health and social services, and to propose some intervention strategies thought to be appropriate to the community of elderly Cuban Americans.

HISTORICAL BACKGROUND OF CUBAN IMMIGRANTS

A significant historical focus for Cubans occurred with the dramatic overthrow of dictator Fulgencio Batista in the late 1950s. Over 215,000 people of Cuban origin were compelled to flee to the United States between 1959 and 1962 (Boswell, 1994). This was primarily due to the major restrictions imposed upon the people by the new leadership of Fidel Castro in 1959. "No longer were free elections possible and a Soviet-type dictatorship was established. Anyone who disagreed with the new regime was either killed or imprisoned. Property, bank accounts, and assets were confiscated. As the economic structure collapsed, food and consumer supplies became scarce" (De Varona, 1996, p. 167).

Many of the Cubans who characterized the exodus during these initial years were well-educated and skilled in a profession or trade (Chabran and Chabran, 1996). The majority of these individuals who left Cuba resettled in Miami, Florida. However, some of them requested to be relocated by the U.S. government to such places as New

York City and New Jersey, with others choosing California, Illinois, and Texas (Olson and Olson, 1995).

After the Cuban missile crisis in 1962, immigration became very difficult. Approximately 250,000 Cubans entered the United States at this time (De Varona, 1996). In 1965, the second wave of Cuban immigration began, precipitated by more internal problems. Castro allowed Cubans to relocate relatives from the port of Camarioca to the U.S. mainland. Approximately 5,000 Cubans emigrated during this boat lift (Chabran and Chabran, 1996). By 1973, Cuban "freedom flights" brought approximately 300,000 Cubans to the United States (Boswell and Curtis, 1984).

The 1980s heralded the third wave of immigration. In response to the group of Cubans who demanded political asylum at the Peruvian Embassy, Castro was obliged to grant permission for others to leave too. From Mariel, the port of exit, many voluntarily chose to emigrate. However, a significant number of criminals and mentally and physically ill persons were among those forced to depart (Kanellos, 1997). In contrast to past emigration from Cuba, these *Marielitos* (so called because they left Cuba through Mariel) were, for the most part, unskilled and uneducated (Gernand, 1996).

With the current governmental restrictions to allow Cubans into the United States, the 1990s have witnessed Cubans still risking their lives to reach America by devising makeshift boats. Many thousands have drowned in this effort. However, courage and determination have been their strengths as they pursued their hopes for a better future.

DEMOGRAPHY
OF ELDERLY CUBAN AMERICANS

In 1990, there were a total of 22,354,059 Hispanic persons living in the United States. Of these individuals 1,043,932 were Cuban born. The median age for females was 38.9 and for males 41.0. This contrasts sharply with the median age for other Hispanic groups, which was 27.7 and 28.8 for females and males, respectively. Specifically, for Mexicans, it was 23.8 and 24.0, and for Puerto Ricans 25.7 and 26.6 (U.S. Bureau of the Census, 1990b).

The older age range of Cubans can be explained to a large extent by their relatively low fertility rates and the past historical tendency for the Cuban government to grant emigration permission to older individuals more readily than to the younger generation (Diaz-Briquets and Perez, 1981). The higher median age of Cuban Americans consequently allows more people of this group to participate in the labor force. This ultimately means that there are fewer unemployed individuals of Cuban origin and more workers at the height of their earning power compared to other Hispanics (Queralt, 1984). Queralt additionally states that conclusions generally made regarding Cubans having higher incomes in contrast to other Hispanics such as Mexicans, Dominicans, and Puerto Ricans generally are not accurately portrayed. The discrepancy in age distributions among these groups requires that incomes be adjusted accordingly.

Whereas the U.S. Bureau of the Census (1990b) *General Population Characteristics* documents that Cuban Americans have a higher occupational level than other Hispanic Americans, this status reflects once again the older age distribution for this group. In 1990, about 20 percent of the Cuban-American labor force were employed in administrative and managerial positions and approximately 18 percent were employed in low-paid work (Boswell, 1994). In 1995 the Cuban-American civilian labor force participation (U.S. Bureau of Labor Statistics, Employment and Earnings, 1995) revealed similar percentages: 22 percent of individuals of Cuban origin were employed in managerial and professional occupations while 14.1 percent of this group were in positions such as technology, sales, and administrative support.

Additionally, Cuban Americans reflect a higher than average educational level compared to other Hispanic Americans living in the United States. However, they also show lower educational levels than the total U.S. population (Boswell, 1994). Educational attainment of elderly Cuban-American immigrants was not likely to go beyond grade-school completion. Educational levels reported from the 1980 and 1990 Census data reflect this situation (U.S. Bureau of the Census, 1990a).

HEALTH STATUS OF CUBAN ELDERLY

In response to the growing number of Hispanics in the United States, a detailed study was conducted from 1982 through 1984 that investigated the health status among Cuban Americans, Mexican Americans, and Puerto Ricans. According to Robert Murphy, director of the Division of Health Examination Statistics at the National Center for Health Statistics, during this time period, blood pressure, obesity, gallstones, and diabetes emerged as leading Hispanic health issues (Marwick, 1991).

Specifically, with regard to Cuban Americans, the Hispanic Health and Nutrition Examination Survey (HHANES) study revealed that 41.8 percent of the men tended to smoke (Escobedo and Remington, 1989). This finding is particularly important due to the high association of cigarette smoking with various cancers (Dollinger, Rosenbaum, and Cable, 1994) and periodontal disease (Akef, Weine, and Weissman, 1992).

The HHANES study also found that 29 percent of the Cuban-origin males and 34 percent of the Cuban-origin females were overweight. This same investigation additionally indicated that 15.8 percent of the Cuban Americans ages forty-five to seventy-four had diabetes. Flegal and associates (1991) found that this relatively low prevalence of diabetes may possibly be attributed to behavioral, genetic, environmental, and/or socioeconomic factors.

Hypertension prevalence was also investigated in the HHANES study (Pappas, Gergen, and Carroll, 1990). Among Cuban Americans who resided in Dade County, Florida, 22.8 and 15.5 percent of males and females, respectively, were diagnosed as being hypertensive. Various health problems have been correlated with being overweight, such as heart disease and diabetes (American Diabetes Association, 1987; Connor and Bristow, 1985). For female persons of Cuban origin between the ages of 55 and 64, 35.6 percent were hypertensive. Among those between 65 and 74, 49.8 percent displayed this condition. Among male persons of Cuban origin ages 55 through 64, 41.4 percent manifested hypertension. For the age span of 65 through 74, 46.3 percent of male Cuban Americans showed this condition (Pappas, Gergen, and Carroll, 1990). Although hypertension knowledge among Hispanics was assessed in the 1980s, Ailinger (1982) did not categorize individuals into their specific ethnic background. Additionally, her sample size was small (330 subjects). Yet, as we approach the year 2000, her work lays the foundation for research still needed in this domain.

For the elderly, dental health is important. In addition to the physical process of eating, the psychological component is of great importance. Dental caries, loss of teeth, ill-fitting dentures, and periodontal disease can all compromise eating, increase weight loss, and lead to inadequate nutrient intake. The HHANES study analyzed the prevalence of total tooth loss, dental caries, and periodontal disease among Cuban Americans, Mexican Americans, and Puerto Ricans (Ismail and Szpunar, 1990). For Cuban Americans, the prevalence of total tooth loss was 6.10 percent in contrast to 2.60 and 2.80 percent among Mexican Americans and Puerto Ricans, respectively. Cuban Americans and Puerto Rican adults additionally had twice as many missing teeth as Mexican Americans. Using comparison data from the National Institute of Dental Research, all Hispanics showed a higher prevalence of gum inflammation and periodontitis (Ismail and Szpunar, 1990) than the general population.

The HHANES study also assessed depression among Cuban Americans (Narrow et al., 1990). Unlike the psychiatric evaluations of Cuban Americans from the 1980 Mariel boatlift, which revealed significant mental disorders, the findings of this survey showed low rates of depressive symptoms and disorder among this population when compared to other Hispanic groups and the U.S. population. The findings additionally indicated that 10 percent of the Cuban-American respondents manifested high levels of depressive symptoms based on the Center for Epidemiological Studies Depression (CES-D) scale, and female respondents reported a significantly higher level of depression than their male counterparts.

Still another component of the HHANES study involved the utilization of health services and health insurance coverage among Cuban Americans, Puerto Ricans, and Mexican Americans (Trevino et al., 1991). Specific to Cuban Americans, this study found that 28.6 percent of this group was uninsured for medical services. However, the individuals of Cuban origin were more likely to be covered by Medicare due to their older age representation. Data from this study showed that among Cuban Americans whose ages ranged from 65 to 74, 5.9 percent reported never having had a routine physical examination.

Angel and Angel (1992) investigated the relationship between age at migration and social connections and the perception of well-being among elderly Hispanics. The 1988 *National Survey of Hispanic Elderly People* (David, 1990) was the data source from which the assessment was derived. Information acquired from the three Hispanic subgroups underscored the unique ethnic differences reflecting migration status, economics, and age. Whereas individuals who emigrate at an older age are likely to manifest greater adjustment problems, Cuban Americans generally showed high interaction with friends and appeared to have benefited from living within their own cultural community. The authors posited that the low childbearing status, when compared to other Hispanic groups, and the higher incomes of these Cuban émigrés played a key role in their reporting better health, less disability, and greater life satisfaction.

Analysis of Health and Psychological Well-Being

We used the data from the 1988 *National Survey of Hispanic Elderly People* (NSHEP) to present some information on health and psychological well-being of Cuban elders (David, 1990). The NSHEP consists of a sample of 704 Cuban elders ages 65 and older. About 29.1 percent of this sample had at least one activities of daily living (ADL) problem. More than half of the sample (53.8 percent) reported having good or excellent health status. A majority of the sample (90.5 percent) was "satisfied" or "very satisfied" with their lives.

Table 7.1 presents the logistic regression analyses of self-rated health, ADL, life satisfaction, and ordinary least-squared (OLS) regression analysis on six selected predictor variables. These variables are stress (i.e., having difficulty with several aspects of life including money, isolation, social relations, and social dependency), language (bilingual versus Spanish only), gender, age, education, and living alone (arrangements). These variables are thought to have direct relationships with the health status of Cuban elders. The findings revealed that stress has significant relationships with both self-rated health (B = .419, p < .001) and ADL (B = .341, p < .001). Elderly Cubans who experienced more stressors were

TABLE 7.1. Logistic Regression of Self-Rated Health, Life Satisfaction, and OLS Regression of Negative Affect

| | Self-Rated Health and Psychological Well-Being | | | | | | | | | |
| Predictor Variables | Self-Rated Health (N = 672) | | ADL (N = 674) | | Life Satisfaction (N = 650) | | OLS Regression of Negative Affect (N = 652) | | |
	B	S.E.	B	S.E.	B	S.E.	B	S.E.	Beta
Health Status					−1.151**	.393	.250**	.098	.096
ADL	.419***	.051			−1.009***	.324	.436***	.109	.150
Stress	−.690***	.189	.341***	.050	−.331***	.076	.293***	.025	.417
Language Bilingual			−.169	.209	.329	.356	.079	.096	.030
Gender Men	−.484**	.179	−.783***	.212	−.158	.335	−.057	.092	−.021
Age 65-74	−.136	.173	−1.081***	.191	−.396	.308	−.062	.089	−.023
Education College	.092	.254	−.345	.287	.196	.481	−.169	.120	−.050
Living Status Alone	−.097	.205	−.248	.227	−.250	.459	.255**	.105	.081
Model χ^2 (6 D.F.)	120.77***								
Model χ^2 (8 D.F.)			113.16***		82.16***		R^2 = .305		

$*p < .05; **p < .01; ***p < .001$

Health Status = 1 for fair and poor, 0 for good and excellent; Life Satisfaction = 1 for very satisfied or satisfied, 0 for dissatisfied or very dissatisfied; ADL = 1 for having problems, 0 for not having problems; Stress scores range from 0 for lowest to 7 for highest; Negative affect scores range from 0 for lowest to 5 for highest; Language = 1 for bilingual, 0 for Spanish only; Gender = 1 for men, 0 for women; Age = 1 for 65 to 74, 0 for 75 and older; Education = 1 for college education, 0 for no college education; Living Status = 1 for living alone, 0 for living with others.

more likely to report poorer health status and have problems with their activities of daily living.

This cross-sectional data set does not allow us to speculate about the causal relationship between stress and health status. However, the findings appear to support the commonsense theory on the negative impact of stress on various dimensions of well-being. Interestingly, bilingual ability has a significant relationship with self-rated health status. That is, elderly Cubans who spoke both English and Spanish were less likely to report a poorer health status than their Spanish-speaking only counterparts (B = −.690, p < .001). This suggests that bilingualism is an important factor in the health status of elderly Cubans. Perhaps bilingual elderly Cubans reported a better health status because they have access to health education in both Spanish and English. They also may have the option of using either Spanish- or English-speaking health care providers and health services. As a result, they may have better health status or at least feel better about their health than those who are limited by their monolanguage ability.

Gender shows significant relationships with both self-rated health (B = −.484, p . 01) and ADL (B = −.783, p < .001). These relationships indicate that elderly Cuban men rated their health better and experienced fewer ADL problems than their female counterparts. It appears that gender is an important factor on the health status of elderly Cuban Americans regardless of their age, education, language skills, and living arrangements. It is important for community health educators, health service providers, and health service researchers to address gender differences in their programs. For example, we need to identify gender differences in health care and health beliefs to better design appropriate programs and services for elderly Cuban Americans. Age had a significant relationship with ADL (B = −1.081, p < .001), indicating that elderly Cubans 65 through 74 years old experienced fewer ADL problems than their counterparts 75 years and older. Education and living arrangements had no significant statistical relationship with either self-rated health status or ADL.

With respect to the psychological well-being of elderly Cuban Americans, the analysis in Table 7.1 shows that health status, ADLs, and stress had significant relationships with life satisfaction.

That is, elderly Cubans who rated their health as poor were less likely to be satisfied with their lives (B = − 1.151, p < .01). Those who experienced ADL problems were less likely to be satisfied with their lives (B = − 1.009, p < .001), and those who experienced more stressors were less likely to be satisfied with their lives (B = − .331, p < .001). Other variables including language, gender, age, education, and living arrangements had no significant statistical relationship with life satisfaction.

Finally, we examined the predictors of negative affects, which are the composition of five negative items from Bradburn's Affect Balance Scale (Bradburn, 1969). These items capture the negative aspect of psychological well-being, measuring a person's feelings of restlessness, loneliness, boredom, depression, and being upset. The findings in Table 7.1 show that self-rated health, ADL, stress, and living arrangements had statistically significant relationships with negative affect. Similarly, elderly Cubans who rated their health as poor (Beta = .096, p < .01) had higher levels of negative affect; elderly Cubans who had ADL problems (Beta = .150, p < .001) had higher levels of negative affect; and elderly Cubans who experienced more stresses (Beta = .417, p < .001) experienced more negative affect. Finally, elderly Cubans who lived alone experienced more negative affect (Beta = .081, p < .01). This is an important finding. Although living arrangements had no significant relationship with self-rated health, ADL, and life satisfaction, this finding indicates that elderly Cubans who live alone were more likely to be at risk of having a poorer sense of psychological well-being than those not living alone. This could be attributed to the fact that they lack social support or social relations.

Our analyses of health and psychological well-being revealed some important findings. It appears that stress has a significantly negative impact on both health and psychological well-being of elderly Cubans. Some of the stressful situations, such as loneliness, anxiety, problems with family relations, or having to depend on others, can be managed, provided there is support from community-based social service agencies or church-based services. The results from our analyses also suggest that if the health status of elderly Cubans were maintained appropriately, they would live happier and more satisfied lives.

HEALTH CARE SERVICES

Siddharthan and Sowers-Hoag (1989) conducted a study comparing the access to health care services and attitudes of Cuban Americans and native-born Americans. From a random survey sample of 1,216 elderly individuals living in Dade County, Florida, Cuban immigrants were identified to be twice as likely to have had health care screening in the past year when compared to native-born North Americans. The investigators attributed the older age of the Cuban immigrants and their perception of health care need due to illness susceptibility as the likely contributors to their greater health care service utilization. The study additionally revealed a preference by the Cuban Americans for long-term care in the home of family or friends rather than in institutional facilities. This finding is not surprising since Hispanics generally favor close family affiliation. The research of Siddharthan and Sowers-Hoag (1989) and Schur, Bernstein, and Berk (1987) shows that Cuban Americans tend to be privately insured. Their research found that of all the Hispanic-American groups, the individuals of Cuban origin maintained the highest rates of health insurance coverage.

Escovar and Kurtines (1983) investigated the factors that predict social service utilization among Cuban-American elderly. Their findings suggest that these elders primarily consult their children as a resource and additionally make use of an informal network of people. These researchers also reported that the social service usage tended to be associated with years lived in the United States (a measure of acculturation). Ecovar and Kurtines recommend that future research incorporate wider use of variables to enhance the predictive ability of social service utilization. A larger sample size, along with random subject selection, was also advised to better characterize the results.

Utilization of Community-Based Health and Social Services

We used data from the NSHEP to provide some empirical information on utilization of community-based social and health services among elderly Cuban Americans. The analysis involved ten services: senior transportation, senior center, meals-on-wheels, senior center meals, homemaker services, health status check by phone, visiting nurse, home health service, food stamps, and church-based social services. The predictor variables capture some basic components of the behavioral model of health service utilization, including need (self-rated health, ADL, and stress), enabling factors (language, education, and living arrangements), and predisposing factors (gender and age). We believe that these predictor variables are important for understanding the pattern of health and social services utilization within the elderly Cuban-American community.

Table 7.2 presents the findings from ten logistic regression analyses of ten utilization variables. It appears that self-rated health status had significant relationships with use of senior transportation (B = .552, p < .05) and use of food stamps (B = .738, p < .001). These findings indicate that elderly Cubans who rated their health as fair or poor were more likely to use senior transportation than were those with good health status. Elderly Cubans with poor health status also were more likely to use food stamps. Language is the significant predictor of the utilization of food stamps (B = − 1.162, p < .001) and church-based social services (B = 1.418, p < .01). ADLs appear to be a significant predictor of the utilization of the meals-on-wheels program (B = 1.305, p < .05), homemaker services (B = 1.303, p < .01), and church-based social services (B = 1.682, p < .001). These findings suggest that elderly Cubans who suffered from ADL problems were more likely to avail themselves of these programs. Stress is not a statistically significant predictor of the utilization of any selected services.

These findings also suggest that bilingual elderly Cubans were less likely to depend on food stamps than those who spoke Spanish only. Nevertheless, an interesting finding shows that bilingual elderly Cubans were more likely to use church-based social services. One can speculate that bilingual Cuban elderly had more opportunities to participate in both English-speaking and Spanish-speaking churches. Thus, services for these elderly are more accessible and available to them. Gender is significantly related to the use of food stamps (B = − .417, p < .05). It suggests that elderly Cuban men were less likely to use food stamps than women. One may raise the question whether Cuban men were more reluctant to accept assistance or to seek help than Cuban women. If this is true, then these findings could have great implications for clinical interventions.

TABLE 7.2. Logistic Regression of Utilization of Community-Based Social and Health Services

Predictor Variables	1 Trans. B (S.E.)	2 Center B (S.E.)	3 Wheels B (S.E.)	4 Meals B (S.E.)	5 Home B (S.E.)	6 Phone B (S.E.)	7 Nurse B (S.E.)	8 Health B (S.E.)	9 Food B (S.E.)	10 Church B (S.E.)
Health Status										
Poor	.552* (.240)	-.321 (.282)	.181 (.522)	-.263 (.296)	.568 (.456)	.550 (.502)	.609 (.332)	.339 (.409)	.738*** (.203)	.135 (.575)
ADL	.379 (.242)	.153 (.331)	1.305* (.518)	-.204 (.330)	1.303** (.446)	.219 (.477)	.444 (.316)	.465 (.396)	.0357 (.219)	1.682*** (.590)
Stress	.024 (.058)	.096 (.75)	-.115 (.134)	.040 (.074)	-.173 (.117)	.163 (.109)	.074 (.078)	.118 (.092)	.003 (.052)	-.026 (.142)
Language										
Bilingual	-.121 (.241)	.148 (.294)	.143 (.499)	.031 (.287)	-.072 (.444)	.035 (.480)	-.542 (.348)	-.105 (.399)	-1.162*** (.207)	1.418** (.545)
Gender										
Men	-.414 (.242)	.297 (.285)	-.042 (.531)	.142 (.278)	-.239 (.464)	.169 (.469)	-.136 (.329)	-.173 (.400)	-.417* (.199)	.753 (.514)
Age										
65-74	-.685*** (.217)	-.672** (.276)	-.788 (.492)	-.611* (.267)	-1.007* (.443)	-1.001* (.453)	-1.378*** (.321)	-.319 (.358)	-.984** (.189)	-.709 (.515)
Education										
College	.311 (.300)	-.057 (.371)	.210 (.634)	.001 (.360)	-.043 (.612)	-.040 (.623)	.203 (.436)	-.423 (.587)	-.548* (.288)	-.402 (.635)
Living Status										
Alone	.673** (.232)	.804*** (.286)	1.402*** (.267)	1.205*** (.267)	.975 (.402)	.158 (.491)	-.175 (.351)	-.208 (.438)	1.390*** (.223)	-.274 (.658)
Model x^2 (8 D.F.)	46.01***	17.37**	22.87**	26.272***	32.85**	12.58	45.50***	11.88	176.623***	22.31**
N	669	668	669	669	669	668	669	667	669	668

*p < .05; **p < .01; ***p < .001

Notes: Service variables: 1 = Senior Transportation; 2 = Senior Center; 3 = Meals-on-Wheels; 4 = Senior Center Meals; 5 = Homemaker Services; 6 = Check Health Status by Phone; 7 = Visiting Nurse; 8 = Home Health Service; 9 = Food Stamps; 10 = Services Provided by Church. Health Status = 1 for fair and poor, 0 for good and excellent; Language = 1 for bilingual, 0 for Spanish only; Gender = 1 for men, 0 for women; Age = 1 for 65 to 74, 0 for 75 and older; Education = 1 for College education, 0 for no College education; Living Status = 1 for living alone, 0 for living with others.

Age is the only variable that had significant relationships with seven out of ten service utilization variables. The results show that Cubans ages 65 to 74 years were less likely to use senior transportation services (B = $-.685$, p < .001), senior centers (B = $-.672$, p < .01), meals-on-wheels (B = $-.788$, p < .05), homemaker services (B = -1.007, p < .01), health status check by phone (B = -1.001, p < .05), visiting nurses (B = -1.378, p < .001), and food stamps (B = $-.984$, p < .01). These findings indicate that the older group (75 and over) of elderly Cubans were more vulnerable because they appeared to depend on others more than their younger counterparts did.

Education is significantly related only to the use of food stamps (B = $-.548$, p < .05). It indicates that elderly Cubans with some college education were less likely to use food stamps than were those without a college education. Education facilitates the process of acculturation among immigrants, especially non-English-speaking immigrants. Education has been found as a strong predictor of economic self-sufficiency among newly arrived immigrant groups (Office of Refugee Resettlement, 1994).

Finally, living arrangements have significant relationships with six utilization variables. The results revealed that compared to elderly Cubans who lived with others, elderly Cubans who live alone are more likely to use senior transportation (B = .673, p < .01), participate in senior centers (B = .804, p < .001), use meals-on-wheels (B = 1.402, p < .001), eat meals at senior centers (B = 1.205, p < .001), use homemaker services (B = .975, p < .01), and use food stamps (B = 1.390, p < .001).

These findings have significant implications for community-based interventions. Elderly Cubans who live alone appear to have different needs for social and health services than those who live with spouses or others. Therefore, service providers may design and offer different services for elderly persons who live alone.

Intergenerational Relations

To understand the potential for intergenerational conflict due to acculturation, De Santis and Ugarriza (1995) investigated a group of thirty Cuban Americans and thirty Haitian immigrant mothers in the Miami-Dade area of Florida. Historically, respect for elders, parents, and guardians has been traditionally offered by the younger generation, not only as a consequence of love but also as a result of the elder's knowledge and experience. This valued consideration sometimes breaks down when children take on adult responsibilities to become translators for their relatives and guardians who do not speak sufficient English. These young people are often asked to become intermediaries in decision making for everyday events, which frequently include health care. The findings of De Santis and Ugarizza (1995) suggest that the family structure is commonly weakened by the obligation of Cuban-American and Haitian children to contribute to household income and chores. The restrictive nature of these demands puts pressure on the younger generation. The authors posit that public mental health nurses have much to offer in assisting elder immigrant groups to integrate into North American society (e.g., by encouraging participation in ESL classes, school meetings, church groups, and community organizations). De Santis and Ugarizza (1995) believe that cultural beliefs and practices can still be maintained in this way while at the same time elderly Cuban Americans can preserve their self-reliance.

Health Care Beliefs

Instead of trying to integrate into mainstream society, a significant number of Cuban Americans rely on the spiritual practice known as Santeria to deal with the various difficulties in their lives. The rejection of the Western approach of consulting psychiatrists often stems from the stigma of being considered crazy or "loco." Moreover, therapists using modern medicine often do not speak Spanish fluently. These professionals are apt to communicate in ways that contrast with Hispanic health beliefs (Ruiz and Langrod, 1976).

Generally, individuals of Cuban origin from all different social-class backgrounds practice Santeria. It is based upon African-American traditions with a Yoruba influence, which integrates beliefs in Catholic saints (Sandoval, 1979). Specific to their health needs, the Cubans who visit *santeros* (priests) often attribute their problems to supernatural causes. According to Sandoval, "the 'santero' obtains the majority of his patients from those suffering from psychosomatic disorders or tensions which do not yield to modern medicine" (p. 53). With the stresses of acculturation and feelings of isolation, the collective approach of dances, chants, and sacrifices is consequently considered a desirable option.

Herbs are essential to Santeria as well (Sandoval, 1979). It is believed that the medicinal properties of wild plants are integral to protecting oneself against evil influences and disease. Amulets and candles are additionally used as a conduit to express spiritual connectedness. Thus, the belief in Santeria ultimately acts as a culturally acceptable coping mechanism. It lends itself to an openness that is often not characteristic of other religions.

CONCLUSION AND IMPLICATIONS

People tend to be drawn to their own ethnicity as aging and illness touch their lives. The security and warmth of their respective culture is conceptualized through language, beliefs, and practices. Consequently, culture may fill the void of life's uncertainties. Ultimately, the underlying expectation is for a supportive environment. The adjustment to American society can oftentimes seem quite daunting to Cuban émigrés. The traditional Cuban value system of respecting the elderly, family cohesiveness, and maintaining a personalized approach to communication is generally perceived as having diminished importance in their new homeland. To help minimize the sense of alienation, Cuban immigrants have commonly chosen to live in areas where other individuals of Cuban origin reside—such as Miami/Dade County. In this way, they artificially recreate the ambiance of a Cuba they wish to remember. Yet, undeniably, the infrastructure of Miami remains North American. Hospitals, pharmacies, social service agencies, governmental organizations, etc., function within an American context, even though designated areas are essentially Cuban in atmosphere.

Many health concerns of Cuban Americans still need to be addressed. Placement in a nursing home is generally not regarded favorably by Cuban immigrants. Their value system assumes that family will take care of the elderly. However, the adult children of these older Cuban émigrés often find that their housing units in the United States are small and their financial responsibilities are considerable. Additionally, they have greater commitments outside the home so that choosing a nursing home for their elderly relatives eventually becomes a viable solution (Hernandez, 1974). In fact, in 1976, the National Association of Spanish Speaking Elderly (Asociación Nacional Pro-Personas Mayores) documented 505 Cuban Americans placed in nursing homes in the Miami/Dade County area. Although no follow-up studies since then have been generated, nursing home placements for these individuals seem to be increasing.

Even though the findings of Tran and Dhooper (1996) showed a lower need for social services by Hispanic elderly of Cuban origin when compared to Puerto Ricans and Mexicans, there are various ways in which the health care system can be sensitive to the unique health care concerns of the Cuban American elderly.

A high priority for Cuban immigrants is to be able to understand and navigate their health care in Spanish. Since Hispanics are becoming the largest minority in the United States (Council on Scientific Affairs, 1991; Current Population Reports, 1990; Ginzberg, 1991), it is consequently important that funds be allocated for Spanish-speaking medical providers and staff in designated areas of need. Thus, policies should be supported to make this goal a reality.

Furthermore, a viable solution to the vital nutritional concerns of the Cuban-American elderly would be to offer a meals-on-wheels program that would deliver culturally prepared foods to their homes by bilingual and bicultural staff. This service would help them to maintain a sense of independence from working families. Still another culturally relevant approach to ensure high-quality health care would be to offer mobile vans with bilingual and bicultural staff to screen for such devastating illnesses as breast, colon, lung, and prostate cancer, as well as heart disease and diabetes.

Also, emergency ambulances affiliated with a Spanish-speaking staff at a 911 station could conceivably save numerous lives. For immediate concerns, bilingual and bicultural home health aides are best utilized in this community. To a certain extent, this particular service does exist. However, an expansion of this service would be extremely beneficial. As elderly become terminally ill, cultural sensitivity becomes more and more essential. Similarly, one's spiritual needs inevitably take on a greater magnitude of importance. Having access to folk healers and herbal medicines can be crucial at this stage of their lives, too.

De Varona (1996) states that Cuban Americans participate in the U.S. political system. Gradually, these individuals have learned to utilize their rights as citizens. Governmental leaders of Cuban origin have been elected through hard work and voting. This avenue of decision making has proven highly effective in supporting the needs of the Cuban-American community.

As individuals of Cuban origin become American citizens, they become a fundamental part of this society. Its multiethnic immigrants have enriched America. They mirror who we are and challenge us to make this country a better place to live. Future research should document unique characteristics of the Cuban-American culture with respect to aging. By designing and implementing culturally appropriate health care programs, health professionals will ultimately utilize our limited resources in most effective ways.

REFERENCES

Ailinger, R.L. (1982). Hypertension knowledge in a Hispanic community. *Nursing Research, 31*(4), 207-209.

Akef, J., Weine, F.S., and Weissman, D.P. (1992). The role of smoking in the progression of periodontal disease: A literature review. *Compendium, 13*(6), 526-531.

American Diabetes Association (1987). *Diabetes in the family,* Revised edition. New York: Prentice-Hall Press.

Angel, J.L. and Angel, R.J. (1992). Age at migration, social connections, and well being among elderly Hispanics. *Journal of Aging and Health, 4*(4), 480-499.

Asociación Nacional Pro-Personas Mayores (1976). The Spanish speaking elderly nursing homes: A Dade County Florida overview. Unpublished working paper, Miami, FL.

Boswell, T.D. (1994). *A demographic profile of Cuban Americans.* Miami, FL: Cuban American Policy Center, Cuban American National Council.

Boswell, T.D. and Curtis, J.R. (1984). *The Cuban-American experience: Culture, images and perspectives.* Totowa, NJ: Rowman and Allanheld Publishers.

Bradburn, N.M. (1969). *The structure of psychological well-being.* Chicago: Aldine.

Chabran, R. and Chabran, R. (Eds.) (1996). *The Latino encyclopedia,* Volume 2. New York: Marshall Cavendish.

Connor, W.E. and Bristow, J.D. (1985). *Coronary heart disease: Prevention, complications, and treatment.* Philadelphia: J.B. Lippincott.

Council on Scientific Affairs. (1991). Hispanic health in the United States. *Journal of the American Medical Association, 265*(2), 248-252.

Current Population Reports (1990). *The Hispanic population in the United States.* Washington, DC: U.S. Dept. of Commerce, Bureau of the Census, Series P-20.

Davis, K. (1990). *National survey of Hispanic elderly people, 1988.* Ann Arbor, MI: InterUniversity Consortium for Political and Social Research.

De Santis, L. and Ugarriza, D.N. (1995). Potential for intergenerational conflict in Cuban and Haitian immigrant families. *Archives of Psychiatric Nursing, 9*(6), 354-364.

De Varona, F. (1996). *Latino literacy—The complete guide to our Hispanic history and culture.* New York: Henry Holt and Company.

Diaz-Briquets, S. and Perez, L. (1981). Cuba: The demography of revolution. *Population Bulletin, 36*(1), 3. Population Reference Bureau, Inc.

Dollinger, M., Rosenbaum, E.H., and Cable, G. (1994). *Everyone's guide to cancer therapy,* Second edition. Kansas City, MO: Andrews and McMeel.

Escobedo, L.G. and Remington, P.L. (1989). Birth cohort analysis of prevalence of cigarette smoking among Hispanics in the United States. *Journal of the American Medical Association, 261,* 66-69.

Escovar, L.A. and Kurtines, W.M. (1983). Psychological predictors of service utilization among Cuban-American elders. *Journal of Community Psychology, 11,* 355-362.

Flegal, K.M., Ezzati, T.M., Harris, M.I., Haynes, S.G., Juarez, R.Z., Knowler, W.C., Perez-Stable, E., and Stern, M.P. (1991). Prevalence of diabetes in Mexican Americans, Cubans, and Puerto Ricans from the Hispanic Health and Nutrition Examination Survey, 1982-1984. *Diabetes Care, 14*(7) (Supplement 3), 628-638.

Gernand, R. (1996). *The Cuban Americans: The immigrant experience.* New York: Chelsea House Publishers.

Ginzberg, E. (1991). Access to health care for Hispanics. *Journal of the American Medical Association, 265,* 238-241.

Hernandez, A.R. (1974). The Cuban minority in the U.S.: Final report on need identification and program evaluation. Washington, DC: Cuban Planning Council, Inc., 148-149.

Ismail, A.I. and Szpunar, S.M. (1990). The prevalence of total loss, dental caries, and periodontal disease among Mexican Americans, Cuban Americans, and Puerto Ricans: Findings from HHANES 1982-1984. *American Journal of Public Health, 80* (Supplement), 66-70.

Kanellos, N. (1997). *The Hispanic American almanac,* Second edition. Detroit, MI: Gale Research.

Marwick, C. (1991). Hispanic HANES takes a long look at Latino health. *Journal of the American Medical Association, 265*(2), 177, 181.

Narrow, W.E., Rae, D.S., Moscicki, E.K., Locker, B.Z., and Regier, D.A. (1990). Depression among Cuban Americans: The Hispanic Health and Nutrition Examination Survey. *Social Psychiatry and Psychiatric Epidemiology, 25*(5), 260-268.

Office of Refugee Resettlement. (1994). *Refugee resettlement program.* Report to the Congress. Washington DC: U.S. Department of Health and Human Services.

Olson, J.S. and Olson, J.E. (1995). *Cuban Americans: From trauma to triumph.* New York: Twayne Publishers.

Pappas, G., Gergen, P., and Carroll, M. (1990). Hypertension prevalence and the status of awareness, treatment, and control in the Hispanic Health and Nutrition Examination Survey (HHANES), 1982-1984. *American Journal of Public Health, 80*(12), 1431-1436.

Queralt, M. (1984). Understanding Cuban immigrants: A cultural perspective. *Social Work,* (March/April), 115-121.

Ruiz, P. and Langrod, J. (1976). Psychiatry and folk healing: A dichotomy? *American Journal of Psychiatry, 133*(1), 95-97.

Sandoval, M.C. (1979). Santeria as a mental health care system: An historical overview. *Social Science and Medicine, 13B*(2), 137-151.

Schur, C.L., Bernstein, A.B., and Berk, M.L. (1987). The importance of distinguishing Hispanic subpopulations in the use of medical care. *Medical Care, 25*(7), 627-641.

Siddharthan, K. and Sowers-Hoag, K. (1989). Elders' attitudes and access to health care: A comparison of Cuban immigrants and native-born Americans. *Journal of Applied Gerontology, 8*(1), 86-96.

Tran, T.V. and Dhooper, S.S. (1996). Ethnic and gender differences in perceived needs for social services among three elderly Hispanic groups. *Journal of Gerontological Social Work, 25*(3/4), 121-147.

Trevino, F.M., Moyer, M.E., Valdez, R.B., and Stroup-Benham, C.A. (1991). Health insurance coverage and utilization of health services by Mexican Americans, mainland Puerto Ricans, and Cuban Americans. *Journal of the American Medical Association, 265*(2), 233-237.

U.S. Bureau of Labor Statistics, Employment and Earnings (1995). No. 662. *Hispanic persons—Civilian labor force participation 1994, 1995.* Washington, DC: U.S. Government Printing Office.

U.S. Bureau of the Census (1990a). *Current population reports.* Washington, DC: U.S. Department of Commerce (Series p-20, Nos. 331, 995, 1045).

U.S. Bureau of the Census (1990b). *General population characteristics.* Washington, DC: U.S. Department of Commerce.

Chapter 8

Mexican-American Elders

Sara Alemán

This chapter addresses the Mexican elders group of Latinos. Included in this designation are three categories of elders. The first includes individuals who were born in Mexico and have not become U.S. citizens; the second group is composed of individuals who were born in Mexico and became U.S. citizens; and the third group consists of those who were born in the United States of Mexican descent. These categories of individuals will be treated under the encompassing category of Mexican American. Although this single category will mask many differences, the category is necessary to provide ethnic group information that includes some common parameters. Many elders of this ethnic heritage who come into agencies for services and/or treatment will share many of the following characteristics or behaviors. Any salient differences will be discussed whenever appropriate so that service providers are better able to deliver culturally appropriate services. Also, service providers should be aware that there are many differences that manifest themselves as a result of different levels of acculturation. It is important to explore those differences with patients and clients.

The chapter presents demographic changes currently underway that partially explain why this population is so important to policymakers and to health and social services personnel. Also, the significance of some of the values of this elder population and how those values play themselves out in the service arena are discussed. The level of acculturation and the interplay with historical values are also considered as important factors. Finally, this chapter identifies changes that may occur among the elders' family systems and implications for service delivery systems.

POPULATION TRENDS AND STATISTICS

Mexican Americans account for over 62.3 percent of all Latinos in the United States (Lopez, 1991). Older Mexican-American group members also account for 54 percent of all elderly Hispanics (Curiel and Rosenthal, 1988; Lopez, 1991). However, the Commonwealth Fund Commission (Andrews, 1989) reported a higher percentage. They report that Mexican-American elderly make up 65 percent of the total Hispanic elderly population. In reality, this number may even be higher given that Mexican-American elders have traditionally been undercounted due to a historical distrust of data-collecting processes.

It is projected that by the year 2010, older Latino elders between sixty-five and seventy-four years of age will increase to 4.7 percent from 3.6 percent in 1990, and the seventy-five and older population is projected to increase from 2.1 percent in 1990 to 3.4 percent in 2010. These percentages reflect a 37.6 percent increase and a 54.1 percent increase respectively (U.S. Department of Commerce, 1989). Also, in 1995, elderly Latinos were 5 percent of the sixty-five-and-over age group. In 2050 they are expected to be 16 percent of this same age group (Treas, 1995). It is important to note that these numbers are not broken down by ethnic group but reflect instead a total number for all Latinos over age sixty-five in the United States.

In spite of the growth in this population, few service delivery mechanisms have addressed specific needs of these elders and their families. Additionally, Mexican-American elders tend to have higher levels of need than do nonminority elders (Trevino, 1988; Weeks and Cuellar, 1981) and also are more likely to underutilize community-based services (Crouch, 1972; Daley, Applewhite, and Jorquez, 1989; Lubben and Becerra, 1987; Sotomayor, 1988; Spearly and Lauderdale, 1983; Woerner, 1979) in spite of higher levels of need (Stoller and Gibson, 1994). According to Juarez (1988), during the period between 1980 and 2000, the population of Mexican elders over sixty years of age is expected to increase by 100 percent. All of these projections indicate an increased need for health and social services among members of this elderly group.

TRAITS OF THE POPULATION

Families generally continue to rely heavily on an extended support system that is intergenerational and includes non-blood relatives, via the system of *compadrazco*. Decisions regarding health
care are family based; that is, the total family makes the decision
not just the individual. Bassford (1995) refers to this as allocentrism. This descriptor refers to the cultural norm of valuing the
group over the individual. This cultural norm is important because
it is at variance with the majority norm that places the value on the
individual. In interactions with majority systems, it is important to
understand this cultural norm, for it dictates how decisions are
made and who makes them. If service providers fail to understand
these family dynamics, it is highly possible that interactions with
majority culture systems will not be productive or will end prematurely.

Many recent immigrants have left their family elders in Mexico,
and thus the young adult family relies on same-age cohorts for
support. The support system includes relatives who may or may not
be blood relatives, for example, *compadres*, but who become part of
the extended family due to traditional religious ceremonies whereby
non-blood relatives accept responsibilities that are usually associated with relatives' roles. These ceremonies create another level of
relationships that provide support in times of need. The *compadres*
become particularly important to the young, immigrant families
who left their older family members in Mexico and are now forced
to experience international family and social systems. In spite of
these geographic distances, many Mexican-American families
strive to maintain traditional extended family ties. There is some
speculation that this intergenerational connection to Mexican relatives left behind is partly responsible for Mexican Americans who
continue to experience low socioeconomic status. This is because
the value of allocentrism requires that those who have resources
contribute to family members who have less than they do. The
result is that workers who earn very little money in the United
States continue to contribute to their families in Mexico. Thus,
limited monetary resources are shared and workers continue to live
in poverty.

Many elders continue to be very religious. Some shifts away from Catholicism are occurring among some Hispanics, but not so much among Mexican Americans (Andrews, 1989). Loyalty to known systems and elements is a very strong characteristic among these elders. Service providers need to know this so that they will cultivate and maintain mutually trusting and loyal relationships between service providers and Mexican-American community members.

An additional important trait is that Mexican-American elders have a view of health that tends to be more holistic than that of the majority culture (Bassford, 1995). Some elders view illness as possibly having natural as well as supernatural origins (Trotter and Chavira, 1981). This provides a view of wellness and illness that involves the total being. Such a cultural value has led many group members to seek help from native healers, both for physical and spiritual well-being. Many Mexican Americans remember the traditional use of *curanderos,* who are native healers and who live in the immediate neighborhood. These traditions contribute to a cultural norm of actively seeking help for health problems from trusted neighbors. Mexican-American elders operate from a strong belief that good health is important. Therefore, it is accurate to expect that these cultural norms and health expectations would lead Mexican Americans to seek help for illnesses when they are physically ill or when they feel "out of balance."

The concept of needing to be in balance is similar to the Native American concept of being one with nature, so that many illnesses are indeed seen as resulting from an imbalance between the physical and natural or the supernatural. Among elderly Mexican Americans there is a strong belief in an inseparable connection between physical and spiritual well-being. Therefore, when an illness occurs and is not easily healed, an elder will seek an answer from the spiritual realm. For example, when an elderly person is unable to quickly recover from a surgical procedure, he or she will seek another cause for the continued illness. The elderly person may seek an answer in emotionally laden relationships: is the person not getting along with someone, did he or she fail to do something, or has he or she hurt someone? If there is a perceived nonphysical reason for the continued illness, the elderly person attempts to correct the illness by seeking relief from the spiritual powers. However, if there is still no relief, the person's culture incorporates a sense of suffering. "This is my cross to bear. We are people born to suffer" (Arizona Center on Aging, 1996, p. 1).

In spite of this cultural value of desiring wellness, the literature documents the underutilization of health and social services (Hopper, 1993; Moore and Hepworth, 1994). Research also supports the finding that Hispanic elders appear to be more frail than their White counterparts when they do come into a nursing home (Bassford, 1995). From a service provider's perspective, these behaviors appear to run against traditional norms. However, behaviors that keep elders from seeking assistance can be traced to a historical distrust and fear of service providers. Many of these elders remember when they were not welcomed into offices and services were segregated. Their current behaviors are an adaptation to a system that is foreign and oftentimes hostile to them.

Another trait that many service providers are generally unaware of is *personalismo* (Alemán, 1997; Arizona Center on Aging, 1996; Ho, 1987). This is a dynamic usually found among all Latinos. In the Mexican-American culture, individuals learn to trust a person by sharing personal information or by getting to know the "total person" (Applewhite and Daley, 1988, p. 11). This behavior is observed when an elder asks the service provider personal questions such as, "Are you married and how many children do you have?" or, "Who are your parents and how often do you see them?" However, most professionals are trained to view these types of questions as inappropriate because it is believed that they impinge on the boundaries of the professional-client relationship. What is little known is that for Mexican-American elders to remain involved in the professional-client relationship, it is important for the worker to self-disclose. Within this culture, self-disclosure is extremely important to the development of the working relationship. Elders feel that it is their right to know their service provider. In this culture, a helper who is not known to the client (i.e., a stranger) does not have an identity by a mere title or agency affiliation. The individual service provider is a person with a family and values that the elder needs to understand to see if this person has compatible internal values. If the worker can disclose personal information, and if the client finds the disclosed information to meet his or her criteria, then the client will more likely return for further information or assistance. If the worker does not self-disclose, it is unlikely that the client will return (Lum, 1986). When a client sees that the service provider is reluctant to share personal information, the elder determines that the worker has no *personalismo*. If the result of this informal assessment by the client is that the provider is not warm and responsive or has no *personalismo*, the relationship may very easily end prematurely. Therefore, in working with almost any elder from a Latino community, *personalismo,* will become an important dynamic to consider.

Great importance is placed by elders on respect that is due them because of their age and position in the family. This respect can be manifested in various ways. For example, they are consulted when problems arise and when an important decision needs to be made. Also, they are asked to accompany younger family members on trips to see other family members or their children and grandchildren. When grandchildren come to visit, they pay their respect to the elders first as they enter a home. The elders are the first to be greeted, and this may include a kiss on the cheek with a tender hug, besides the traditional handshake. Among new immigrants, the grandchildren may tenderly kiss the hand of the grandparent instead of shaking it.

ISSUES RELATED
TO LEVEL OF ACCULTURATION

Some behavioral domains are impacted when immigrants adjust to the social systems and environment of the majority culture but maintain some traditions of their ethnic culture (Torres-Gil and Villa, 1993). This process, identified as acculturation, varies and depends on time in the United States, reason for being here, economic level enjoyed by the family, and ability to not remain segregated within their community (Alemán, 1997). Other factors that are also important in assessing level of acculturation include English language skills, educational levels above the five years of education that this cohort of elders currently average), income levels, and the use of services (Pousada, 1995; for a complete discussion, see Alemán, 1997. All of these domains are impacted by external factors. For example, if the elder has historically had difficulty in earning more than a minimum wage, any bilingual abilities may not have improved since, most likely, their co-workers were also monolingual. However, acquisition of bilingual language skills plays a crucial role because English language skills are necessary in interactions with the larger society. In the past, elders who worked in low-wage employment situations were simply unable to break any part of the cycle to move out of poverty. Hence, they were unable to increase their level of acculturation. This unskilled level of employment is described by Popple and Leighninger (1993) as the secondary labor market that is identified with low wages, poor working conditions, considerable variability, harsh and often arbitrary discipline, and little opportunity to advance. If one asks any elder, this is how they describe employers and employment situations (Bernat et al., 1997).

A phenomenon that is becoming common in more assimilated families is the geographic distance between young adults and their parents because the younger generation has moved to find employment. This event creates a fragmentation of family systems that isolates elders in their homes and denies the children and grandchildren the ongoing support and exposure to the traditional culture that only the grandparents can provide. The consequences for all generations can be alarming: the grandparents lose their role as the transmitters of the culture and family history and the adult children lose their role of supporting the elders. Further, the adult children lose support and advice from the elders, and the young children lose the benefit of the wisdom and learning of cultural norms that the elders usually transmit.

The monolingual, Spanish-speaking elder experiences a world that is small in access to new and current modes of service provision and general information. Elders are forced to stay within a world that can only be negotiated in Spanish. The inability to speak English dramatically impacts their ability to interact with the external world and, hence, limits their ability to acculturate and use needed services. However, Andrews (1989) found that even when they speak and understand English, the majority of Hispanic elders maintain a preference for speaking in Spanish. This preference for their native language may be based on an instinctive comfort level.

Many elders are also very fatalistic and accept the fact that there are things that they cannot control (Arizona Center on Aging, 1996). If something adverse happens, they believe there is nothing that they can do. This cultural approach is likely to present itself to outsiders as a reluctance to do anything about problems. In fact, the lack of willingness to take on an issue and try to resolve it may appear to be a passive acceptance. For many Mexican-American elders, however, this fatalistic view is not a mentality of "giving up." Rather, it is a belief that God wills it and, therefore, mere human beings who are frail and have limitations cannot change the circumstances (Alemán, 1997; Arizona Center on Aging, 1996).

The complex nature of the interrelated health-seeking behaviors and fatalism present unusual challenges to the service provider. One must understand the dynamics of this deeply ingrained belief in order to impact behaviors. Given the modern medical view that is scientifically rooted and held by the majority of service providers, these cultural behaviors may be frustrating. Service providers should not become frustrated but rather should recognize they can still impact passive attitudes by seeking assistance from a religious leader or respected and trusted family member. Ultimately, the goal is for the service provider to be trusted by the elder and the family.

IMPLICATIONS FOR HEALTH
AND SOCIAL SERVICE PROVIDERS

The following section provides some insights that, coupled with the previous discussion, will be of value to service providers. It is very important to recognize that Mexican-American elders are very unlikely to come into community-based agencies to receive services, even though they may be very frail (Lopez, 1991; Weeks and Cuellar, 1981). Because of this dynamic, as well as their unique culture, it is imperative that health and social service providers take pains to understand some of these peculiarities. Information is discussed that will assist the service delivery person to understand some behaviors that may be encountered. Hopefully, comprehensive services can be provided to older Mexican-American clients who usually have multiple needs.

Acculturation

Why is the client's level of acculturation important in assessing client needs? The level of acculturation provides information that guides the service provider. The client is the best source of information to determine the acculturation level. An effective service provider facilitates the opportunity for clients to articulate who they are and what they need during the assessment. By being patient and willing to learn about the elder, the client and worker will be able to determine the method by which to best provide services. Given time, elders and their families will have the opportunity to fully identify themselves to service providers, and this will give them some control over their situation. It is important for the service provider to allow plenty of time and private accommodations to complete the assessment process. However, the notion of privacy may include grandchildren and neighborhood children playing while the interview is taking place. In these situations, look to the family members and elders to determine if the level of activity is acceptable. If that cannot be determined by their reactions, ask the older person if they need to move to another location. This respect for the individual's and family's privacy will be interpreted as a sign that the worker is sensitive to the family.

The level of acculturation will also be an extremely important factor in other areas. For example, newer immigrants will be even less likely to use formal medical and social facilities. Various factors play a role in this phenomenon. One is the impact of current anti-immigrant rhetoric and attitudes. Mexican Americans, who historically have been distrustful of majority-culture medical and service providers, feel more distrustful given the current political climate. The result may be that elders will resort to the more traditional use of *curanderos* and trusted religious systems. In some instances, a delay of treatment with modern medical technology will lead to negative health consequences. Should the elder die or not receive timely medical services, this could heighten the level of distrust between the elder's family and the professionals. The service provider may need to remember that "All human life takes place in a historical, social, and cultural context" (Lidz and Arnold, 1990, p. 65). Among other factors, the service provider may need to realize that current fears, passive behaviors, and distrust may be rooted in many years of negative interactions. By contrast, there may also be some quiet acceptance of whatever the professionals say or recommend. This behavior also results from an ingrained respect for professionals. In summary, despite levels of acculturation, culturally traditional behaviors and attitudes may be very prevalent.

Respect

The respect that elders expect from their family members also extends to service providers. Older Mexican Americans expect that service providers will show respect, extending from how they expect a professional to dress to how they are addressed. Service providers should dress professionally when working with these elders. Also, older people should be addressed as "Mr. Gonzalez" (Señor Gonzalez) or "Mrs. Gonzalez" (Señora Gonzalez) instead of by the first name. Respect that is shown to a Mexican-American elder leads to respect given by the elder to the worker. All of these dynamics lead to a sense of trust and positive expectations.

The boundaries of *personalismo* extend to knowing a service provider from a personal point of view. It does not extend to other formalities. These elders expect respect to be demonstrated by how people greet them, address them, treat them and their family members, and dress when they come to pay a professional call. All these factors give service providers opportunities to be respectful and subsequently to build positive, long-lasting professional relationships.

ANTICIPATED CHANGES
AND RECOMMENDATIONS

Information that is currently available on elderly Mexican Americans and their family systems, as well as current demographics, reflects changes in those systems (U.S. Department of Commerce, 1989). While the Administration on Aging (1997) predicts that the age structure of future populations will affect the social and economic condition of the nation, the major cause of the family-systems changes may be attributed to family dislocation within a larger and demanding foreign environment. Another possible cause is the isolation and fearfulness that elders experience. The source of the isolation that they experience is twofold: they are isolated from their younger and more mobile family members and from the social systems as well. The first source is the movement away from the parents as younger families relocate to meet economic responsibilities. The second source is the social systems and the larger environment that may be hostile to elders who are not bilingual. Their fearfulness comes from having to negotiate an oftentimes hostile and foreign environment that they have never found to be particularly helpful. Without the bilingual voices of their children and grandchildren to advocate for them and to lead them through the maze of that foreign environment, it is possible that their levels of fear will only increase.

Given these elders' traditional reluctance to use community-based services, it is possible that by the time they finally come in for services, they will have high levels of need. With this potential, it is important that service providers be more alert to ways of helping these elders. If at all possible, agencies need to develop programs and outreach efforts that encourage the utilization of services. This can be done by contacting the communities where these elders may be found, such as places of worship, Spanish-speaking radio and television stations, and social clubs. Another approach that is very effective in reaching these elders, but is also very time-consuming, is the process of going door-to-door and leaving pamphlets that advertise services, hours, costs, and locations. These pamphlets should be in both English and Spanish. This same information should also be provided through the spoken media since some of these elders will be unable to read or write in English or Spanish. The more that a community hears about an agency or services, the more likely people are to believe that it will continue to exist when they need it. Stability of agencies and their continued presence in the community are extremely important to Mexican-American elders.

These strategies are important to operationalize because eventually these elders are going to come into health and social service agencies for assistance. In many cases, service providers will treat these elders when they are extremely frail, so it may be wiser to provide services to them and become familiar with them prior to the deterioration of their health.

In summary, health and social service providers need to learn about the traditional Mexican-American culture. Also, they need to be aware that many changes are evolving in these family systems. For example, the advent of unmarried mothers is a recent phenomenon that, during the adolescent years of these elders, was unheard of. For young women to become parents without marriage was not only a personal disaster but also a horrific shame for the entire family. Therefore, the elders are experiencing events that formerly brought sanctions to the individual as well as the family. Service providers need to be aware that if they are familiar with the traditional culture and norms, they can be more effective with elders who are at different stages of acculturation. However, if they do not take the time to learn about the culture and the elders' values, it will be more difficult to develop working relationships with the elders and their families.

Following is a vignette that depicts the importance of knowing the Mexican-American culture and family system.

> Mrs. Rodriguez is an eighty-year-old Mexican-American widow who was hospitalized with pneumonia and asthma for one week. She lives by herself and keeps her home clean except for the fact that she has four cats and, prior to being hospitalized, she had not let them out as much as they wanted.
>
> The nurse case manager at the hospital who planned the discharge agreed to let her go home even though she lives by herself. It was agreed that her daughter, son, and in-laws would come by every day and check on her at various times throughout the day.
>
> On the second day that she was at home, Loretta, an English-speaking community health worker, came by to check on her to make sure that she was following the medical discharge plans. As soon as Loretta entered the home, she wrinkled her nose and her facial expression was one of disgust. She smelled cat urine and was aghast that Mrs. Rodriguez was living with the stench. She immediately called her supervisor and said that the plan was not working out, as Mrs. Rodriguez was in a horrible

situation. She recommended that they find a nursing home that would immediately take Mrs. Rodriguez.

Loretta then went back to Mrs. Rodriguez and told her what was going to happen. As soon as Mrs. Rodriguez heard the phrase "nursing home," she became very agitated. She did not know exactly what Loretta had said but she did not like the tone of her voice or the way that she was talking to her. The more that Loretta tried to calm Mrs. Rodriguez, the more agitated she became. Finally, Mrs. Rodriguez made herself understood and Loretta brought her the telephone. Mrs. Rodriguez called her daughter, Patricia, and let her talk with Loretta. Ten minutes later the daughter was there to get an explanation of what was going on. She realized that the stench from the cats was the cause of Loretta's concern for her mother's health.

Patricia agreed to clean the cats' litter box and to keep it clean so that her mother would be in a safe environment. Loretta agreed that she may have overreacted and exercised her power over Mrs. Rodriguez' safety based on her sense of proper home environment. Because Patricia and Loretta were close to the same age, and because Patricia was bilingual and bicultural, she explained to Loretta that the family would never allow their mother to go to a nursing home unless something drastic happened. Patricia further said that she and her sister-in-law had planned to clean the house and keep it clean but that the first time they could do it was the following day when both would be able to do it together. They would clean the house as well as the kitty litter box very regularly from then on.

Patricia also explained that her mother's inability to speak English made it difficult and scary for her when she was by herself. Also, she asked that if anyone had to come to visit Mrs. Rodriguez, they should call Patricia's brother so that he could plan for someone to be present with their mother. This would reduce Mrs. Rodriguez' fear of strangers and would help her understand what needed to be done for her well-being.

As a result of this interaction, Mrs. Rodriguez learned to make sure that someone who was bilingual was with her when the health providers came to visit. As time went on and Mrs. Rodriguez's health improved, the need for outsiders to visit became less frequent. However, because of this experience, she learned that when the health providers came, they were looking out for her best interests and that she could trust them to be more understanding of her desire to stay at home. Nevertheless, she preferred to have a translator with her every time a health provider visited.

Lessons to be learned from this vignette include the fear that elderly Mexican Americans may exhibit toward English-speaking professionals whom they do not know. The fear is compounded when these professionals act without consulting with the family to ensure that the safety of the elder is a family priority. Although many family dynamics are in a state of transition, decisions regarding the health care of elderly women is usually reached by consensus among the family members, with the males in the family usually making the final decisions. However, if a daughter is available, she is usually the one who will diligently take the daily responsibility for the elder's care.

Another important concept is the trust that needs to exist even when the elder cannot speak English. The idea of trusting a stranger who speaks only English is new to elders, and usually they will not readily trust outsiders. Trust develops slowly and with much patience on the health or social services provider's part. Just because the intentions are good does not mean that they are in the best interest of a person who belongs to another culture. Sometimes, they may be in the person's best interest, but unless there is trust and mutual respect, the elder will not abide by the provider's recommendations. They will also feel threatened and vulnerable since they do not know why things are happening to them.

In summary, it is very important that a service provider develop trusting communication with a Mexican-American elder and his or her family and not assume that what they think is best is in fact so. In the majority of situations, the family will remain involved with the elder; therefore, they need to be involved in all of the developments and decisions as the elderly person progresses through health and social services systems.

REFERENCES

Administration on Aging (1997). Aging into the 21st Century. <http://www.aoa.dhhs.gov/aoa/wn.html>. Available AoA Home Page.

Alemán, S. (1997). *Hispanic elders and human services.* New York: Garland Press.

Andrews, J. (1989). *Poverty and poor health among elderly Hispanic Americans.* A Report of the Commonwealth Fund Commission of Elderly People Living Alone. Baltimore, MD: Commonwealth Fund Commission.

Applewhite, S. and Daley, M. (1988). Cross-cultural understanding for social work practice with the Hispanic elderly. In S.R. Applewhite (Ed.), *Hispanic elderly in transition: Theory, research, policy and practice.* Westport, CT: Greenwood Press, 3-16.

Arizona Center on Aging (1996). *Working with Hispanic elders.* Tucson, AZ: University of Arizona.

Bassford, T.L. (1995). Health status of Hispanic elders. In David V. Espino (Guest Ed.), *Clinics in geriatric medicine.* Philadelphia: W.B. Saunders Company.

Bernat, F., Alemán, S., Gitelson, R., and Cartsonis, S. (1997). *A bi-cultural study of victimization.* Paper presented at the meeting of the American Society of Criminology, San Diego, CA.

Crouch, B.M. (1972). Age and institutional support: Perceptions of older Mexican Americans. *Journal of Gerontology, 27,* 524-529.

Curiel, H. and Rosenthal, J.A. (1988). The influence of aging on self-esteem: A consideration of ethnicity, gender, and acculturation level differences. In M. Sotomayor and H. Curiel (Eds.), *Hispanic elderly: A cultural signature.* Edinburg, TX: Pan American University Press, 11-31.

Daley, J.M., Applewhite, S.R., and Jorquez, J. (1989). Community participation of the Chicano elderly: A model. *International Journal of Aging and Human Development, 29*(2), 135-150.

Ho, M.K. (1987). *Family therapy with ethnic communities.* Newbury Park, CA: Sage Publications.

Hopper, S.V. (1993). The influence of ethnicity on the health of older women. In Fran E. Kaiser (Guest Ed.), *Clinics in Geriatric Medicine.* Philadelphia: W.B. Saunders Company.

Juarez, R.Z. (1988). Current and future long-term care needs of Mexican American elderly in Arizona. *Renalto Rosaldo Lecture Series Monograph,* Volume 4. Tucson, AZ: University of Arizona, 69-93.

Lidz, W. and Arnold, R.M. (1990). Institutional constraints on autonomy. *Generations* (Supplement), 65-68.

Lopez, C. (1991). *On the sidelines: Hispanic elderly and the continuum of care.* Washington, DC: National Council of La Raza, Policy Analysis Center and Office of Institutional Development.

Lubben, J.E. and Becerra, R. (1987). Social support among Black, Mexican, and Chinese elderly. In D.E. Gelfand and C.M. Barresi (Eds.), *Ethnic dimensions of aging.* New York: Springer Publishing Company, 130-140.

Lum, C. (1986). *Social work practice and people of color: A process-stage approach.* Monterey, CA: Brooks-Cole Publishing Company.

Moore, P. and Hepworth, J.T. (1994). Use of perinatal and infant health services by Mexican-American Medicaid enrollees. *Journal of the American Medical Association, 272*(4), 297-304.

Popple, P.R. and Leighninger, L. (1993). *Social work, social welfare, and American society.* Second edition. Boston: Allyn and Bacon.

Pousada, L. (1995). Hispanic-American elders. In David V. Espino (Guest Ed.), *Clinics in Geriatric Medicine.* Philadelphia: W.B. Saunders Company.

Sotomayor, M. (1988). Introduction. In M. Sotomayor and H. Curiel (Ed.), *Hispanic elderly: A cultural signature.* Edinburg, TX: Pan American University Press, 1-7.

Spearly, J.L. and Lauderdale, L. (1983). Community characteristics and ethnicity in the prediction of child maltreatment rates. *Child Abuse and Neglect,* 7, 91-105.

Stoller, E.P. and Gibson, R.C. (1994). Inequalities in health and mortality: Gender, race, and class. In E.P. Stoller and R.C. Gibson (Eds.), *Worlds of difference.* Thousand Oaks, CA: Pine Forge Press, 209-223.

Torres-Gil, F. and Villa, V. (1993). Health and long-term care: Family policy for Hispanic aging. In M. Sotomayor and A. Garcia (Eds.), *Elderly Latinos: Issues and solutions for the 21st century.* Westport, CT: Greenwood Press, 45-58.

Treas, J. (1995). Older Americans in the 1990s and beyond. *Population Bulletin, 50*(2), Washington, DC: Population Reference Bureau.

Trevino, M.C. (1988). A comparative analysis of need, access, and utilization of health and human services. In S.R. Applewhite (Ed.), *Hispanic elderly in transition: Theory, research, policy and practice.* Westport, CT: Greenwood Press, 61-71.

Trotter II, R.T. and Chavira, J.A. (1981). *Curanderismo, Mexican American folk healing.* Athens, GA: The University of Georgia Press.

U.S. Department of Commerce (1989). *Statistical abstract of the United States 1989,* 109th edition. Bureau of the Census. Washington, DC: Author.

Weeks, J.R. and Cuellar, J.B. (1981). The role of family members in the helping networks of older people. *The Gerontologist, 21*(4), 388-394.

Woerner, L. (1979). The Hispanic elderly: Meeting the needs of a special population. *Civil Rights Digest,* (Spring), 3-11.

Chapter 9

The Yaqui (Yoeme) Elderly

Sara Alemán
Juan Paz

The Yaqui people are an indigenous population with origins in Mexico. Not unlike the indigenous populations of the United States, they suffered at the hands of their government. The Yaqui escaped from persecution in Mexico to the United States, where they hoped to live in peace.

During the end of the 1800s and the early part of this century, the Yaqui migrated to the United States because in the Rio Yaqui area they were being persecuted and killed by the Mexican government. The dictator Porfirio Díaz implemented a policy that sought to exterminate the Yaqui so that their fertile land could be taken from them. According to Turner (1986), in his historical accounts of Mexico, 15,700 Yaquis were sold into slavery to work in Yucatán on the henequen plantations during 1905 alone. They were sold at the price of 65 pesos each. Of these, two-thirds died within the first year of slavery (Chassen-Lopez, in press). Some Yaqui individuals left their villages and went to live in the larger towns, learning the Spanish language and Mexican culture to avoid persecution. Some intermarried with Mexicans while others migrated to the United States and founded several communities in Arizona. In Tucson, people first moved into Old Pascua Village at the turn of the twentieth century. It was officially founded in 1921.

In Arizona, the Yaqui experience is one of marginalization and historical oppression. They have also experienced inequities and barriers to social services (U.S. Commission on Civil Rights, 1982a). Similarly, they have also experienced the injustices faced by Mexican Americans in the Southwest border area.

Due to their desire to live a peaceful and safe life, they learned Spanish and intermingled their traditional religious beliefs with those of the Catholic Church. They also learned Spanish as a means of self-protection and survival. In spite of these extensive accommodations, they sought to maintain their independence and to preserve their cultural traditions. Another accommodation that impacted their cohesive approach to survival was the necessity to be recognized as a tribe in order to obtain needed medical and social services. Subsequently, they sought to be recognized as a legally identified tribe. On September 18, 1978, Public Law 95-375 was signed into law, granting the Pascua Yaqui of Arizona the same status as all other federally recognized Native American tribes in the United States (Spicer, 1984, 1985).

Today, most Yaquis are integrated into the majority culture to some extent and enjoy the comforts of modern urban living: running water, electricity, natural gas, television, shopping, etc. However, the Yaqui remain fiercely independent and distinctive in their observance of their traditional medicine and spirituality, their wariness of outsiders, and their work ethic.

Members of the Pascua Yaqui Tribe in Arizona number approximately 10,000. This figure includes enrolled Yaqui and those who are pending enrollment as tribal members, and excludes descendants who are not registered with the tribe. There are six traditional Yaqui communities in Arizona (U.S. Department of Commerce, 1992), of which Old Pascua Village is the oldest. This Yaqui barrio is located in central Tucson. The other villages, located throughout the southern part of Arizona, are Barrio Libre, Guadalupe, Yoeme Pueblo, High-town, and Penjamo.

THE CURRENT COHORT
OF THE YAQUI ELDERLY

The Yaqui elderly population of Old Pascua comprises a generation of Yaqui who are first-generation United States born. Their parents migrated to Old Pascua Village in Tucson from their coastal villages in Sonora, Mexico. Due to historical oppression and racism, this cohort of elderly has been marginalized since childhood. Their parents, who sought safety from persecution by the Mexican government, found it only within their villages. However, they did not escape the hostility and nonacceptance from the majority culture. Therefore, their families developed strong patterns of self-reliance and a need to remain invisible to avoid being singled out. Their historical experiences ingrained in the Yaqui a distrust of government intervention in their lives. Family members in need sought help within the community to avoid government intervention (Holden, 1991). However, it was understood by community members that the poor were individuals who had exhausted all their resources and were in need of basic assistance.

In spite of their federal tribal recognition and the receipt of some social services, the Yaqui continue to experience severe poverty (Kossan, 1996). This is particularly true among the elders, and this poverty leads to the potential for poor health among this age cohort.

YAQUI CULTURE

The culture is one that recognizes the worth and dignity of all individuals and, within the society, Yaqui elders are highly respected and hold high status. They play a significant and powerful role in their society. This is traditional but is further reinforced by the fact that the migration patterns of the Yaqui have not been favorable to the continuation or development of a complex, stable, and large kinship system (Spicer, 1984). Because the Yaqui were forced to migrate from their homeland to the United States and various parts of Mexico and Central America, many tribal members live separated from their blood relatives, especially their extended families. When tribal blood relatives do live near each other, the Yaqui do not emphasize whose relative they are, or how distant their kinship ties may be. Rather, it is simply important that the person is a blood relative. These factors reinforce the roles that elders traditionally occupied in their extended culture.

Rituals, and even origins in the same river town in Mexico, are often the identifiers for tribal membership (Spicer, 1985). Within the Yaqui community, kinship terms are used to refer to most individuals. For example, all older women are referred to as mothers or grandmothers and treated with the traditional respect accorded that position (Spicer, 1984). Further, all relationships in the Yaqui system are based on respect and authority. The older the individuals are, the more respect and authority they have. The decision about who will be accepted as head of the household is not based on gender or other qualities, although these may be taken into consideration. In learning and giving respect and authority to their elders, the Yaqui are similar to other Native American tribes (Devore and Schlesinger, 1996) and Mexican Americans (Alemán, 1997).

Social service agencies, for the most part, have been located outside the Yaqui community, making transportation and access to services a significant barrier. In 1982, the United States Commission on Civil Rights (1982a) noted the existence of barriers to senior citizen programs in Tucson. Participation by Latinos and Native Americans was minimal in relation to their representation in the county's population. Not until 1988 was a senior citizen center created within Old Pascua Village, adjacent to the neighborhood youth center, and services became more readily available with this structure.

Roles of Yaqui Elders

The elders' role is essential to the spiritual core of the community. Because their communities are far from the Rio Yaqui homeland in Mexico, the elderly assume the role of educating the following generations regarding the roles and responsibilities of members of the various societies within the culture. The Yaquis have managed to preserve their cultural/spiritual practices similar to the way of the *penitentes* of New Mexico. One significant difference is that the *penitentes* were marginalized and remained covert until recently. The Yaquis, on the other hand, have always been fiercely independent and openly practiced their religion. Another major reason for their openness with their religion is that their culture and their spiritual beliefs are the core of the community. Current practices continue to be celebrated in an open community setting, and the Yaqui spiritual beliefs are a mix of their traditional rituals and the influence of the European missionaries. According to Sheridan (1996), this combination of beliefs created a "culture that is a vibrant fusion of the European and Native American" (p. 36).

This section describes how the elders are integral in preserving the ceremonies and the three societies that make up Yaqui culture. The first society is the Ceremonial Society, which is in charge of the

Easter ceremonies. This society includes the *fariseos,* calvary, and *chapyekas.* The *caballeros* and the infantry are headed by a *capitan.* Members of this society vow to serve Jesus.

Elders organize all of the activities for all of the ceremonies. The elders lead the prayers and all of the processions that precede the different ceremonies. In all of the activities, the elders teach certain younger individuals the prayers, processions, and the rituals that accompany each part of the ceremony. The training and teachings illustrate in a visual and emotional manner the role that the elders occupy in the transmission of Yaqui culture.

The second society is the Church Society and the components include the *maestro,* who is the spiritual leader and a lay priest. An elder who is called the *maestro mayor* (the elder teacher) occupies this important role. That elder is aided by the sacristans in caring for the crucifixes and the male holy figures. Young and unmarried women, *cantoras,* also assist the maestro and sing during the ceremonies. Elderly women are in charge of the upkeep of the altars. These elderly women also select younger women to train in the care of the altars since the altars are only used on special occasions.

The third society is the Fiesta Dancers Society, and it includes two types of fiesta dancers who dance at the Lenten activities, as well as other spiritual events. Although these dances require a great deal of stamina and energy, it is the older Yaqui men who lead the dances and train younger men to do the best known dances, the Pascolas and the Deer Dances. These dances are accompanied by music and song that are special forms of prayer to the Spirit. Therefore, this dance predates any influence from the Catholic Church, since it is considered a special form of spiritual prayer (Rebeca Tapia, personal communication, April 5, 1997). Because the dances are historical, it has always been the elders who teach the younger Yaqui men to dance and thus preserve the traditional dances, music, and song.

Each society performs important and vital tasks in the spiritual life of the community during the year. Some of the celebrations take place during the entire Lenten Season, as well as during the celebration of each community's patron saint, the Day of the Dead, and fiestas for funerals, baptisms, and death anniversaries, among others. Some of the spiritual tasks are performed in Latin, Spanish, or Cahiti, the Yaqui language.

The elderly remain involved in performing the ceremonies and in training the younger generations to continue the culture that is based on these teachings and values of community cohesiveness. These leadership roles provide a high visibility for the elders and lead to an incentive for respect and value that is given to these elders by their entire community.

Self-Identity

The vast majority of the Yaqui elders at Old Pascua identify as either Hispanic or Yaqui and speak Spanish only; a smaller number speak Cahiti. This dual identity is understandable because, in the past, some elderly identified themselves and their families as Mexican American for survival and safety. Still others identified as Native American because their experiences were similar to those of the Tohono O'Odham. The Tohono O'Odham, like the Yaqui, have roots in Mexico and are a bi-national, trilingual group. Consequently, both tribes share a strong bond with Mexico.

DEMOGRAPHICS THAT IMPACT ROLES

In the village of Old Pascua (see Alemán and Paz, 1998, for a complete discussion of the demographics), the majority of the elders (60 percent) have six or fewer years of education and only eight persons had more than a high school education. In today's complex society, the more education one has, the higher the income. A large percentage (80 percent) had an annual income of less than $7,000 per year and another significantly large percentage of individuals (74 percent) were dependent on Social Security benefits for their incomes. These data strengthen the notion that a significant number live in poverty with few sources of income. In addition, almost one-fifth (21 percent) are receiving Supplemental Security Income benefits, and only twelve of the elders in Old Pascua had income from earnings. Of the remainder, 15 percent receive money from retirement pensions.

The majority of elders reported that they live with family members. In spite of these intergenerational living arrangements, the household income level is consistently low. Only one person reported receiving financial assistance from other household members on a regular basis. This striking fact indicates two important pieces of information. First, in most Yaqui families the elderly are a major source of economic support for the family system. Second, most intergenerational families live in poverty. The second fact is consistent with other Native American and Mexican family experiences. Overall, these data suggest that a large number of Yaqui households survive in conditions of poverty. Income data reveal that in one-third of the households the income of one person supports two persons. Close to half (48 percent) of households have three or more persons dependent on one income.

In the exploration of factors that may contribute to poverty, the related issues of receipt of Social Security and marital status cannot be disregarded (Popple and Leighninger, 1996). Some researchers (Atchely, 1991; Hopper, 1993) have found that being married is an important factor in staying out of poverty; others have found that elders who live alone are most likely to live in chronic poverty. This is consistent with studies that show that Native Americans and Hispanics in single-headed households are more likely to be in poverty (Arizona Community Action Association, Inc., 1994; U.S. Department of Health and Human Services, 1987).

These data demonstrate that the elderly and their families possess limited economic resources and live in intergenerational families to cope with the hardships of chronic poverty. The variables of income and living arrangements must not be confused with housing preference. Some Hispanic researchers state that the elderly have a preference for intergenerational living. Not so; *la necesidad,* the need to live with a minimally decent quality of life, often forces them to live in intergenerational households (Paz, 1986). In fact, an earlier study conducted by Greta Glugoski (personal communication, 1995) of Hispanic elderly in California found that, if given the option and if it were economically feasible, a majority of the elderly would elect to live in their own homes.

These data strengthen the theory that Yaqui elders experience triple jeopardy, (i.e., they are old, poor, and members of an ethnic minority group). They face social and historical barriers that prevent their participation in programs designed for senior citizens. This cohort of elderly live in an urban setting and in some cases they are excluded from receiving health care and social services because they do not live on a reservation. Historically, issues of language, transportation, and mistrust of government prevent their access to needed services. For example, during the 1980s the umbrella agency the Pima Council on Aging and Tucson Metropolitan Ministries operated a meals program for Yaqui elders. For over ten years, Yaqui participants in the meals program were obliged to accept a diet of foods designed for white senior citizens. Nine years ago, the tribe took over the nutrition program and hired Yaqui individuals to prepare nutritional meals that incorporated their dietary preferences.

The Yaqui elderly find themselves in a state of social services limbo, where they are often denied services and forced to go without them. Originally, they were denied services because they were thought to be Mexican nationals, which made them ineligible to receive state health and social services. On the other hand, some health care planners categorized them as Native American, thus making them ineligible to receive these same services. For example, the state-managed health care system for the poor, known as the Arizona Health Care Cost Containment System, often excluded Yaqui elders from receiving services. These individuals were compelled to apply for services financed by the Indian Health Services (IHS). Nevertheless, when these senior citizens sought services financed by IHS, they were denied services because they were not enrolled Native Americans. When older individuals received services from a community health center, they encountered several days of waiting for an appointment and frequently were met with a dehumanizing amount of bureaucratic red tape. Some individuals elected to do without services due to negative experiences with the system as well as their historical experiences. As a result, avoidance of the health and social service network is often seen as a way to preserve their dignity.

LANGUAGE DISCRIMINATION

Spanish is the language of choice for the majority of the Yaqui elderly. Some do speak Cahiti and English. When the data-collection process was underway for this project, some discussion was held with the elderly about their experiences with agencies serving senior citizens. The majority of the elderly indicated that many agencies still do not have bilingual workers and still other agencies required them to bring their own translator. This often discouraged them from seeking services, since getting to the agency with a translator in tow alone was a challenge.

IMPLICATIONS FOR HEALTH AND SOCIAL SERVICES PRACTICE

Health and social services practice with elderly Yaqui clients requires practitioners to plan a period for development of a trusting relationship. In this stage, the service provider will work with the client to prepare for interaction with a health care and social services network that is often hostile to persons from diverse cultural backgrounds (Chestang, 1972). In other words, they need to prepare the client to deal with agencies that do not value diversity. If this preparation is not done, the distrust of the Yaqui elderly client can easily be heightened by exposure to an agency that is culturally insensitive. For example, an agency may require a person to bring a translator to an interview or may not provide any privacy to discuss personal problems; however, this population requires a strict code of silence and confidentiality, given their fearfulness of government interference in their family systems.

The initial stage may include preparing a client for rejection of eligibility for services as well as the aforementioned intrusions into private matters. In cases where services are denied, clients need to be informed of options such as filing an appeal, challenging a decision, and/or involving the assistance of a legal aid center or other possible advocates. Preparing a client for possible rejection from services is vital, especially in cases where persons have not previously asked for assistance. Rejection of services may have serious social and psychological effects on clients by making them feel increasingly vulnerable. The trauma of rejection is compounded by their loss of dignity and respect. The initial stage helps to minimize these problems by acknowledging that eligibility determinations are not always final, may be in error, and can be challenged.

Professionals who provide services to Yaqui elders must take into account several variables. The first major variable to consider during the initial stage of conducting an assessment is to include the total family when planning the delivery of services. Instead of viewing the elderly as separate from their families, they should be viewed as inextricably intertwined with their families. In other words, instead of providing only individual-based services, the focus should be on providing family-based services that take into consideration the family context in which the elder lives.

This research has uncovered intergenerational poverty among families. Another professional role entails facilitating the ability of the family to ameliorate its economic status by linking them to services. This requires workers to develop extensive knowledge of elderly and family services available in the community and to function in the role of a broker. This may be necessary in the case of facilitating access to an array of services from medical care to food stamps. The broker role will also require the social worker to develop an extensive knowledge of programs and policies that are targeted to Native American, Mexican American, and other elders. The broker will have to develop skills at helping the client population negotiate the myriad red tape that is required to participate in programs for the elderly. The task of the professional worker is to minimize the negative impact of the red tape and to facilitate the flow of information and services in an expeditious manner.

Culturally competent services to Yaqui elderly necessitate a tricultural approach to service delivery. This includes determining the acculturation level of the client. Some Yaqui elders may identify more with the Yaqui culture while others may identify more with the Hispanic culture. Still others may identify with other Native American cultures. An added dimension of their cultural identity is how positive they feel about their own culture. Do they have a positive sense of worth? Are they proud or are they embarrassed about their culture? How long has the client been in the United States? What is the primary language of the client? Some individuals may be Spanish dominant, some may be English dominant, and others may be bilingual. Another group may speak the original Yoeme language of their ancestors in addition to their adopted languages. How comfortable is the client dealing with non-Yaqui systems and their representatives? How comfortable is the client dealing with non-Yaqui persons? Some elderly Yaquis may continue to refuse services from outside their community. For example, an eighty-year-old woman was recently taken to the hospital to receive health care services from a registered nurse. However, the woman's illness was already advanced to such a stage that she died within a week. This woman had previously refused to go to a hospital for health care. It was only through the skilled and convincing persuasion of a Yaqui nurse that she finally agreed to go to the hospital. A subsequent discussion with the nurse revealed the elderly woman to be a classic example of an individual who did not trust the health care system and chose to go without needed care.

In recognition of the fact that a high level of distrust exists toward outsiders, service planners and service providers must also determine to what extent a client is willing to trust direct services personnel. From a cultural vantage point, the service providers must begin from the outset to establish bonds of mutual trust, or *confianza*, with the client.

YAQUI HEALTH BELIEFS AND PRACTICES IN ACTION

The Yaqui believe that there are many causes of illness, including spirits, lunar eclipses, intraclan marriages, vow breaking, dishonoring taboos, witches, and negative energy. During the 1930s, research within the Yaqui community revealed many traditional medicine cures for a variety of ailments, including dysentery, typhoid fever, smallpox, and rabies. Many of the remedies found among the Yaqui in the 1930s were still reported as being used in the 1980s, for example, preventing illness in children by tying a string or bracelet around the wrist (Spicer, 1984).

Many Yaqui beliefs about health are in conflict with those in the dominant culture. For example, the Yaqui believe in the power of personal and family energy to effect a cure of illness. This energy is transferred to the ill person by their family members and community through touching, verbal and nonverbal communication, and close proximity to family and sacred objects (Rebecca Ponder, personal communication, April 1994). In modern health care facilities, especially hospitals, this is not possible. Patients are taken away from the community, their family is only allowed to visit at certain times, and their belongings are removed, especially if they are valuable. In the Yaqui belief, patients are taken away from the only environment that can heal them.

The concept of female modesty is another example of the dominant cultural values conflicting with those of the Yaqui. Yaqui morality dictates that it is taboo for a female to be without coverings on the intimate parts of her body for an extended period of time. Many times, health care workers ask Yaqui women to break this taboo by removing their undergarments (R. Tapia, personal communication, April 5, 1997).

Also, many Yaqui still believe in going to a *curandero* (a lay person who cures illnesses with herbs and prayers) for health treatment (Vicenta Muñoz, personal communication, February 12, 1994). Many Yaqui health professionals encourage the use of both approaches among their patients. An example of this was a recent blessing ceremony at the home of a couple where the husband was diagnosed with terminal cancer. While receiving treatment from modern medicine, he still felt the need for a blessing ceremony. He stated that he needed to strengthen his spirit as his body was being bombarded with chemotherapy. He believed that if the spirit is made strong, it will eventually cure the body of its illness. This combination of traditional with Western medicine is not unusual and, in fact, provides the combination that many elders need to deal with their physical and spiritual well-being.

In sum, professional delivery of services to the Yaqui elderly poses a challenge. To be bilingual and bicultural in the Southwest is no longer sufficient. The dynamic interaction of the Yaqui elders with other populations of the Southwest demonstrates the necessity to be multicultural and to have the requisite skills to assess the impact of poverty and barriers on health status and life situation. To be professional and culturally relevant with the Yaqui elderly further requires time to develop a sense of trust, patience, awareness, and respect for cultural differences and a holistic approach to healing.

Several recommendations arise. First is the need to have a planning stage during the traditional health or social services assessment. The purpose is to prepare the client to deal adequately with a potentially hostile system and for other contingencies. The second recommendation is to develop a comprehensive approach that identifies resources available in the community and matches them to the client system. The third recommendation is that Yaqui elders must be provided services within the context of their total family system. Service providers must be flexible in instituting action modalities that require engaging in the broker role on behalf of their clients. Finally, the influence of a client's culture must be considered during all stages of the helping relationship.

Yaqui Traditional Medicine

The following is a list of common medical situations and corresponding herbal cures that are still practiced by many Yaqui:

Ailment	Cure
Dysentery	goma de Sonora, cominos (cumin), cinnamon bark, and mint
Diarrhea	molanisco
Headaches	beilburia root, mesquite leaves, bark of cuhuca
Typhoid fever	"immortal plant" (probably contains quinine)
Scarlet fever	mochi plant, lia plant
Rattlesnake bites	milkweed, rattler's gallbladder mixed with alcohol
Cuts and bruises	yerba del manzo, rosemary, yerba coloraga, and alucema seed
Whooping cough	string or bracelet is tied around a child's wrist and is never removed
Smallpox	amapa (dye wood), black insect-pinocate
Coughs	torote
Lung trouble	snake grass
Gas	mesquite bark
Fainting spells	Brazil wood and mesquite trees

Pinkeye	haicocoa berries
Abortion	corcho, roots of the "immortal plant"
Ant bites	wax from the mesquite tree
Rabies	fresno tree tea and atole, beans and water taken until it is thrown up every day for up to three days, milkweed plant and savila

REFERENCES

Alemán, S. (1997). Case management and Mexican American elders. *Journal of Case Management, 6*(2), 69-76.

Alemán, S. and Paz, J. (1998). The Yaqui elderly, cultural oppression and resilience. *Journal of Aging and Ethnicity, 1*(2), 113-127.

Arizona Community Action Association, Inc. (1994). *Poverty in Arizona: A shared responsibility.* Phoenix, AZ: Author.

Atchely, R.C. (1991). *Social forces and aging,* Sixth edition. Belmont, CA: Wadsworth Publishing Company.

Chassen-Lopez, F. (In press). *Juana Catarina Romero, Porfirian Cacica: The Woman and the myth.* University of Kentucky.

Chestang, I. (1972). *Character development in a hostile environment: Occasional paper number 3.* Chicago: University of Chicago School of Social Service Administration.

Devore, W. and Schlesinger, E.G. (1996). *Ethnic-sensitive social work practice,* Third edition. New York: Macmillan Publishing Company.

Holden, K.J. (1991). *Yaqui women: Contemporary life histories.* London: University of Nebraska Press.

Hopper, S.V. (1993). The influence of ethnicity on the health of older women. In F.E. Kaiser (Ed.), *Clinics in geriatric medicine.* Philadelphia: W.B. Saunders Company, 231-259.

Kossan, P. (1996, August 24). Yaquis' reservation bid created rift in Guadalupe. Phoenix, AZ: *The Arizona Republic,* A1, A24.

Paz, J. (1986). *Housing issues and the Hispanic elderly.* Washington, DC: House Subcommittee on Housing and Community Development, Subcommittee of the House Banking and Commerce Committee.

Popple, P.R. and Leighninger, L. (1996). *Social work, social welfare, and American society,* Third edition. Boston: Allyn and Bacon.

Sheridan, T.E. (1996). The Yoemem (Yaquis): An enduring people. In T.E. Sheridan and N.J. Parezo (Eds.), *Paths of life: American Indians of the Southwest and northern Mexico.* Tucson, AZ: The University of Arizona Press, 35-49.

Spicer, E.H. (1984). *Pascua: A Yaqui village in Arizona.* Tucson, AZ: The University of Arizona Press.

Spicer, E.H. (1985). *The Yaqui: A cultural history.* Tucson, AZ: The University of Arizona Press.

Turner, J. (1986). *Barbarous Mexico*. Tucson, AZ: University of Arizona Press.

U.S. Commission on Civil Rights (1982a). *Minority elderly services: New programs, old problems, Part I*. Washington, DC: Author.

U.S. Commission on Civil Rights (1982b). *Minority elderly services: New programs old problems, Part II*. Washington, DC: Author.

U.S. Department of Commerce (1992). *Pascua Yaqui Indian Reservation Community Profile*. Washington, DC: Author.

U.S. Department of Health and Human Services (1987). *Aging America: Trends and projections*. Washington, DC: Author.

Chapter 10

Navajo Elders

Sara Peña
Sara Alemán
Charlotte Beyal

The following is an example of modern-day aging on the Navajo Reservation:

This morning I went to visit my mother. I usually visit her every other day to have breakfast, lunch, or just for conversation. Today, I needed advice on a certain matter so I got up earlier than usual hoping to see her before she left the house but I was late according to her schedule.

My mother recently retired after thirty years with the Indian Health Services. Now she spends each day sheepherding and on this particular morning she was out with the herd early because the weather forecast predicted light showers and breezy conditions.

As I looked for her and saw her, I noticed that she was approximately half a mile away from home. I drove part of the way then I got out of my car and proceeded toward her. We walked and talked for awhile and when I was ready to leave, my mother noticed one of the sheep was giving birth to a set of lambs. She went on over to help the sheep and I stayed up on the hill watching the rest of the herd.

As I sat there, a breeze of crisp air blew across my face and the scent of the fresh vegetation surrounding me took me back in thought to my childhood years when I used to herd sheep with my brothers and sisters.

I continued to watch my mother, though not intentionally. This was a moment that I was able to observe the woman who is not only the person who gave birth to me, but also the person who has guided me and taught me ways of survival in life as a Navajo woman. She has been my teacher for thirty-eight years and I believe she will continue to be just that for the rest of hers and my life.

Her hair is not gray, thanks to Clairol, and her skin is not wrinkled but very soft. She stands approximately 5′4″ and weighs close to 155 pounds. Her physique appears to be of one who has walked many miles. Although she is overweight by Western medical standards, she does not appear to be in need of a diet. Her face, her dark brown eyes, her thin lips, and her high cheekbones lay the foundation of her beauty as a teenager and continue to remain in her perfect form after many years.

I catch myself staring when she calls me over to help her. The newborn lambs need assistance in nursing so we hold the sheep; doing this creates a bond between the mother and her offspring. At this time my mother begins to talk to the sheep in Navajo and tells her of the responsibilities of parenting. The tone in her voice reminded me of the way she spoke to me when I gave birth to my baby eleven years ago. "The role of parenting will not be easy," she tells the sheep. "You will continue to graze with the rest of the herd; this will build up your strength. You will be back with your babies when it is feeding time this afternoon." Her voice remains gentle as always without a tone of harshness as she speaks using words of encouragement.

When my mother first announced her plans for what she wanted to do after retirement, one of her wishes was to raise sheep and goats and to one day return to her homeland (sheep camp) to continue to run the family homestead. I was not sure if she could handle sheepherding. She had not tended to sheep since she was a teenager. I also was not sure if she was physically prepared. I always thought she would not last over thirty days only because of what I had observed in her daily routine before retirement.

With a bath each day, a beige tone of Cover Girl smoothed gently across her face with a light touch of rose-colored blush, I was wrong. She has not ignored her daily cosmetic ritual nor has she neglected her attire. In fact, she continues to visit the salon to have her hair styled and treated and she continues to maintain a positive and healthy attitude.

She has spoken very little of her childhood, but through her guidance and success as a single parent of six children, it is evident that she is also a role model and a good parent. The turmoil and hardships she endured as a child might be reasons as to why she is the strong-willed person that she is today.

Her aunt and uncle adopted my mother when she was four years old. Her birth mother was taken from her in 1969 by tuberculosis. Her biological father passed away in 1991, and at 102 years of age most recently her adoptive father lost his life after he was diagnosed with Alzheimer's disease.

Being an adopted child taught her to be a loving mother. After a few years of boarding school in Shelako, Oklahoma, she was forcibly returned home at the age of sixteen to marry a stranger. Years of physical abuse led to their divorce in 1969. After her divorce she vowed never to give up any of her children and to always be available in their time of need.

She is kind in many ways. She enjoys having small intimate family dinners as well as large family gatherings in her home and she makes note that her relatives never go unrecognized for their accomplishments. Many people respect her for who she is and not for what she has.

Thank the stars for giving us, along with our friends and relatives, a person who has and will continue to share her love, kindness, and wisdom with whomever is willing to accept it without asking for anything in return. (Connie Hudgins, Tuba City, Arizona)

This chapter addresses some areas of concern to individuals who work with elders who are Navajo, or Diné, as they call themselves. As in other nonmainstream cultures, the Diné are experiencing some very dramatic changes in their cultures, family systems, and in the traditional ways of viewing the world. They have a unique and complex culture that is changing to accommodate the majority culture. They also have a complex language, and this compounds the issues related to service accessibility and delivery. For example, Hassell (1972) writes, "The Navajos have a name for only one day in the week—Sunday. Other days are counted as so many days to or from Sunday" (p. 5). There is also an intricate family system that is only somewhat replicated among other Native groups. Therefore, family systems that non-Natives are familiar with generally do not provide a basis for understanding the complex family system that operates among the Diné. This chapter addresses the needs of Diné elders who still adhere to their traditional values, healing approaches, and family systems. The vignette describes a changing world and it also depicts the world in which elders are the most comfortable and secure.

The history of the Indian Health Service (IHS) is also presented in this chapter. This is of paramount importance because the IHS delivers health services based on the Western medical model to the Navajo, and the majority of professionals are non-Native. The importance of evaluating health care from the perspective of those who are treated cannot be emphasized enough when looking at the Navajo elder. The room for misunderstanding between elders and the predominantly non-Native medical staff employed by IHS is great. These are people from two different worlds who are separated by language, culture, religion, and way of life.

The following is a brief historical backdrop for understanding the history between the Diné and the United States government, which has fundamentally defined how many Diné elders deal with systems and individuals that are supposed to provide services to them and their families.

THE DINÉ

The Diné, a nomadic people and part of the NaDene language group, have language relatives in Alaska, Canada, Washington, Oregon, and California. Part of the Athabaskan ethnic group (Downs, 1972; Wood, Vannette, and Andrews, 1982), the Diné are centered in Arizona and New Mexico but can also be found in numbers over 1,000 in California, Colorado, Texas, and Utah. In

1990, 212,000 Diné registered with the Navajo Tribe and they made up 11.7 percent of the total American Indian population (U.S. Census Bureau, 1992). The majority of tribal members live on the Navajo Reservation, which consists of 27,000 square miles and spans the three states of Arizona, New Mexico, and Utah.

As a colonized minority group, the Navajo have been assigned the curious position of outsiders in their own world. Effects of colonization in the form of boarding schools, hospitals, and churches have taken their toll on the Navajo people. Despite many difficulties, however, the Navajo have survived, and to understand where they are today, one must understand where they came from.

THE BEGINNING

The Navajo people believe in the four-world structure. The worlds are described as the black, blue, yellow, and white or glittering world. The First World was black, and four holy beings were created to run this new world. These holy beings were Water Monster, Blue Heron, Frog, and Lightning. These leaders were to govern the people in positive ways in order to promote good moral character and to prevent adultery and incest from occurring among the people.

However, a struggle for power began among the four leaders, and the result of this bitter rivalry was the creation of witchcraft. This power dispute brought an end to the first world because witchcraft took over the holy beings. The First World was destroyed and the Diné began a struggle with incestuous behavior and other types of sinful activities.

The Second World, the blue world that is also known as the bird world, was a new start for the Diné, with new holy beings. These new deities were the Wolf, Coyote, the Mountain Lion, and the Bear. These beings were given the task of keeping a sense of order among the Diné. The First World beings that had moved to the Second World, as well as Coyote, who was mischievous, remembered the powers of witchcraft from the First World. The new deities began to struggle over power in the Second World, and Coyote used witchcraft to try and gain power over the others. The other holy beings tried to protect themselves from Coyote by using witchcraft, and the holy beings of the Second World once again destroyed the world they were entrusted with protecting.

The Third World, the yellow world, had leaders in the Deer, Badger, Skunk, and Porcupine. In the beginning of the Third World, everything went well. But after some time, greed and jealousy took over. Coyote gave the Third World deities the idea of using witchcraft against one another, and the Third World was consequently destroyed. After the destruction of the First, Second, and Third Worlds, the Fourth World was formed. The Fourth World is the white or glittering world; the Diné are currently in this world. The leaders of this world are the Talking God, the Hoghan God, Born for Water, and Monster Slayer. These leaders introduced new rules to the Diné to promote good moral character, and their leadership has been successful to date.

Fourth World

The way in which two of the Fourth World deities became leaders is quite important. In the Third World, the First Man and First Woman began to argue and soon all men and women in the world were against each other. The dispute between the sexes originated out of undefined duties and responsibilities. The two groups agreed to separate and for the next four years they were not allowed any contact. During these four years, men became like women and women became like men in order to survive. (This is why today it is said that the Diné are not to be prejudiced against gay or lesbian people.) Separation also resulted in offensive behavior, and monsters were born out of this behavior. The men and women agreed to unite, but following this, the monsters began to prey on them and soon many of the people were gone. The monsters came into the Fourth World when it was created and soon all hope was lost, because the people had no way to fight against the monsters.

Around this time, a baby was found on Choo'li, or Gobernador Knob. This baby grew to be a woman in twelve days, and on the twelfth day, a *Kinall'da,* or puberty ceremony, was held for her, and she became known as Asdzaa Nadleehe' or Changing Woman. Changing Woman soon afterward became pregnant with twins for the Sun and for Water. After the birth of Born for Sunlight and Born for Water, Changing Woman kept them underground for most of their youth, hidden from the monsters. The twins grew up and wanted to protect their people from the monsters, so they went to see their father the Sun, who had the means to create or destroy any life on earth. After passing a series of tests, the Sun gave the twins weapons with which to destroy the monsters and the twins began a campaign wherein they killed the terrible monsters. Once all these monsters were killed, the twins happened upon five more monsters: Dichin Hastiin (Hunger Man), Te'i'i' Hastiin (Poverty Man), Bil Hastiin (Sleep Man), Yaa' Hastiin (Lice Man), and Sa' (Old Age). These monsters pleaded for their lives by arguing that the Diné needed them to make their lives worthwhile, and after some convincing, the twins agreed to let them live. Consequently, today "people eat to nourish their bodies and are interested each day in food; they make shoes and clothing and wear them out; they enjoy sleep when they are tired; they keep clean to live more comfortably; and babies are being born daily while older people are closing their eyes forever in death," (Yazzie, 1982, p. 70).

After the majority of monsters were slain, the twins went to live with their mother on the mountain of Choo'li. It was from this point on that laws began to develop from the deeds of Changing Woman, Born for Water, and Monster Slayer (Born for Sunlight's name changed after fighting with monsters). They set rules, procedures, and a system of social order and the duties of women and men were defined. Women were put in charge of the clan system, children, the home, the fields, the livestock, and the property. Men were put in leadership positions and had an important part in ceremonies. For the Diné, Monster Slayer represents the aggressive or male part in humans and Born for Water represents the gentle or female part. The laws are based on a gender code and were made to provide *hozho*, a balanced way of life, for the people. The chaos of the previous worlds taught the Diné and the Holy Beings to always work toward the balance of *hozho*. The area in which the Diné were meant to live was able to provide this balance.

Diné Bikeyah

The Fourth World was created within a certain area, and the Holy People gave this land area to the Diné. The area designated for the Diné was the area within the six sacred mountains and the four sacred directions. One mountain to the east is Blanca Peak, known to the Diné as Sisnaajini'. This mountain represents the white shell and the thinking process, and offerings are made to Sisnaajini at dawn with white cornmeal. The mountain to the south is Mt. Taylor or Tsoodzil, which is known to represent the turquoise stone and the planning process, and offerings are made with corn pollen at noon to this mountain. The mountain to the west, Dook'o'oosliid, also known as the San Francisco Peaks, is represented by the abalone shell, and offerings are made with yellow corn meal at dusk. The meaning behind Dook'o'oosliid has to do with the necessity of family and importance of social relationships. The mountain to the north is Happiness Through the Black Jet Stone, and dark blue corn meal is offered to the mountain in the night. Herfano Mesa, the second mountain in the east, is called Dzilna'oodilii, and this mountain represents the center of the universe. Offerings of corn pollen are given to this mountain. Gobernador Knob, known as Ch'ooli, is the third mountain in the east. This mountain represents the earth and its gifts of life through Changing Woman, such as water, air, and soil. The Diné lived within these sacred mountains on the land known as Diné Bikeyah (Dick, 1977).

Clan Systems

Within these mountains, Changing Woman created a means to *hozho* through social order. One of the ways she created social order was through the clan system. The Diné, a matrilineal people, are born into their mother's clan and for their father's clan. The clan system determines whom a Diné can marry. It was, and continues to be, taboo to marry into one's own clan. The purpose of the taboo is to have healthy offspring. Clanship determines land-use rights, and these are given to a woman and her female descendants.

Traditionally, the Navajo groom separates from his family to move into his in-laws' residence. A family includes a female head of household, her female descendents, and their sons and/or husbands. Women hold land in common for their lineage, and today the land is still held in common by the descendants of the women landowners of 1924 when the newly established Tribal Council documented land allocations (Beyal, personal communication, October 10, 1998).

GOVERNMENT

Prior to colonization, the Navajo tribe was not centralized under one leader. Instead, a clan headman called a Naa'tani' represented the individual clans. Ceremonial meetings brought the Naa'tani headmen together every three to four years for a *naachiid,* or ceremonial meetings, which were held as late as 1863.

The Spanish and, after the Treaty of Guadalupe Hidalgo, the United States governments formed treaty agreements with Diné, with no knowledge of the Naa'tani organization. The agreements between European governments and the Navajo were actually agreements between one or two bands of Navajo, not the entire tribe as it is currently organized.

During the 1800s, the U.S. government worked on thousands of treaty agreements with Native American tribes. One reason the U.S. government attempted to form a treaty agreement with the Navajo was to prevent the bands from raiding homesteads of non-Navajos. The Navajo tribe at this time was widely dispersed, and many bands were unaware of treaties that other bands were signing. The raiding continued in spite of all the treaties because the United States government continued to sign treaties with individual Naa'tani'.

In 1863, General James H. Carleton arrived in New Mexico and was given the task of keeping his impatient men busy. After meeting with the territorial governor, Carleton decided to put an end to Navajo raiding by "gathering them together, little by little, on to a reservation, away from the haunts, and hills and hiding-places of their country" (Kelly, 1968, p. 6). Kit Carson was given the duty of bringing in the Navajo tribe. The Diné were given until June of 1863 to surrender without harm, but only a few bands agreed to the demand.

Carson then invaded Navajo country, burning crops, taking sheep, and shooting Navajo men whenever resistance was offered (Kelly, 1968). In the spring of 1864, the Diné began what is now known as The Long Walk. It was the walk from central and eastern Arizona to a fort called Bosque Redondo in eastern New Mexico (Kelly, 1968).

By December, 8,500 Diné were at Fort Sumner/Bosque Redondo, and the Diné were held as prisoners for four years. Supplied with rations such as coffee and flour, but without cooking instructions, many people became ill from eating uncooked flour and other staples. Illnesses that the tribe had never experienced began to kill their members. In addition, many taboos were broken because the army did not understand Native culture. For example, the Diné believe that living people should have nothing to do with dead people; at Bosque Redondo, the Diné were at times forced to live on or near burial sites.

The Treaty of 1868 was born out of the imprisonment at Bosque Redondo. The Diné were told that if they agreed to sign the treaty they would be released. The Treaty of 1868 was signed, and the Diné were released after four years of imprisonment.

With the majority of their homes destroyed and their livestock gone, the Diné were given two sheep each upon the time of their release. In the years to follow, family status became linked to "the size and well-being of their herd" (Parezo, 1996, p. 22). In 1868, an estimated 7,500 Diné were released after the signing of the treaty, which stated that the federal government would give the Navajo people a land base in the eastern part of Arizona. This reservation land expanded in the years to follow with the addition of the Chenille Valley in 1878; the Ganado, Window Rock, and New Mexico areas in 1880; the Navajo-Hopi Joint Partition Land in 1882; and Tuba City and southern Utah in 1884. The relationship between the Diné and the federal government also expanded in the years following the signing of the Treaty of 1868.

FEDERAL-TRIBAL RELATIONSHIP

In the 1700s, America's newly arrived Europeans did not initially establish any Indian law or policy. Instead, the Supreme Court made up Indian law as cases were brought to court, and policy developed out of a few words in the Constitution.

The Constitution, under Article I, Section 8, Clause 3, otherwise known as the Commerce Clause, mentions tribes briefly, stating that the government's position is to regulate commerce with foreign nations, among states, and with tribes. This clause did not give much precedent for the standing of tribes in the newly formed country.

Three cases in tribal law, known as the Marshall Trilogy, established the concepts that define the situation of tribes in the United States today. Chief Justice John Marshall presided over each case. *Johnson v. McIntosh* in 1823 was the first case, a dispute in which both Johnson and McIntosh had purchased the same land from different sources. One source was the Illinois and Piankeshaw Indian Nations, and the other was the U.S. government. The Supreme Court had to consider whether tribes could sell land. The Marshall decision revolved around the concept of the Doctrine of Discovery: "That discovery gave title to the government by whose subjects, or by whose authority it was made, against all other European governments" (Getches, Wilkinson, and Williams, 1993, p. 73). This decision meant that Native people did not have title to the land; Indian tribes were instead rewarded with areas to use because they were not a European power. This decision began the legal framework for extinguishing Indian title to land.

The next case, *Cherokee Nation v. Georgia* in 1831, occurred when the state of Georgia enacted laws which seized Cherokee lands that had been guaranteed to them by a treaty with the U.S. government. This case asked the court to define tribes and whether or not they are foreign nations or states (see Clause 3). The court decided that the tribes were "distinct political societies," but since they were located within the U.S. boundaries, they could not be considered foreign nations, and were then named "domestic, dependent nations." In addition, the court defined the relationship between the tribes and the federal government as one of a "ward to his guardian." The Cherokees won the case because state laws have no effect on tribes. Only the federal government can enact laws that affect tribes; this established the federal trust responsibility that is still in effect.

In *Worchester v. Georgia,* a case decided in 1832, a missionary named Worchester was living on Cherokee land without a permit from the governor of Georgia. He was arrested and sentenced by the State of Georgia to serve time in a prison work camp. Marshall used the 1785 Cherokee treaty (the Treaty of Hopewell), the Trade and Intercourse Acts, and Article I, Section 8, Clause 3 of the Constitution to make his decision. The court held that the "Cherokee nation . . . is a distinct community, occupying its own territory, with boundaries accurately described, in which the laws of Georgia can have no force" (Getches, Wilkinson, and Williams, 1993, p. 146).

Cases that followed the trilogy reestablished tribes as quasi-sovereign peoples ruled by treaty agreements, federal policy, and tribal law. Today, federal policy over Indian tribes is the responsibility of the Department of Interior.

Department of Interior

The Department of War regulated North American tribes from 1786 until 1849, when the Department of Interior took over. The Bureau of Indian Affairs (BIA) was founded in 1824 under the Department of War and was reestablished under the Department of Interior. The Secretary of the Interior, the Bureau of Indian Affairs, and appointed Indian commissioners experimented with a variety of policies to try and "fit" the Native American into the newly established United States. One of the approaches was the reservation policy of the 1850s, which allowed the federal government to contain tribes and attempt to assimilate them to the European way of life. The majority of the public in the 1800s viewed the Native American through ethnocentric eyes, and physical containment allowed these views a voice.

President Ulysses S. Grant in 1870 assigned religious denominations to tribes "to civilize the Indian" (Getches, Wilkinson, and Williams, 1993, p. 178). Captain R. H. Pratt, the first superintendent of the Carlisle Indian Boarding School, stated, "A great general had said that the only good Indian is a dead one. I agree with that sentiment, but only in this: that all the Indian there is in the race should be dead. Kill the Indian in him and save the man" (Getches, Wilkinson, and Williams, 1993, p. 209). The 1928 Merriam Report, which was a study of federal Indian policies, stated its objective: "Work with or for the Indians is to fit them either to merge into the social and economic life of the prevailing civilization as developed by whites" (Getches, Wilkinson, and Williams, 1993, p. 217). The federal government agreed that Native Americans could stay in the United States but only if they assimilated.

In 1949, the Hoover Administration demanded a change in federal Indian policy, stating, "Complete integration of Indians should be the goal so that Indians would move into the mass of the population" (Getches, Wilkinson, and Williams, 1993, p. 229). A new policy, known as House Concurrent Resolution 108, included the termination of hundreds of tribes. Although the policy did not terminate the Navajo Tribe, the majority of children under eighteen were sent to boarding schools away from home to achieve the goals of the Hoover Administration. The termination period was followed by the self-determination period, which is the current Native policy.

NAVAJO-FEDERAL RELATIONSHIP

The relationship between the federal government and the Navajo Tribe continued to develop in the years following the signing of the Treaty of 1868. Native Americans became citizens in 1924 under the Indian Citizenship Act. Unfortunately, under Arizona and New Mexico law at that time, one had to speak English to vote, and in 1952 two-thirds of the Navajo population could not speak, read, or write English (Hassell, 1972).

The official beginning of the Navajo tribal government occurred in 1922, when oil was discovered on the Navajo reservation. The same year the Bureau of Indian Affairs appointed a Navajo business council; this council formed without the authorization of the Navajo population. The bureau invented this council to approve oil leases. In 1924, Indian Commissioner Burke questioned the Business Council and invented the Navajo Tribal Council. In 1927, John C. Hunter invented chapter governments, and this system continues to be in use today. The chapter government is similar to a city council and the tribal council is analogous to a state government.

In the years between 1868 and 1928, the Navajo sheep flocks flourished so much that in 1928 the federal government ordered a livestock reduction on the Navajo reservation. The *dibe'*, or sheep, were killed or sold due to overgrazing and erosion. John Collier, commissioner of the Bureau of Indian Affairs at the time, was instrumental in the livestock reduction and, to this day, Navajo elders remember Collier's name with contempt. In 1934, grazing districts were established and the sheep permit was introduced to limit sheep. In 1934, Congress passed the Indian Section 16 of the Indian Reorganization Act (IRA), which authorized any tribe on a reservation to form and adopt a constitution, with the approval of the Secretary of the Interior. In 1937, 200 Navajo headmen met, discussed, and approved a constitution, but the Department of Interior refused to recognize it. The Navajo Tribe, with 45,000 members, rejected the IRA (Getches, Wilkinson, and Williams, 1993). Because the Navajo Tribal Council is not organized under the IRA, the tribe does not have a constitution and they must seek the approval of the Department of the Interior on most types of ordinances. For instance, if a Navajo tribal member wants to start a business on the reservation, the business lease can take up to three years to obtain because the forms have to be signed by the Secretary of Interior. In comparison, a non-tribal member's business lease can take as little as two months to process, since the tribe approves this exclusively.

The Navajo people are highly regulated. Because of the trust relationship, the policy efforts of the late 1800s and early 1900s, and the tribe's rejection of the IRA, the tribe does not exist outside of the federal government context. Nevertheless, the Diné continue to exist and continue to govern with an elected Tribal Council.

Indian Health Services

The federal government provides health care to recognized tribes because of the trust relationship established by Article I, Section 8, Clause 3 of the U.S. Constitution. Health care policy did not develop out of solicitation by the tribes; it was granted because the federal government decided that it was what tribes lacked. It should be remembered that Native people had long-established systems of health care that served them well and the indigenous health care system was extremely different from what the government offered them.

Although Army physicians in the nineteenth century did provide medical assistance to Native peoples, it was limited. Official health care on reservations did not occur until after the Snyder Act of 1921. Comprehensive health care on reservations did not begin until the 1950s.

Established in 1955 as an agency of the Department of Health and Human Services, the Indian Health Service provides health care to federally recognized Indian tribal members and their descendants.

The IHS policy states that it is responsible "for providing federal health services to American Indians and Alaska Natives" (Trujillo, 1998, http://www.ihs.gov/AboutIHS/general/IHS.intro.asp).

Initially, the Indian Health Service experienced difficulties in recruiting physicians and medical staff to work on the reservation. The Navajo reservation is an example of a remote and isolated area where medical staff refused to move. However, the medical draft during the Vietnam War brought physicians to the reservation. They served with the Indian Health Service for two years in exchange for paying off student loans (Tom-Orme, 1988). The physicians came and went during a period of establishing health care on the reservation. This, in addition to the continuous problems of federal funding and lack of proper facilities or equipment, contributed to how Indian Health Service has been conceptualized by residents of reservations.

The IHS is the primary health care provider on reservations, but with insurance benefits, large urban populations, and traditional healing, the IHS served only 65 percent of the Native American population in 1993 (Getches, Wilkinson, and Williams, 1993). Nineteen percent of the total services offered are in Navajo areas. As members of a federally recognized tribe, the Diné and their descendents are eligible for services provided by IHS (Trujillo, 1998, http:www.ihs.gov.aboutIHS/general/thisfacts.asp).

Under the Self-Determination Act and the public law agreements P.L. 93-638 and P.L. 94-437, tribes were given the option of administering or contracting their own health programs. In 1977, the Navajo Tribal Council passed resolution CFR 20-77, establishing the Navajo Division of Health Improvement Services. In 1989, under resolution CS-57-89, the agency became the Navajo Division of Health. This agency supplements the Navajo Area IHS and provides a variety of health-related services.

In 1998, Dr. Taylor McKenzie, the Navajo Nation's first physician and surgeon, was asked to head the Navajo Division of Health. Dr. McKenzie's interest in the health field started when "he noticed the lack of communication between non-Indian physicians and Navajo patients" (NavajoToday, 1998, http:www.navajos.com/navajotoday/mckenzie.shml). McKenzie says that it is time the Navajo Nation contracts with the Navajo Area Indian Health Services using the Indian Self-Determination Act.

The lack of communication between health facilitators and the members of the Navajo tribe is changing because many people who are fifty years old and under know how to speak English. However, for those tribal members who are older, the problems associated with language continue to exist. In addition, issues of culture may contribute to divisions in understanding when an older person experiences health services provided by non-Natives. In 1990, Native American elders over sixty-five years of age made up 5.8 percent of the total American Indian population. Though small, this is the population that has witnessed the most dramatic changes in their way of life and in the delivery of health and social services.

NAVAJO ELDERS

The majority of Navajo elders live in rural areas. Sources of income for the rural Navajo include livestock, weaving, silver-smithing, pawning, employment wages, or welfare (Lamphere, 1977). Job opportunities for younger family members are, for the most part, found in populated reservation communities or off the reservation in border towns. The lack of employment opportunities in rural areas may leave elderly persons living alone there. In many of these instances, they may only be visited once or twice a month by their children, grandchildren, and great-grandchildren.

The 1990 census reported that 31 percent of all Native Americans live below the poverty level. Also, in 1990, 89,978 Diné lived on the Navajo reservation, and of these, 48,968 or 54.4 percent were at or below the poverty line (Arizona Community Action Association, 1993). Although these reports say that the Navajo are a poor people, the older people say that they are not poor. Wealth to the Navajo is different than wealth to the majority of America. For the Navajo, wealth is found in livestock, turquoise and silver jewelry, and children (Hassell, 1972). In addition, neither poverty nor great wealth are socially acceptable, and "the attainment of wealth as a chief aim in life is universally condemned and a successful man will take steps to prevent too great an accumulation of material good for fear of being called a witch" (Kelly, 1968, p. 30).

Demands on elders who live in the rural areas vary by season. In the winter, a family must have access to coal and wood for heating the home and they must also have or be able to purchase hay for the sheep, goats, and other livestock. The majority of rural areas on the huge Navajo reservation do not have access to running water, electricity, telephones, or gas lines. As a result, finding transportation and day-to-day maintenance activities are a large part of rural life. These include having access to a truck in order to go to town or to a relative's home to haul water back to the hogan, the traditional elders' home. In the summer, hogans have to be repaired with mud and outhouses have to be dug and rebuilt periodically.

Concern for the livestock and the value of the sheep and goats can be seen in every elderly person. If there is no one to watch the sheep, elders do not leave home. It is said that Navajo women know their sheep, even if there are 100 of them (Hassell, 1972). Generally, elders' lives revolve around care of the family and the animals.

Rural life has many responsibilities, including codes that everyone must live by. These codes of behavior include working hard, being generous, helping the elderly, and not being mean, jealous, or stingy (Lamphere, 1977). If one does the opposite of these things consistently, people may consider that a person is a witch or is using witchcraft to hurt other people. Elders live by these codes, which enable rural life, as they know it, to continue. However, their world is changing in many ways, and these codes are continually challenged by the intrusion of Western values.

For the Diné in the rural environment, health is very important. Medicine men and women are used to both prevent and cure illnesses. Medicine people are educated and must be respected for their knowledge. Medicine men and women are not general practitioners; they instead specialize in certain cures and can refer patients to other healers for various ailments. Medicine people are reimbursed for their efforts with an amount depending on the patient's income and the complexity of the ailment. Payments can range from one penny to a sheep. This is why elders say the IHS hospital does not help them. They give nothing to the doctor, no transaction occurs, and it is impersonal. Additionally, in traditional medicine, the belief that a person can heal certain parts of the body separately is wrong. To truly heal, the whole body must be evaluated and cured (Kelly, 1968). This belief is also in opposition with whatever medical treatment elders receive at the hands of medical doctors. The discrepancies between what elders expect and what they receive create multiple avenues for miscommunication as well as mistrust.

Also, the Diné believe that disease occurs when there is an imbalance between a Diné person and the Holy People, nature, or another person (Kelly, 1968). This belief reinforces the "oneness" of elders with their total environment. In support of this, Kunitz and Levy (1991) argued that the Navajo belief system changed little after the incorporation of Western medicine, Christianity, and peyotism (see also Tom-Orme, 1988).

The Navajo reservation is over 27,000 square miles, and on this land there are seven major medical facilities. With the majority of elders in rural areas, some live 70 to 100 miles away from these medical facilities and very few have access to personal transportation. This is due to lack of an automobile or the inability, particularly of elders, to drive. In rural areas, the neighborhood is usually a compound composed of clan relatives. If an elderly person wants to go to a medical facility, he or she might leave home at four or five in the morning to try and catch a ride with a relative going to work in the closest town—and this is only if there is someone to watch the sheep.

Without the benefit of a telephone or knowledge of English, the elder will go to the hospital without an appointment. At Indian Health Service facilities, people are served on a first-come, first-served basis. Many people wait the whole day and at the end of the day are told to come back the next day. For the elder, the process is more complex. They have to find someone returning to the rural areas so that they can get a ride. If someone is able to take care of the sheep the second day, they can return to the medical facility. Generally, visits to the hospital become complicated activities without the benefit of reliable transportation or money.

TRADITIONAL AND MODERN MEDICAL CARE

Lifestyle

Depending on the size of the family and its members' ability to be employed off of the reservation, an elderly person may often reside on the reservation alone, with someone coming to check on them periodically. Health providers on the reservation include the native healers as well as the hospitals and clinics operated by the Public Health Service. There are also private, nonprofit providers such as Christian missionaries.

A traditional healer may be used because he or she would be more accessible to the people. The whereabouts of the healer are known so that this person is available day or night. The patients do not need an appointment. If they find the healer at home, fate is on their side. If they find the healer is not home, they may try to find someone else to help them. In any ceremony there is always a social and recreational component as well as the health component.

Usually, the patient and healer have established kinship through clan and previous visits. The healing event may last several days and may involve the patient, healer, and all the participants sharing meals together. However, if the patient were to present with broken bones or bleeding of any kind, he or she would automatically be referred to the hospital or clinic because native healers do not set bones or deal with blood. For colds or coughs, the healer may try homeopathy and herbs that he or she has harvested. In these instances the native healers deal with patients without the use of doctors or pharmacies. If the illness does not improve, the caretaker may take the patient to the hospital.

It should be noted that most patients travel approximately 50 to 70 miles to be seen by a doctor and then another 50 to 70 miles to return home. Since most elders do not drive, this distance often causes patients and their families extreme hardships.

In the past, hospitals were viewed as death houses. The hospital was a place of last resort. Since the Navajo have a fear of the dead, they would not come to the hospital until their illness was quite severe. However, within the last fifty years hospitals have become more acceptable due to political involvement of such persons as Councilwoman Annie Wauneka. Now there is much demand for health services. Hospital settings continue to be very impersonal on the reservation and unlike the traditional health care system that elders know and respect.

Patients are warehoused in waiting areas to be seen in an assembly-line style. First they sign in. Then they sit and wait to be called by a receptionist or nurse's aide who will check their weight, temperature, and so on. Patients sit and wait again until they are seen by the doctor who may ask for more information, depending on the need, lack of medical history, or miscommunication. At the end, there is no conclusion to the visit and many patients do not know what was decided regarding their presenting problem. Sometimes they must wait while the whole hospital closes for lunch. If patients have the funds, they will go out into the community to purchase a meal. However, in the majority of situations, the elderly have little, if any, expendable cash and they go without food until they return home in the evening. For the elderly, this is a long and strenuous day in a foreign environment with little, if any, comprehension of what is transpiring.

In some instances, patients are sent from one health care provider to another. Often, the patients are not given any paperwork nor are their medical records readily available. In these cases, the following may happen: "They don't communicate well among each other. If someone tells me to go to X place and writes me a note to take from here, the clinic over there never knows why I'm there. They don't know anything about me or don't have papers on me. I sit all day (waiting) when this happens" (Tom-Orme, 1988, p. 178).

The rural, old-fashioned physician was more like the traditional Navajo healer. The old-fashioned physician made home visits and knew the entire family, the history of each family member, who they were, where they came from, and their health history. Today, the traditional Navajo healer has the same relationship with the patients and the same depth of family history. The differences between modern doctors and traditional healers create a chasm between an elder and a doctor.

TRADITIONAL AND CURRENT
HEALTH CARE BEHAVIOR

In the traditional medical approach, the patient would go to all the neighbors and tell them that he or she was having a healing ceremony. The neighbors would bring food and come to help build the temporary shelters that serve to hold the ceremony. This inclusive ceremony became a social event in the community. In days past, many of the participants would gamble and have horse races as well as other social activities during the healing ceremonies, which could last up to nine days. The belief was that the energy from everyone helped the patient to heal. The healing ceremonies were for all willing participants, so it was not uncommon for neighbors to bring all their children and, in the old days, this is how young people met and later married.

Traditional healing is reciprocal. During certain times in the ceremony, all of the attention is on the patient. Yet, during times of relaxation, the healer talks about himself or herself. By the end of the ceremony, the participants and the patient know the healer very well.

Many of the traditional approaches to health care continue in modern times among the elders. Healing is an inclusive process that, in fact, needs all community members for the individual's well-being. This belief is not commonly known to many of the Indian Health Service doctors that come in to pay off their medical loans but are not equipped to provide culturally appropriate care.

Current health care delivery methods in a hospital setting are based on communication between doctor and patient. Due to elders' inability to adequately describe their symptoms, young children are often the translators for both the grandparent and the doctor. In spite of some translators being very young, children become the conduit for exchanging and sharing life-saving or life-threatening information.

In the Navajo way, health care decisions are oftentimes made individually. However, what needs to be discussed with the family is the care of the sheep should the elder have to be hospitalized. Because sheep are so important to the very existence of the Diné, their care is paramount in importance. In daily life, livestock is referred to as their mother and father and the animals are the foundation for the whole family. Continuation of the Diné is based on the family's ability to have sheep. Therefore, medical plans are not made unless someone can care for the sheep. These dynamics are difficult for some health care providers to understand, since to them sheep are seen as livestock with no personal connections.

If medical doctors really want to be effective with the Navajo community, they will have to practice medicine the way the rural doctor of yesterday did. This approach involves one-to-one contact and home visits. Unfortunately, most doctors and nurses do not see the value of spending so much time with their Navajo patients since, as pointed out earlier, many patients have to travel seventy miles one way to get health care. Additionally, learning about the Navajo is not important to the health care provider because he or she usually will not gain recognition or be promoted based on work on the Navajo reservation. Since doctors and nurses do not see themselves as being promoted to higher-level positions in this setting, there is little incentive to invest time and energy in knowing their patients and their culture.

In the Navajo way of life, it is a given that life is hard. When children are young they are told to get up early and run because when they run, the gods will see them and know them later on. They become familiar to the gods, who will say, "There goes my child." In many families, mothers will throw cold water on children and pull the covers off them early in the mornings to wake them up so they can run. They do not want their children to become poor or dependent. The children need to strengthen themselves. Children are taught that gods are everything but that they are also weak so they need the childrens' and adults' prayers. When life is difficult, the gods need prayer. Once people pray, things will be better. Prayer is important to prevent disease and illness. The Navajo culture emphasizes well-being within their traditional norms.

In modern medicine, credentials are used as a shield to prevent the patient from knowing the doctor as a person. Patients are supposed to accept the credentials that are bestowed upon medical professionals from faraway universities. There is no effort by the professionals to become personally acquainted with patients. Because they have to deal with an unknown doctor, many elders will go "shopping" around to find the provider who will help them feel comfortable. The end result is that the patients then try to keep all of the appointments with several doctors and get medicine from every doctor so easily that they can quickly become overmedicated.

Because of the transitions that the culture is experiencing, elders may be traditional in all aspects of their lives but be bicultural in their acceptance of medical care. They will use traditional healers and Western medical care for the same symptoms. Much of this dual-system utilization comes from the encouragement of younger Navajos who have been exposed to modern medical miracles.

Theories of Aging

Current theories of aging do not address Native Americans in general or Navajos in particular. There is no social science theoretical framework that applies to this population. Dynamics of Navajo aging include a deep-rooted respect for elders, a oneness with the environment, a need for harmony between people and Mother Earth as well as between individuals, a oneness with their animals (sheep), and a daily existence that is lived out in harmony. For example, one of the authors was at a ceremony dressed in jeans. She found a rock to sit on and tried to "clean" the rock before sitting down. From where she sat, she observed an old Navajo woman dressed in the beautiful traditional velveteen attire. The old woman simply sat down on the ground with no attempt made to "not get dirty." This harmony with Mother Earth exemplifies the oneness that is a daily way of life.

The Diné's sense of time is another dynamic that impacts how aging is viewed. To age is to grow in wisdom. To the Diné, time does not hold the meaning that it does to others. Given their sense of harmony, time does not control their lives; it simply comes. Events happen in due time. One need not try to fit into a schedule; therefore, age simply happens as is natural. The rhythm of life brings age as a reward.

The Diné believe in staying healthy, but health is a consequence of living by their codes of behavior and in harmony. For example, it is not uncommon to see the oldest family members sheepherding. This activity is important for the continuation of life. Sheepherding is done, not for the sake of staying active and healthy, but for the continuation of their total existence.

Implications for Health Providers

As previously mentioned, the Diné have a very complex culture, and this includes many beliefs that are grounded in lifetimes and generations of practice. Some Western medical professionals ignore many of these beliefs and practices. Additionally, age is associated with wisdom and many elders experience difficulties in trusting medical decisions when treated by young professionals. Language differences and culturally insensitive behavior may accentuate this mistrust. Therefore, it is important that health professionals listen intently to how symptoms are described and acknowledge with respect any attempt to deal with the symptoms via traditional methods.

REFERENCES

Arizona Community Action Association (1993). *Poverty in Arizona.* Phoenix, AZ: Arizona Department of Economic Security.

Dick, J. (1977). *Stories of traditional Navajo life and culture by twenty-two Navajo men and women.* Tsaile, Navajo Nation, AZ: Navajo Community College Press.

Downs, J.F. (1972). *The Navajo.* New York: Holt, Rinehart and Winston, Inc.

Getches, D.H., Wilkinson, C.F., and Williams, R.A. (1993). *Cases and materials in federal Indian law* (Third edition). St. Paul, MN: West Publishing.

Hassell, S.W. (1972). *Know the Navajo.* Estes Park, CO: Vic Walker, Indian Trader.

Kelly, L.C. (1968). *The Navajo Indians and federal Indian policy.* Tucson, AZ: University of Arizona Press.

Kunitz, S.J. and Levy, J.E. (1991). *Navajo aging.* Tucson, AZ: The University of Arizona Press.

Lamphere, L. (1977). *To run after them.* Tucson, AZ: The University of Arizona Press.

NavajoToday. (1998). <http://www.navajos.com/navajotoday/mckenzie.html>.

Parezo, N.J. (1996). The Diné (Navajo). In T.E. Sheridan and N.J. Parezo (Eds.), *Paths of life.* Tucson, AZ: The University of Arizona Press, 3-34.

Tom-Orme, L. (1988, March). Diabetes in a Navajo community: A qualitative study of health/illness beliefs and practices. A dissertation submitted to the faculty of the University of Utah, College of Nursing.

Trujillo, M.H. (1998). <http://www.his.gov/index.asp>.

U.S. Bureau of the Census (1992). *Statistical Abstract of the United States* (112th edition). Washington, DC: U.S. Government Printing Office.

Wood, J.J., Vannette, W.M., and Andrews, M.J. (1982). *"Sheep is life": An assessment of livestock reduction in the former Navajo-Hopi joint use area.* Flagstaff, AZ: Northern Arizona University.

Yazzie, E. (Ed.). (1982). *Navajo history.* Rough Rock, AZ: Navajo Curriculum Center.

Chapter 11

Views and Visions: Moving Toward Culturally Competent Practice

Mary Damskey

Culturally competent practice implies much more than obtaining basic knowledge about a specific population group. It involves a commitment to create a society in which all members are valued for their particular and distinctive talents, contributions, and abilities. In an increasingly multiracial, multicultural, and multiethnic society it also implies an unwavering determination to work toward social and economic justice. The preceding chapters offer the reader an opportunity to explore and consider the perspectives of several groups of ethnic elders. The goal of this book is to increase and enhance the reader's knowledge base of the historical context, value system, and cultural variables that influence elders' behaviors in seeking and utilizing health and social services, and to provide direction in the form of models of intervention and strategies for culturally competent practice. As stated in the beginning of this work, the aging population in the United States necessitates incorporation of the particular needs of the ethnic elderly into our health and social service programs. The increase in the number of elderly, coupled with a growing minority population, suggests that practitioners, agencies, and institutions can no longer ignore the unique characteristics of this population when providing services.

This chapter examines and delineates some of the common themes. The intention is not to dilute the sharp and varied perspectives offered in the book, but rather to highlight the shared, collective, and prevailing concepts and theories that will be useful to both health and social service professionals. As such, this chapter provides an overview of the common themes and their implications for assessment and practice; directions for policy, program, and research development; and educational objectives.

COMMON THEMES

Several themes repeat themselves throughout the work of most of the authors. Although a primary strength of the book is showcasing the specifics of each ethnic group, it is also important to note the many shared (universal) concerns and problems. Along with identification of these shared concerns are ideas for assessment and interventions that may be appropriate across different ethnic groups.

Historical Context

It is essential for health and social service providers to be as familiar as possible with the historical contexts that have shaped the ethnic elders' experiences in their countries of origin and that in turn shape their current experiences, patterns of behavior, and interactions. This work's authors point out that many of the ethnic elderly underutilize health and social services, and those who do seek services frequently drop out or prematurely terminate such services. Much of the existing research contends that underutilization and ineffective programs are the result of the biased nature of the services themselves and the inadequate training that health and mental health workers receive (Sue and Sue, 1990).

Underutilization of services can also often be directly tied to the fear and distrust that many elders feel toward the U.S. government and its various institutions. Understanding how this mistrust developed can offer invaluable insight into behaviors related to elders seeking or not seeking social and health services. An example of this is offered in Chapter 10, on the Navajo. To examine the history of this tribe's experience with the U.S. government is to understand the reluctance of the people to trust its institutions and the white representatives of those institutions. It is an easy leap then to comprehend why a Navajo elder may not follow a white health provider's advice or might even refuse to seek services from mainstream institutions. Understanding these issues helps us to view the ethnic elder's behavior as purposeful and not merely noncompliant.

A common theme among elders is the overwhelming stress, grief, and loss associated with the immigration experience, or in the case of the Navajo, the immigration of Europeans into their homeland. Furthermore, assimilation and acculturation place additional psychological strains on the elders and their families. Ethnic elders experience significant stress from intra- and interpersonal loss, role shifts, changing family structures, and problems related to language ability. All of these factors combine to place these elders at greater risk for health and mental health problems (Angel and Angel, 1997).

Stress of Immigration

The process of emigrating to a new country means giving up that which is known and familiar, that which is loved and held dear, and in some cases that which is feared and distrusted. To leave one's homeland often means leaving family, friends, and relatives, as well as home, profession, job, school, church, spiritual or religious sites, ancestral burial grounds, a known climate, diet, and a rhythm of life to which the individual and the family have been accustomed. These changes incur psychological, emotional, social, and economic costs (Angel and Angel, 1997). Ethnic elders who did not immigrate, but rather were born in the United States, face challenges related to ongoing discrimination and oppressive political and social policies. They also inherit the shared history of the preceding generations, which directly affects how they engage and interact with the dominant culture and its institutions.

Elderly immigrants who left their homeland because of persecution came to the United States hoping to find a peaceful place to live. Many Vietnamese, Japanese, Russian Jewish, Cuban, and Yaqui elders who faced adverse and oppressive conditions in their countries of origin have in turn been subjected to harsh and traumatic experiences as the result of political and social policy here. Oftentimes, instead of safety and peace, they have been confronted with age discrimination and racism. Freed (Chapter 2) remarks on the Japanese elderly and their experiences in U.S. relocation camps during World War II. She states that the experience "left an indelible mark upon them and their families. To understand and work with them today, counselors must know about the trauma they suffered, which many do not even share with their sansei children or yonsei grandchildren, just as many survivors of Nazi concentration camps with-hold their degradation."

For the Navajo, European settling of the United States meant destruction of their way of life, a devaluing of their beliefs, and loss of their land, autonomy, and freedom. Looking back at the history of how Native Americans were treated reveals a sad legacy of broken treaties and false promises. Is there any doubt that the elders would be careful of trusting a representative from the U.S. government?

In turn, Bossè (Chapter 6) discusses the changes that Puerto Ricans encounter when they immigrate to the United States from the island; they enjoy a majority status there that must be relinquished when they migrate to the mainland, "where they constitute just another immigrant minority with all the negative stereotypes along with the racial and ethnic prejudices that implies."

Alemán (Chapter 8) also refers to the uneasiness that many Mexican-American elders experience when using formal services. "Many of these elders remember when they were not welcomed into offices and services were segregated" (p. 143). Many elders' fears and distrust are fueled by current anti-immigrant activities that erode trust toward the majority culture.

It is not uncommon for practitioners to lack information or fail to inquire about the elder's experience of immigration or acculturation. Inexperience or lack of exposure to a particular ethnic group may preclude the professional from having specific knowledge about the historical antecedents that have shaped the ethnic elders' present perspective. Additionally, there is a tendency to focus only on the here and now when providing services. Time limits, an ethnocentric orientation, and an emphasis on efficiency often discourage the practitioner from taking the time necessary to obtain a detailed history; yet, acquiring knowledge about the elders' past history can make a difference in whether or not the service provided will be accepted and effectively delivered.

Acculturation, Loss, and Grief

Being subject to political and ethnic persecution, coupled with the day-to-day challenges associated with acculturation, can pose serious health and mental problems for the ethnic elder. Bossè reminds us: "The global nature of the change in cultural surrounding can seriously affect an older person's well-being because it severs ties to familiar networks, institutions, and lifelong values, beliefs, and expectations." The concrete tasks associated with acculturation are numerous: learning a new language and securing economic resources, housing, education, and health care are just a few. The psychosocial tasks are equally daunting: coping with social isolation and family adjustment issues, understanding and navigating new social structures while relinquishing old, and simultaneously dealing with new crises while coping with unresolved issues can present overwhelming challenges (Angel and Angel, 1997).

Moreover, the changes and challenges associated with immigration and acculturation often involve significant losses for the ethnic elder: loss of social status, profession, roles of authority, ability to communicate readily and easily, and traditions and customs. In addition, the process of acculturation may have evoked changes in the makeup of the family household; changing economic and social conditions may result in an increased distance between the elders and their children as young adults move away to seek increased employment opportunities. This shift in family living arrangements can mean losses not only for the elderly but for their families as well. Alemán (Chapter 8) refers to the fact that geographic distance can create a

> fragmentation of family systems that isolates elders in their homes and denies the children and grandchildren the ongoing support and exposure to the traditional culture that only the grandparents can provide. The consequences for all generations can be alarming: the grandparents lose their role as the transmitters of the culture and family history and the adult children lose their role of supporting the elders. Further, the adult children lose support and advice from the elders, and the young children lose the benefit of the wisdom and learning of cultural norms that elders usually transmit. (p. 145)

The total impact on social and cultural systems can be extremely significant and potentially devastating.

For others, shifts in previously held roles result in intergenerational conflict, as cited in Tran and Melcer's chapter on Cuban-

American elders (Chapter 7). He suggests that when adult children are forced to serve as translators for their elderly parents, respect is broken down and family structure is weakened. Ngo and Tran (Chapter 3) cite a similar concern: ". . . due to the lack of adequate English, many parents and grandparents heavily rely on their young children's language skills for tasks such as translation and filling out paperwork. The loss of authority due to role reversal generates much distress among the elders. These individuals often feel help-less and useless. This is particularly demoralizing for those who once held respected positions in Vietnam" (p. 43). Similarly, Freed suggests that the high rate of suicide among Japanese elders is the result of loss of traditional family roles and conflict between cultures over the role of women.

The psychosocial effects of the multiplied losses that each ethnic group has experienced is significant in view of the effect that repeated loss has on the individual psyche (Beiser, 1988, as cited in Chapter 3). Much of the literature on the elderly in general focuses on loss, which occurs more frequently as one ages (Tirrito, Nathan-son, and Langer, 1996). For the ethnic elderly, that number is compounded. The cumulative number of losses that these groups of elders may have experienced is overwhelming. A thorough understanding of the theories and dynamics of loss and grief will enhance the practitioner's ability to work cross-culturally. Grief manifests itself physically, cognitively, emotionally, and behaviorally (Worden, 1991); this should be taken into consideration when assessing and working with an elderly client. Being knowledgeable about specific cultural norms for expressing sadness and grief will enable the practitioner to intervene more effectively. Simply acknowledging that many of these individuals have experienced excessive and repeated loss has the likely effect (outcome) of increasing respect and empathy for the elders and all that they have survived.

Family Structure

Without exception, every author emphasizes that family structures and roles for ethnic elders are different from the majority culture's. Although there are some unique differences between groups, what seems to be universal is a broader definition of family. Also, the focus on individualism, independence, and self-efficacy in the dominant culture is often in direct contrast to the ethnic elder's family experience, where the family is viewed as the primary locus of authority, control, and personal fulfillment. Puerto Rican families are described as having strong family bonds with patterns of frequent interaction and a deep sense of family obligation. African-American and Mexican-American families oftentimes include non-biological members, who are perceived to be as important to the functioning of the family as blood relatives. For Vietnamese, the family is considered the most important social as well as spiritual unit; it is the primary locus of affective as well as concrete support. Russian families have a tradition of three generations living together in a single dwelling, and established friends are relied upon as closely as family members. Navajo families also rely on expanded kinship systems that are extremely elaborate.

Yaqui families have an extended form of kinship that includes all tribal members. In Japanese families, loyalty to family comes before all else and the group is perceived as more important than the individual. The traditional Cuban-American family also stresses the importance of family cohesiveness.

The significance of family is not unique to ethnic elders, but the broader definition of family, and sensitivity to the importance of family in decision making, will help practitioners plan and provide services. This is particularly true with nursing home placement. Many authors referred to a cultural value expectation that the elderly person should be cared for within his or her own family system. However, social and economic stresses are forcing families to make decisions about extended care that are painful for everyone. They may be especially conflictual for families of ethnic elders who have a strong prohibition against such an option yet feel that they have limited choices. As noted by Freed in Chapter 2 (p. 22): "Until recently, elderly Japanese rejected nursing homes, assuming that they would be cared for by their families. It was considered shameful for children to place a parent in a nursing home" (Yeo, 1993). Yet in recent years some Japanese communities have established nursing homes. While a community-based nursing home may increase the acceptability of such an arrangement, for some groups of elders this may not be feasible. Clearly the issue of nursing home placement is a sensitive one. Cultural prohibitions against institutionalized care, combined with variables related to language, diet, problems with health care coverage, and a distrust of mainstream institutions may also factor into the reluctance of various groups to use extended-care facilities. Home and community-based services, for as long as possible, will likely be a more effective way to help ease the strain placed on overburdened families.

Another common family structure theme is the fact that the elders are highly respected for their wisdom, knowledge, and experience. They are viewed within their cultures as keepers of family history, lore, customs, traditions, ceremonies, and beliefs. It is their wisdom that helps guide future generations and ensures that the group's values and traditions continue. This norm of high esteem and respect accorded to the elders within their family, group, or community may not be offered outside that protected group. Dominant-culture views of the elderly are often associated with negative experiences, such as physical disability, mental decline, aging bodies, death, and lack of productivity and usefulness. Elders are frequently seen as a homogeneous group; their individual strengths and abilities are often overlooked, discounted, and ignored (Angel and Angel 1997; Schneider and Kropf, 1992). The current aging of American baby boomers may result in changing attitudes toward the elderly, but ethnic elders and dominant-culture elders alike may experience a lack of respect for their status, individuality, and experience. Recognizing the valued role of the elderly member within the family, and according that member the respect that their position entails will help develop trust toward the professional and provide comfort for the elder.

POLICY, PROGRAM, AND RESEARCH DIRECTIONS

The culture of Western medicine and Western institutions can often conflict with the needs of a multicultural society. Traditional or medical models of health and wellness that focus on the client as a symptom to be treated, a disease to be eradicated, or a problem to be attended to may fail to take into account the whole person. A monocultural view of health and social service delivery that subscribes to a one-size-fits-all philosophy of care will do much to inhibit ethnic elders from seeking and utilizing those services.

Policy and administrative mandates that emphasize cost effectiveness, time-limited or managed care, and speed and efficiency at the expense of individualized and specialized care only serve to further isolate elders from formal support systems.

Other barriers to service delivery and effectiveness common to ethnic elders include access, eligibility, language, transportation, level of acculturation, stigma, fewer and poorer quality services, lack of knowledge about existing services, lack of knowledge about the process of obtaining services, delays, and rejections. In addition, agency and institutional settings that do not reflect a varying cultural landscape—and consequently are devoid of multicultural diversity such as music, art, dietary preferences, written information in the language of the client (when available and appropriate), bilingual and bicultural staff, and use of traditional and folk healers, medicines, and ceremonies—can further alienate ethnic elders and their families.

Many agencies and institutions have a written mission statement that denotes their philosophic commitment to diversity; however, demonstrating this commitment requires that administrators and institutional leaders take an active role in ensuring that the mission is carried out. When an agency administrator, hospital director, or nursing supervisor communicates to the rest of the staff a sense of urgency and recognition of the importance of developing a culturally competent system of service provision, it is likely that one will evolve (Tirrito, Nathanson, and Langer, 1996). Operationalizing this belief would necessarily include community outreach, proactive policies that directly reflect the needs of the particular community, culturally appropriate service delivery, continuing staff education and training, and ongoing assessment and evaluation of effectiveness. In light of the fact that many agencies and institutions may not be culturally sensitive, Alemán and Paz, in their chapter on the Yaqui (Chapter 9), discuss how to help elders who come into contact with agencies that are often inhospitable and antagonistic. The reader is referred to that chapter for specific suggestions that may be useful for many populations.

Further suggestions include the development of programs that are community based and that utilize the expertise of the ethnic community and its leaders in delivery partnerships. This involves seeking out and establishing a network of consultants who can help ensure that services reach those who are in need and that reflect the cultural needs of that community. Members of the ethnic community could serve as hospital consultants, agency advisors, and program and policy planners. An example of such a partnership is one that was recently established at the Indian Health Service (IHS) in Winslow, Arizona, a small rural community that serves many Navajo clients. In addition to providing mainstream medical treatment, funding was recently secured to hire a traditional Navajo healer as a member of the staff. This enables tribal members to use the combined resources of traditional and Western healing in one setting. Such a partnership also demonstrates a true commitment to meeting the diverse needs of the community and providing holistic care.

Future policy and program emphasis should be placed on development and enhancement of home and community-based services. These are more likely to be successful because they allow for greater utilization of natural helping networks, such as family, friends, churches, folk healers, and support of the larger community.

RESEARCH

Research on the medical and mental health needs of ethnic elders is limited. Greater knowledge of how specific medical and mental health problems differentially affect ethnic groups will contribute toward prevention efforts that can aid in the early identification and treatment of those who are at risk. Also, research efforts that help to pinpoint how environmental, educational, economic, social, and cultural variables intertwine in relation to the health status of ethnic elders will help steer policy and program direction.

Further evaluation of culture-specific intervention strategies and models of treatment that guide professional education and training are needed, as well as further evaluation of the use of Western therapeutic techniques on minority cultures. There is currently a limited amount of information about the effectiveness of such strategies as well as limited efforts to develop new and innovative methods of working with the culturally diverse. Research efforts in these directions will benefit both clients and practitioners.

EDUCATIONAL OBJECTIVES
FOR HEALTH AND SOCIAL SERVICE PROVIDERS

Structural, institutional, and individual biases and stereotypes all serve to create barriers to effective, culturally competent practice. The authors here have sought to illuminate a pathway for caring professionals which encourages a respectful curiosity, moving us to learn more about the diverse populations that we serve. Ethnic identification offers information that can be extremely useful in working with various clients; however, having particular knowledge about a group or community does not necessarily correlate with understanding the individual. The belief that ethnic or group identification is the sole determining factor in understanding a person or group could lead to incomplete and biased assessments. Ethnic identification provides us with a general direction from which we can further explore, but does not provide us a detailed, specific map.

What we can do is employ the information we have available to carefully examine ideas and perceptions that arise when working with a member of a particular ethnic group. We are then free to use or discard those perceptions as they reveal themselves to be accurate or inaccurate. The key issue is for the practitioner to be cognizant and knowledgeable not only about group differences and diverse views, but, perhaps most important, about our own ways of seeing, perceiving, feeling, behaving, and relating. Understanding how our worldview may enhance or hinder our work with people we perceive as different from ourselves is a key to culturally sensitive practice. When our personal, social, economic, cultural, and spiritual realties are diverse, there is a likelihood of attributing different meanings or values to similar behaviors or events (Barrera, 1994). To be aware of that likelihood enables us to consciously work toward building stronger bridges of understanding.

Health and social service professionals bring not only their own personal worldview but also the view of their profession. Providers of service are socialized into a professional culture, including beliefs, practices, norms, and rituals (Spector, 1991), that directly influences our ways of seeing, doing, and believing. Understanding the duality of how our personal and professional belief system affects our interactions with others is vital to culturally responsive practice.

It is the responsibility of the culturally competent professional to look for unique strengths in the client that can serve as resources for problem solving; this is an inherent part of professional social work practice. This strengths approach is a useful tool that recognizes clients as "experts" on their situation, with the ability to make good decisions about their lives. "Seeking out strengths of individuals and groups is one way to discover the stories, narrative and systems of meaning that guide clients. This puts practitioners in the position of discovering the language, the symbols, the images, the perspectives that move clients—for good or for ill" (Saleebey, 1997, p. 50). Inherent in this model are three primary principles:

- Given the difficulties they have, and the *known* resources available to them, people are often doing amazingly well—the best they can at the time.
- People have survived to this point—certainly not without pain and struggle—through employing their will, their vision, their skills, and as they have grappled with life, what they learned about themselves and their world. We must understand these capacities and make alliance with this knowledge in order to help.
- Change can only come when you collaborate with client's aspirations, perceptions and strengths and when you firmly believe in them. (Saleebey, 1997, p. 49)

Our goal in seeking and utilizing strengths is to recognize and respect the elder's worldview, which may include differential use of formal and informal support systems, and reliance on folk and traditional healers, herbal medicines, ceremonies, and ritual for diagnosis and healing. Their perspective may also encompass a broader, more holistic view of health and illness that encompasses the spiritual, physical, and emotional aspects of the person, along with differing views on the meaning of life and death. Employing an ecological model of assessment that takes into account the individual, family, group, and community, as well as the biological, psychological, social, cultural, and spiritual aspects of the person will enable the professional to obtain a more accurate picture of the client. This holistic perspective increases the likelihood that services offered will be appropriate to the needs of the client.

Communication between the client and the helping professional is obviously a key factor in any assessment and intervention. It has been well documented that language and communication barriers are one of the primary deterrents to use of social and health care services (Furino, 1992). Barriers to communication are verbal as well as nonverbal. Differences in language, dialect, slang and jargon, and paralanguage aspects of communication such as vocal tone, volume, and speech patterns can all contribute to a failure to communicate. The use of translators or interpreters may be necessary and helpful, but is not without complications that can range from problems with misinterpretation to incorrect translations involving alteration of the message by adding or deleting key components. Other problems can occur when young children are used to convey information, or if the interpreter is not well versed in the health and medical aspects of the problem being discussed.

Although it may not be realistic to expect that most providers will be bilingual, some emphasis must be placed on the recruitment and retention of bilingual and bicultural health and social service providers. Partnerships between institutions of higher education and ethnically diverse groups, tribes, and communities can be formed to encourage ongoing education of group members who can serve as vital links between their communities and the larger society. An example of such a partnership is that of Northern Arizona University and the Navajo Nation. A joint commitment by the university and tribe resulted in the delivery of professional programs in nursing, social work, and education on the reservation, thus enabling tribal members to obtain professional educations without having to leave their families and home community. Many of these students plan to work on the reservation after completing their studies or seek employment in bordering communities that provide health and social services to tribal members. These professionals in turn can help to make formal services more responsive to the needs of the community and be instrumental in encouraging those who are fearful of utilizing services that may be helpful to them.

We live and work in a diverse and complex society that continually challenges us to move beyond narrow and rigid ways of thinking and responding. Working with ethnic elders affords us the opportunity to use the best of our creative energies and ideas. It also enables us to learn more about alternative ways of health and healing and offers the chance to experience the world through the eyes of another. These opportunities stretch our personal and professional boundaries; they help to move us to new levels of understanding and encourage us to challenge existing institutions and prescribed ways of doing things. When we look at our programs, policies, and practices with new eyes and a fresh vision we see possibilities and promise, and replace fixed and inflexible ways of thinking and doing. Our willingness to open ourselves up to new knowledge, differing beliefs, and innovative ways of problem solving will do much to ensure the health and well-being of each client we are privileged to serve.

REFERENCES

Angel, R. and Angel, J. (1997). *Who will care for us? Aging and long term care in multicultural America.* New York: New York University Press.

Barrera, I. (1994). Thoughts on the assessment of young children whose sociocultural background is unfamiliar to the assessor. *Zero to Three, 14*(6), 9-13

Furino, A. (1992). *Health policy and the Hispanic.* Boulder, CO: Westview Press.

Julia, M.C. (1996). *Multicultural awareness in the health care professions.* Boston: Allyn and Bacon.

Saleebey, D. (1997). *The strengths perspective in social work practice,* Second edition. New York: Longman.

Schneider, R.L. and Kropf, N.P. (Eds.) (1992). *Gerontological social work: Knowledge, service settings, and special populations.* Chicago: Nelson Hall Publishing.

Spector, R. (1991). *Cultural diversity in health and illness,* Third edition. Norwalk, CT: Appleton and Lange.

Sue, D.W. and Sue, D. (1990). *Counseling the culturally different: Theory and practice,* Second edition. New York: John Wiley and Sons.

Tirrito, T., Nathanson, I., and Langer, N. (1996). *Elder practice: A multidisciplinary approach to working with older adults in the community.* Columbia, SC: University of South Carolina Press.

Worden, J.W. (1991). *Grief counseling and grief therapy: A handbook for the mental health practitioner.* New York: Springer.

Index

Order Your Own Copy of
This Important Book for Your Personal Library!

THERAPEUTIC INTERVENTIONS WITH ETHNIC ELDERS
Health and Social Issues

_____ in hardbound at $39.95 (ISBN: 0-7890-0272-8)

_____ in softbound at $24.95 (ISBN: 0-7890-0273-6)

COST OF BOOKS_____

OUTSIDE USA/CANADA/
MEXICO: ADD 20%_____

POSTAGE & HANDLING_____
*(US: $3.00 for first book & $1.25
for each additional book)
Outside US: $4.75 for first book
& $1.75 for each additional book)*

SUBTOTAL_____

IN CANADA: ADD 7% GST_____

STATE TAX_____
*(NY, OH & MN residents, please
add appropriate local sales tax)*

FINAL TOTAL_____
*(If paying in Canadian funds,
convert using the current
exchange rate. UNESCO
coupons welcome.)*

☐ **BILL ME LATER:** ($5 service charge will be added)
(Bill-me option is good on US/Canada/Mexico orders only;
not good to jobbers, wholesalers, or subscription agencies.)

☐ Check here if billing address is different from
shipping address and attach purchase order and
billing address information.

Signature_____

☐ **PAYMENT ENCLOSED:** $_____

☐ **PLEASE CHARGE TO MY CREDIT CARD.**

☐ Visa   ☐ MasterCard   ☐ AmEx   ☐ Discover
☐ Diner's Club

Account # _____

Exp. Date _____

Signature _____

Prices in US dollars and subject to change without notice.

NAME _____

INSTITUTION _____

ADDRESS _____

CITY _____

STATE/ZIP _____

COUNTRY _____ COUNTY (NY residents only) _____

TEL _____ FAX _____

E-MAIL_____
May we use your e-mail address for confirmations and other types of information? ☐ Yes   ☐ No

Order From Your Local Bookstore or Directly From
The Haworth Press, Inc.
10 Alice Street, Binghamton, New York 13904-1580 • USA
TELEPHONE: 1-800-HAWORTH (1-800-429-6784) / Outside US/Canada: (607) 722-5857
FAX: 1-800-895-0582 / Outside US/Canada: (607) 772-6362
E-mail: getinfo@haworthpressinc.com
PLEASE PHOTOCOPY THIS FORM FOR YOUR PERSONAL USE.

BOF96